Toward an Archaeology of Buildings

Contexts and concepts

Edited by

Gunilla Malm

BAR International Series 1186
2003

Published in 2016 by
BAR Publishing, Oxford

BAR International Series 1186

Toward an Archaeology of Buildings

ISBN 978 1 84171 552 0

Typesetting and layout: Darko Jerko

BAR Publishing is the trading name of British Archaeological Reports (Oxford) Ltd.
British Archaeological Reports was first incorporated in 1974 to publish the BAR
Series, International and British. In 1992 Hadrian Books Ltd became part of the BAR
group. This volume was originally published by Archaeopress in conjunction with
British Archaeological Reports (Oxford) Ltd / Hadrian Books Ltd, the Series principal
publisher, in 2003. This present volume is published by BAR Publishing, 2016.

Printed in England

BAR
PUBLISHING

BAR titles are available from:

BAR Publishing
122 Banbury Rd, Oxford, OX2 7BP, UK
EMAIL   info@barpublishing.com
PHONE   +44 (0)1865 310431
FAX   +44 (0)1865 316916
www.barpublishing.com

CONTENTS

FOREWORD

This BAR-volume is an exposé of building archaeological research works and building restorations. It is a well known truth that buildings as and restorations mirror the dynamic of societies. Either as a single monument, as conglomerat in cities or towns or as single rooms or spaces, building and restoration is a result of socio-economic, political or ideological power or expressions. But there are many different ways of looking at building and restoration in this respect as the authors of this volume show.

Geographically the volume covers the area of parts of Europe and West Asia, Spanish Town in Jamaica and Cape Dutch Tongaat in South Africa. The chapters are presented in chronological order from Ancient Times up to Modern Times.

It is a hope the the reader will find the volume interesting and enjoyable and that the contents will be used as a base for futher discussions either at home or at international meetings.

Gunilla Malm

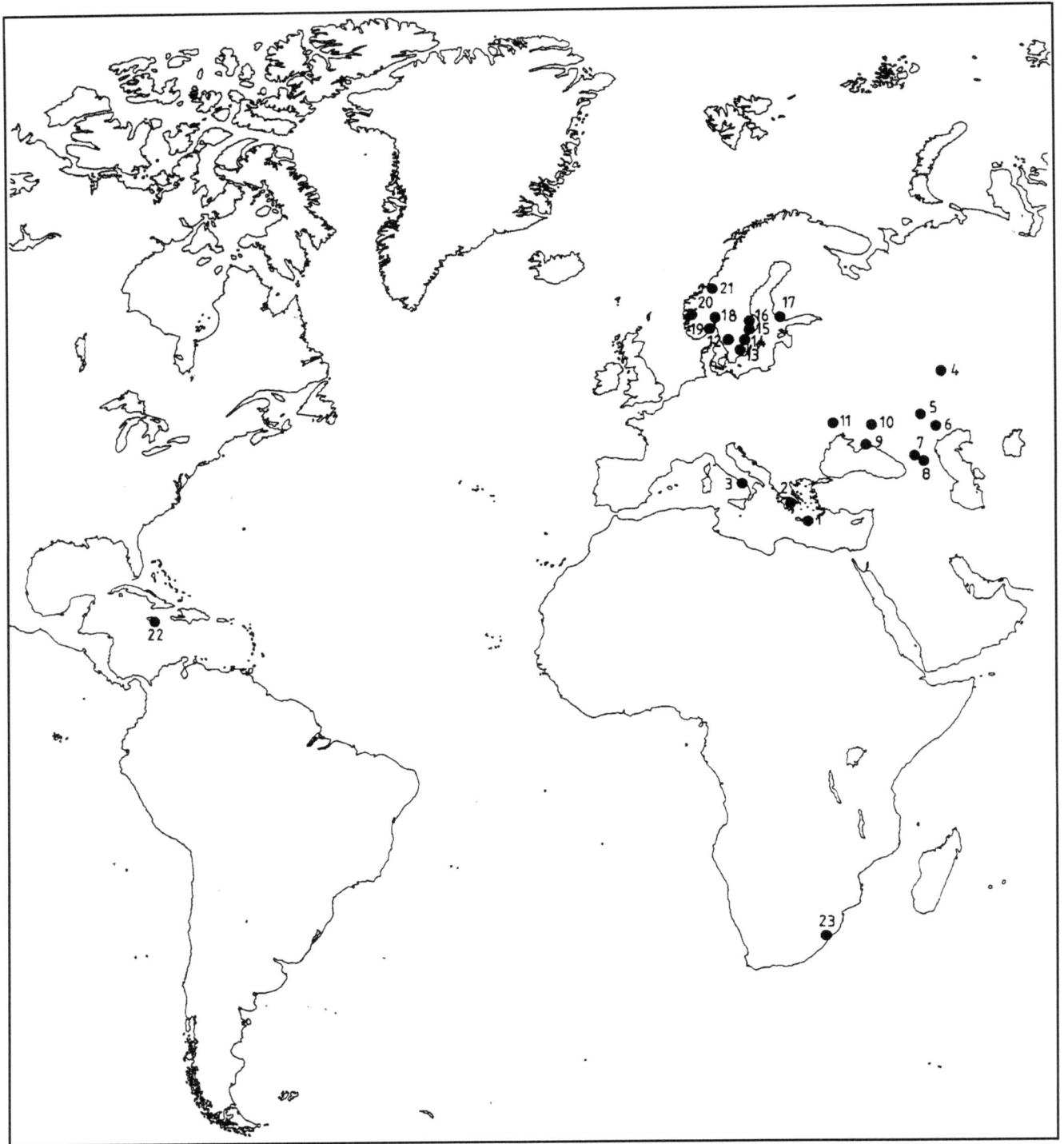

Map of sites mentioned in the chapters.
1. GREECE: CRETE. Phaistos, Knossos, Mallia, Gournia and Kato Zakro.
2. GREECE. Mycenae.
3. ITALY. Pompeii.
4-11. EUROPE/ASIA: 4. Bulgar, 5. Vodianskoe site, 6. Sarai, 7. Upper Julat, 8.
        Lower Julat, 9. Krym, 10. Kuchugury site and 11. Old Orkhey.
12-16. SWEDEN. 12. Skara, 13. Växjö, 14. Linköping, 15. Strängnäs and 16,
        Uppsala.
17. FINLAND. Abo.
18-21. NORWAY: 18 Oslo, 19. Tönsberg, 20. Bergen and 21 Trondheim.
22. JAMAICA. Spanish Town.
24. SOUTH AFRICA. Tongaat.

SPACE 1999 (B)CE:
POST-PROCESSUAL APPROACHES TO MINOAN ARCHITECTURE

Louise A. HITCHCOCK

Abstract: Minoan buildings possess a "Labyrinthine" layout, which includes a variety of room types grouped around a central court. Variability in their arrangement is created through distinctions in the placement of doorways and corridors. Previous scholarship has arbitrarily assigned functions to Minoan rooms based on form or on analogies with Egyptian architecture. Such methods are rooted in universalist assumptions that neglected the complexity and regional diversity of Minoan buildings. With multiple entry ways, passageways, and varying degrees of accessibility, these buildings were experienced by different people in different ways.

This paper analyzes the function of Minoan monumental buildings in Late Bronze Age Crete using contextual analyses and the introduction of comparative evidence from elsewhere in the Near East in order to examine room function and meaning on multiple levels. These levels include movement, experience, visual access, and regional differences. Previous arguments for variability, polysemy, and ambiguity in ancient art and archaeology have been suspiciously regarded as advocating an anything-goes relativism with regard to the interpretation of the past. Counter-claims argue that the evidence limits relativistic interpretations. In support of the claim for emphasis on variability I argue that emphasizing similarities with regard to style, form, and function limits what we can know about the past by placing limitations on how we study the evidence. Instead of placing limits on the interpretation of evidence, the evidence should place limits on us. I present the case for polysemy with several examples of Minoan monumental buildings as non-verbal communicative systems that signify on multiple levels.

INTRODUCTION

Minoan buildings possess a "Labyrinthine" layout, which includes elaborate halls and ceremonial spaces, storage areas, and industrial quarters grouped in similar locations around a central court. Previous scholarship has arbitrarily assigned functions to Minoan rooms based on form or on analogies with Egyptian architecture (e.g. Evans 1921; 1928; 1930; 1936; Graham 1987). Furthermore, the significance of superficial similarities in the layout and design of these buildings has been magnified to the extent that these buildings are assumed to have had similar if not identical functions. Such methods are rooted in universalist assumptions that assigned identical functions to every structure, neglecting the complexity and diversity of Minoan buildings.

This diversity was created in several ways: in the distribution and quantity of particular features, in construction details, in the placement of doorways, stairways, and corridors; and through change over time. I have termed my approach to reading these different types of distinctions contextual, because I analyzed differences in the spatial or syntagmatic relationships of the Minoan architectural vocabulary.

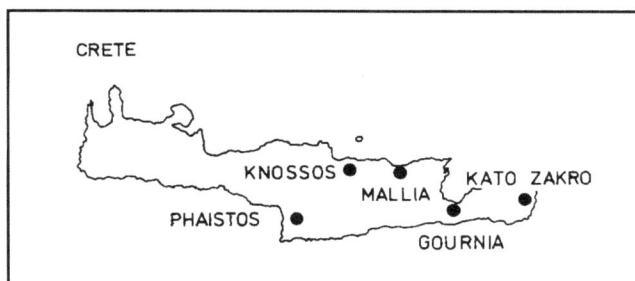

Map

Syntagmatic refers to the spatial and temporal relationships that monuments and objects are placed in. Understanding these connections through relational thinking emphasizes a cognitive style that tends to be non-Western in that there is a greater tolerance for ambiguity.

In contrast to syntagmatic signs, paradigmatic signs acquire meaning and definition through opposition to what they are not so that meaning comes about through a process of opposition (both are detailed in Samovar and Porter 1997). Oppositional thinking forms the basis of paradigmatic relationships in structuralism and can be related to a certain cultural orientation and cognitive style that is particularly Western. This style is believed by some to be controlled mainly by the left hemisphere of the brain. Past approaches to the understanding of Minoan society have been grounded in paradigmatic relationships. These relationships take the form of simplistic and essentializing oppositions such as "Villa" : "Palace"; Burgher : King (or Priest); Rural : Urban; Female : Male; smaller : larger; Nature : Culture; Mycenaean : Minoan; Greek : 'Other'; symmetrical : agglutinative; logical : irrational; simple : complex; clear : confused; orderly : chaotic; fortified : defenseless; and warlike : peaceful.

In addition to analyzing relational differences as outlined above, I have also detected patterns in the distribution of and relationship between certain features, which I have termed structured distribution. Structured distribution is based on the concept of "structured deposition" formulated by Colin Richards and Julian Thomas (1984). Structured deposition is a method for recognizing ritual behavior in the archaeological record. It relies on the detection of rule-bound or deliberate patterns in the deposition of archaeological remains. These patterns indicate formalized repetitive actions on the part of social actors who created the deposit over time. Structured distribution is basically a formal term for recognizing repetitive behavior in an architectural context as structured by patterns in the distribution of artifacts and/ or architectural features as we will see later.

Previous "post-processual" studies emphasizing variability, polysemy, and ambiguity have been suspiciously regarded as advocating an anything-goes relativism with regard to interpreting of the past (e.g. Shanks and Tilley 1989). Counter-claims argue that the evidence limits the interpretations made by post-processualists. In support of this counter-claim, I argue that emphasizing universal similarities with regard to style, form, and function places limitations on how we study the evidence, how much we can learn about the past, and which types of evidence we privilege. Instead of placing limits on the interpretation of evidence, the evidence should place limits on us as readers, authors, and interpreters. I view what Umberto Eco (1994: 40-42) calls Authorisation as an ongoing process that is enabled and constrained through dialog and discourse.

CONTEXTUAL SEMIOTICS

My approach to the Minoan built environment might best be understood as the development of a contextual semiotics. Contextual semiotics requires shifting the level of analysis from "language" to "text" (for example, Moore 1985). Traditionally archaeologists have used types as indicators of contact, cultural affiliation, and diffusion, but the question of meaning is not pursued (cf. Hodder 1982:9). For example, how often have you read a catalog that told you what each object was found with, what kind of room it was found in, and what was found in connecting rooms? Including this information would enable the reader to know something about how the object was encountered and circulated by the particular culture that used it. Thus, the experiences of an object or a room type in space and the relationships between them, whether random or patterned, is eliminated from the construction of typological categories.

The detection of minimal units based on morphological characteristics and reoccurring syntactic relationships serves a similar descriptive purpose and has been used to demonstrate regularity in the planning and execution of Minoan buildings (for example, Preziosi 1983). However, as Mathew Johnson (1993:31ff; also Eco 1994: 48) has observed, an architectural semiotics derived from linguistic semiotics does not address the economic and social realities produced by architectural space that takes on ever more complex meanings, through being experienced by many different social actors.

Explanatory, contextual analysis reintegrates Minoan room types with their associated features. Such reintegration enables the critical analysis of the internal relations between these things (Moore 1990). For example, Jameson (1992:105) sees rooms as the words or minimal units of built space with corridors, doorways, and staircases functioning as spatial verbs and adverbs, which are modified by adjectives in the form of paint, furnishings, decoration, and ornament.

Altogether, he takes these as architectural "sentences," that are read through embodied experience as users fill various subject positions. This textual metaphor for built space implies that interpretation takes place as a practice of reading and re-reading which can change based on the historical conditions of the reader (cf. Moore 1985; 1990). A contextual approach shifts the emphasis of analysis from object category to the built environment as a unit made up of sub-units including rooms, objects, decoration, and other types of spaces.

ARCHAEOGRAMMATOLOGY

Such relational readings of archaeological material might be understood as an "Archaeogrammatology" (e.g. Hitchcock 1997: esp. 47). By this, I mean an examination of the relationship between space and material culture in the production of and interpretation of meanings where the meaning of a single object or room type is spatially deferred throughout a host of associations. The associations between things are inscribed in space and this constitutes the relationships, which we experience. It is from these experiences that we assign meaning.

Just as a word can take on different meanings depending on its context in a sentence, the meaning or function of a particular type of room might be changed by modifying its relationship to other rooms through the arrangement of doors and/or corridors. It is the variability of spacing in relationships between architectural forms, this *différance*, which I call the archaeo-gram that contributes to different and complex functions/meanings for those forms. Hence, the daily routines of individual agents were enabled or constrained in a process that was continuously re-negotiated through movement, experience, and the modification of rooms and artifacts to each other (e.g. Giddens 1993). To the extent that these relationships can be experienced different ways and from different frames of reference, a surplus of meanings will emerge from the reading of the material record (e.g. Yates 1990a: 221ff).

What follows are selected examples (further detailed in Hitchcock 2000) of how each of the concepts I have summarized might affect our understanding of how the Minoan "Palaces" functioned. Although I will present a selection of the patterns I have detected, the emphasis will be on differences as inscribed in spatial relationships. These differences are deemed significant to the production of meanings following Derrida's (1968: 26) observation that every process of signification is constituted by a "play of differences."

DISTRIBUTION AND QUANTITY OF PARTICULAR FEATURES

At the "Palace" at Phaistos (Pernier and Banti 1951), located in south central Crete, a significant amount of space was given over to workshops on the ground floor, grain storage on the upper floor, and the use of a kiln in the East Court (Fig. 1). The substantial remains of grain that were stored on the upper floor above one wing of workshops are largely dismissed in earlier formalist interpretations that interpret the upper floor as a platform for viewing bull games that supposedly took place in the Central Court (Graham 1957; 1987). Such rigid interpretations have been complicit in fabricating an idealized and ahistorical Minoan past that speak volumes about present fantasies, but diminish ancient realities.

Popular as well as scholarly accounts that reduce hundreds of rooms to a few inches on the page further trivialize our understanding of these structures. A careful analysis of the circulation system on an enlarged plan reveals that as many as two thirds of the existing rooms and courts in the building were devoted to halls and related spaces traditionally seen as ritual, residential, or ceremonial (Figs. 2-4) (cf. Graham 1987). An unusual recurring feature at Phaistos is a room known as a "Lustral Basin." This is a small rectangular room sunken below the floor level and reached by a short flight of

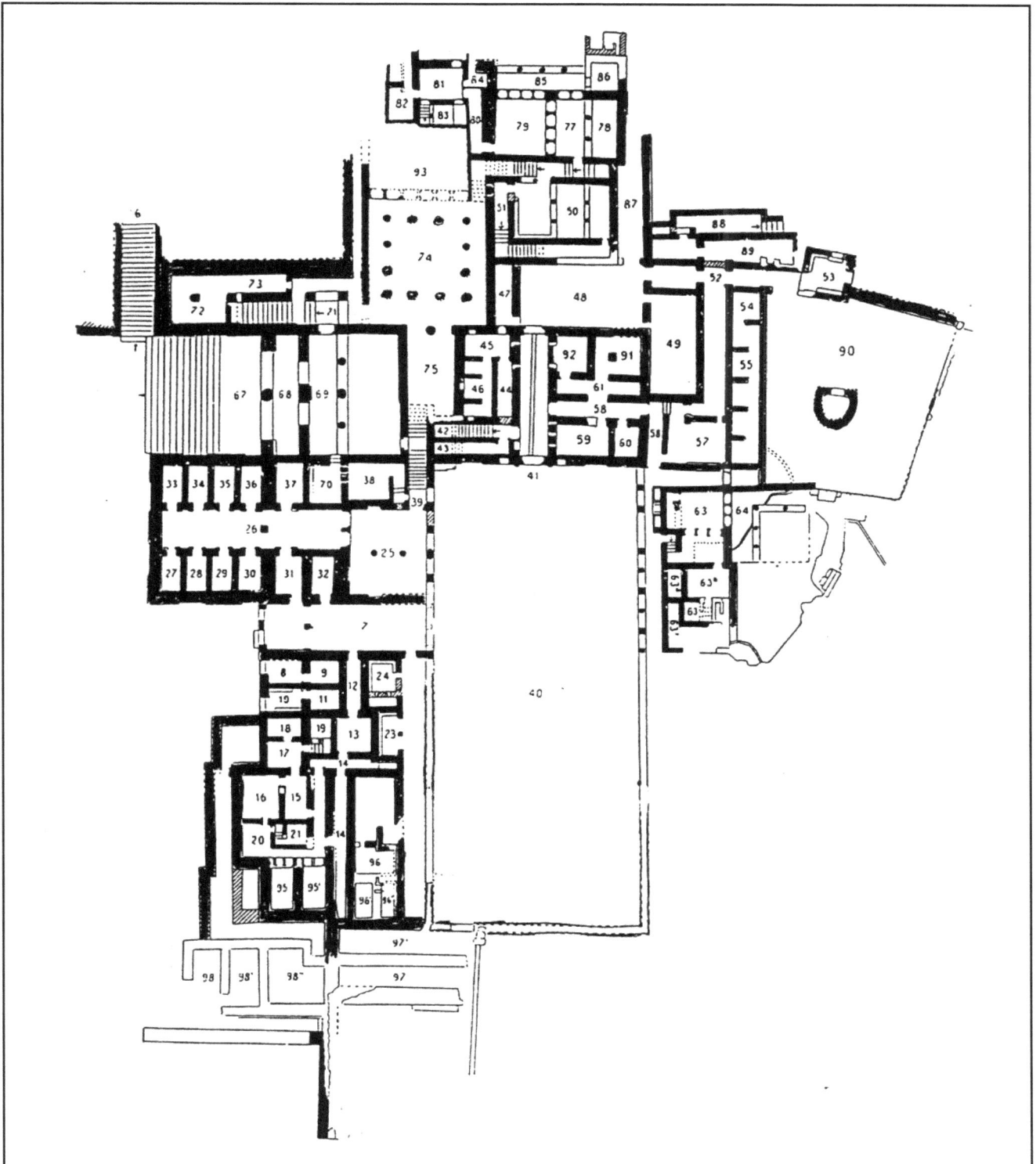

Fig. 1 Phaistos, Second "Palace" (after Pernier and Banti 1951)

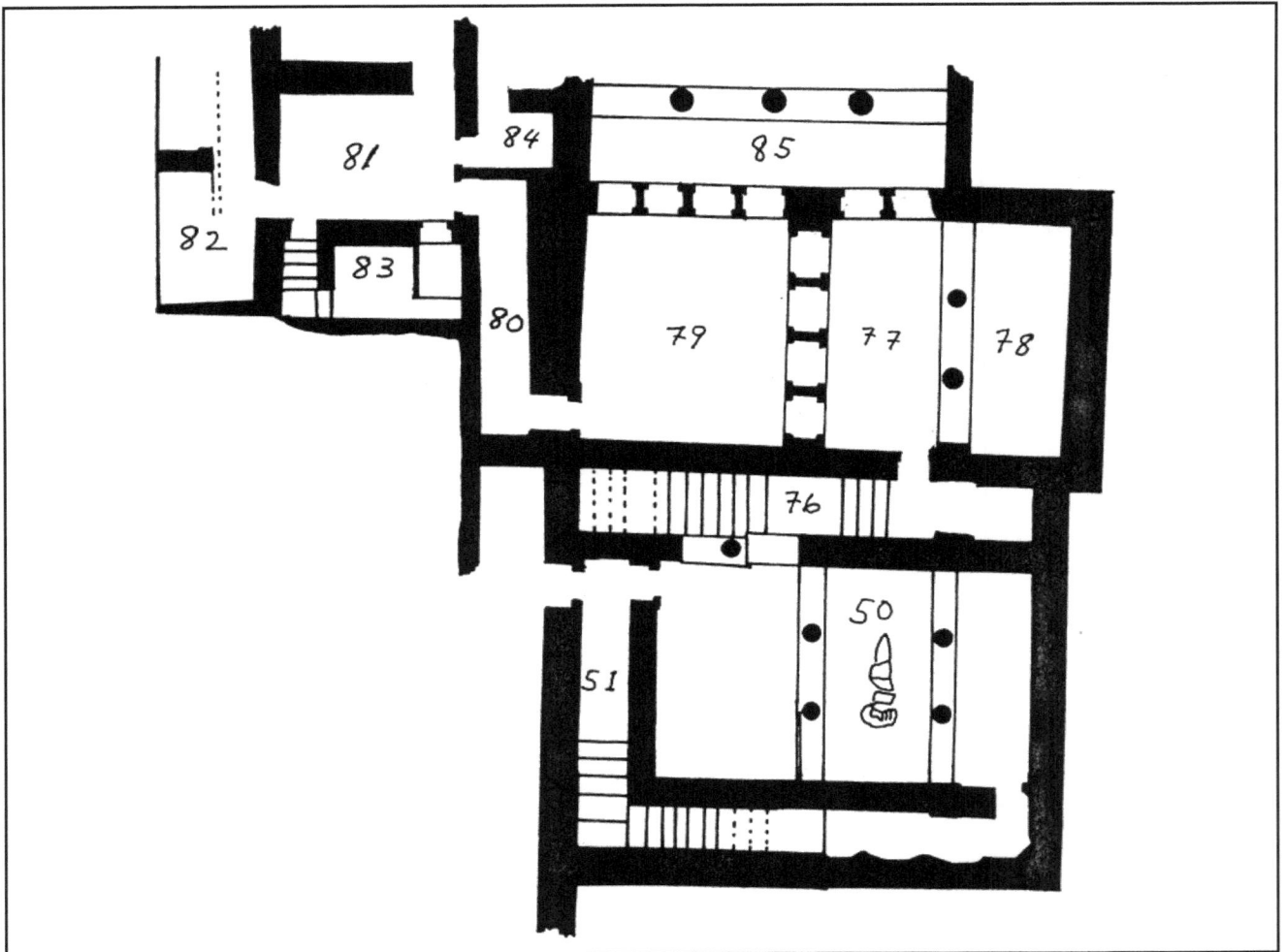

Fig. 2 Phaistos, Second "Palace," detail of North Hall (after Pernier and Banti 1951)

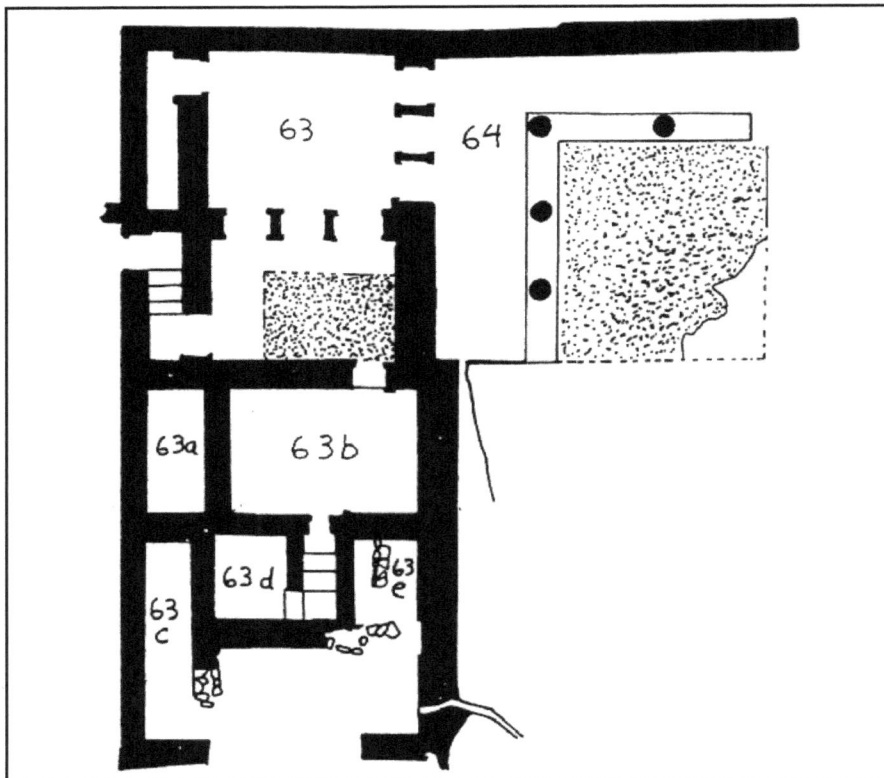

Fig. 3 Phaistos, Second "Palace," detail of East Hall (after Pernier and Banti 1951)

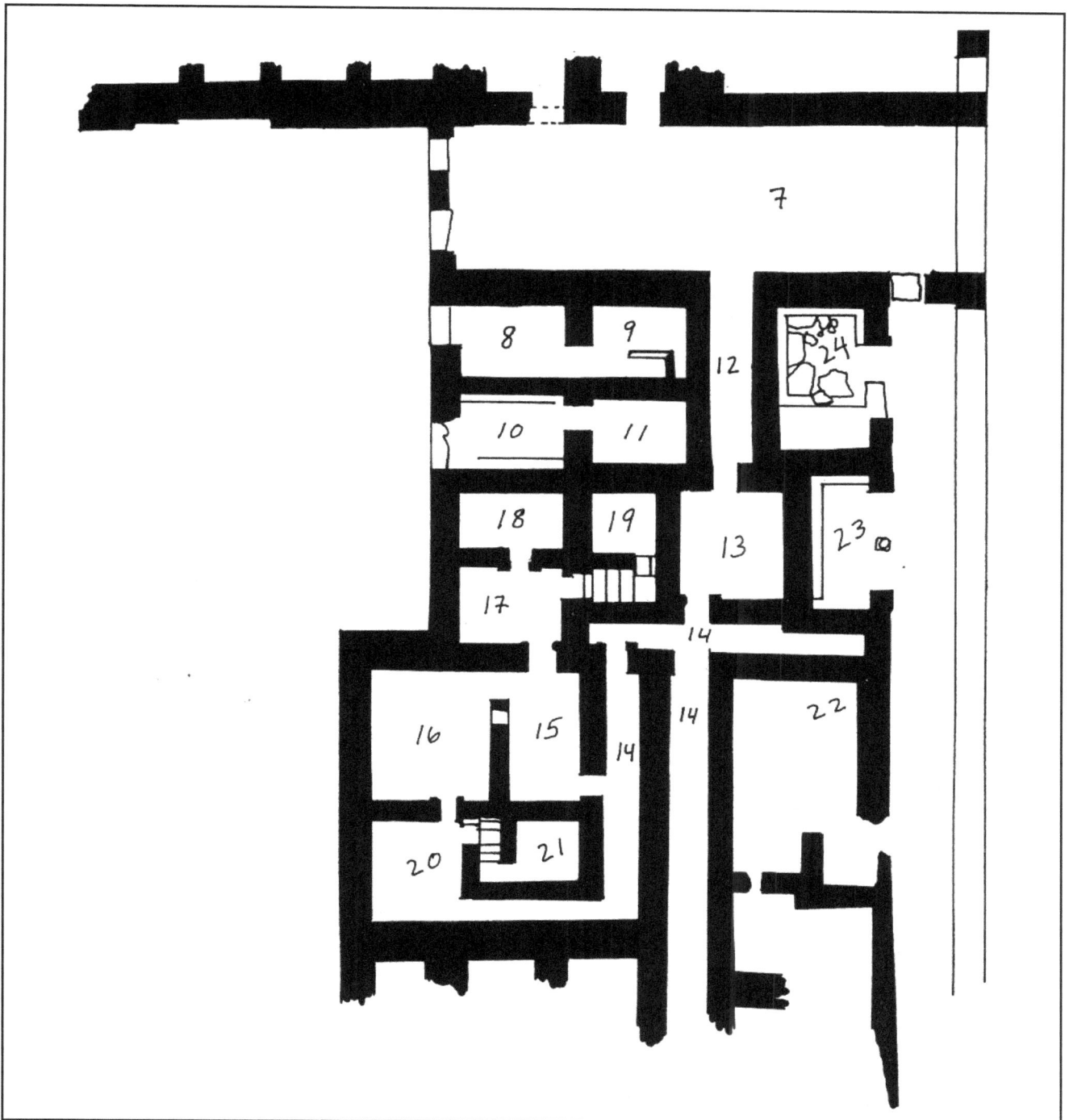

Fig. 4 Phaistos, Second "Palace," detail of "Lustral Basins" in West Wing (after Levi 1981)

stairs, making a turn and running along a parapet. It should be noted that these rooms lack drains while at one site a drain was actually blocked where a basin was constructed as a later addition (Gesell 1985: 118). This basin has been associated with ritual initiation (Marinatos 1984; 1993; Marinatos and Hägg 1986) and purification (Evans 1921; 1928; 1930; 1935), symbolic descent into the earth, and less plausibly with bathing (detailed Hitchcock 2000: 160-181). At Phaistos there are four such rooms, two to four times the number found at the other Minoan "Palaces."

Two of these "Lustral Basins" and their ante-rooms, 17 and 19; and 20 and 21, are located in the West Wing behind the west facade, an area typically associated with storage (Fig. 4). They are only accessible with great difficulty. The "Basins" and the routes of access to them take up most of the south half of the West Wing. Each is located six thresholds from either the exterior of the "Palace" or from the Central Court. This long winding route begins in entry corridor 7, turns south through corridor 12, passes through vestibule 13, turns west and again south through corridor 14, then west and north through room 15, and finally branches off to the west for complex 20-21 or north for 17/19. The route was decorated with incised double-axe marks, the dominant Minoan religious symbol, and maroon or red painted plaster, perhaps symbolizing blood, the substance of life giving sacrifice.

Other than gaining access to the "Basins" there is little other purpose to this lengthy journey, which must be repeated to leave or go to other parts of the "Palace." This arrangement might be seen as orchestrating the symbolic recreation of a journey in an artificial landscape (cf. Tilley 1994, 30-31). Landscape played a significant role in Minoan religion and a number of features in the landscape may have been symbolically represented or referenced architecturally (Hitchcock 2001). Along the architectural route at Phaistos, one would be drawn along the corridor, then might remain in one of the small adjoining halls for a while to meditate, talk to fellow participants, or experience something, then continue down another corridor, and so on, until reaching the "Basin."

The other two "Basins" were found in the north (Fig. 2, room 83) and east (Fig. 3, room 63d) wings in a close association with elaborately appointed halls that structured different patterns of movement and experience that might be connected to different activities. Given that most of the building was

taken up by these features and their associated halls and pathways, the entire structure might be read as a center for the performance of purification, initiation, or contemplation in the "Basins" on a scale unattested elsewhere on Crete. Such use need not exclude other uses for the halls such as gatherings of "Palace" elites or sleeping at the end of the day.

PLACEMENT OF DOORWAYS AND CORRIDORS

The main entrances to the "Palaces" at Phaistos, Knossos, Mallia (Fig. 5), and Gournia (Fig. 6) are located on the west. The west facades formed the main public front of these structures, incorporating finely dressed ashlar blocks, and they have been interpreted as concealing the public food supply for their respective regions (cf. Branigan 1987). Paved

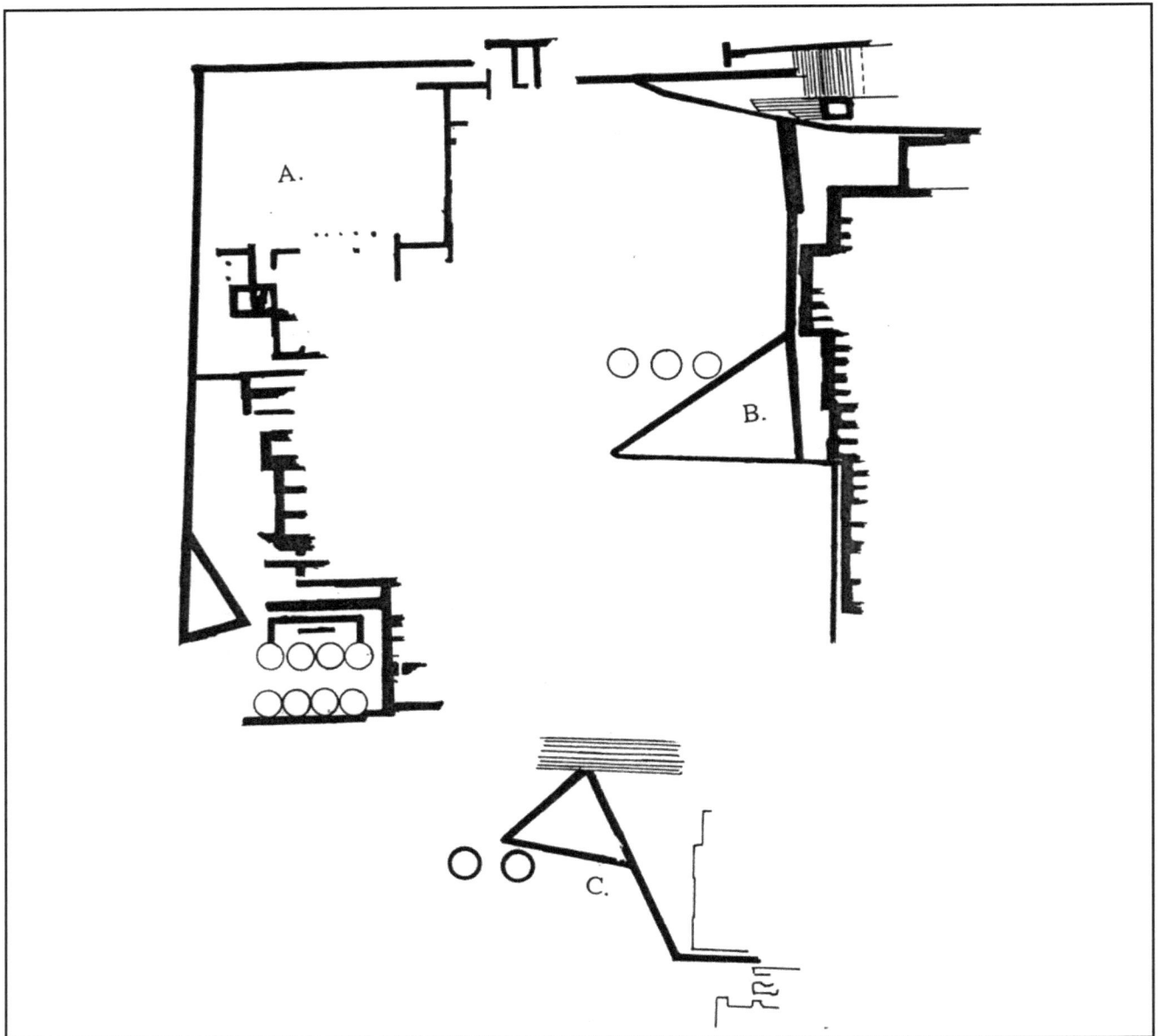

Fig. 5 West Courts of "Palaces:" a. Mallia 2, b. Knossos 1, c. Phaistos 1 (after Marinatos 1993)

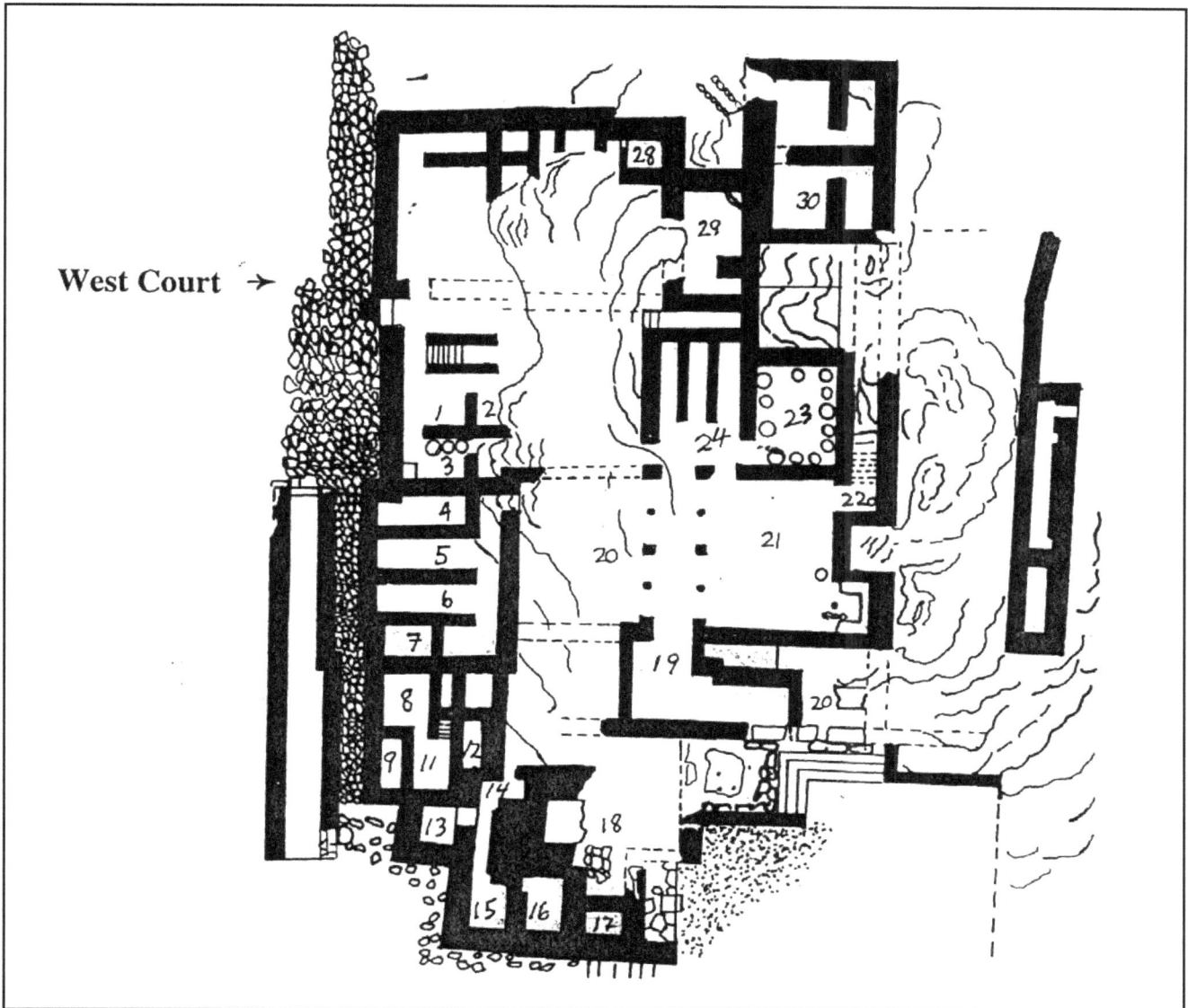

Fig. 6 Gournia, "Palace" (after Boyd-Hawes 1904)

external courts, also on the west, have been interpreted as the site of public gatherings, possibly connected with the harvest (Marinatos 1987).

The "Palace" at Kato Zakro (Fig. 7) (Platon 1985) on the east coast of Crete is distinct in several ways: 1. its west facade was constructed out of megalithic or rough, unfinished limestone blocks (Shaw 1973: 80, 191); 2. the scanty remains of a west court were covered over with an annex of rooms used for dying fabrics; 3. its main formal entrance is on the northeast and connected with the road leading to the harbor; and 4. it contains an elaborate system of built pools and springs not replicated elsewhere.

The location of the main entrance in relationship to the harbor road and imported finds such as elephant ivory and copper ingots indicates that Kato Zakro was constructed to facilitate trade with the east (e.g. Wiener 1987). The absence of a West Court, the megalithic facade, and a diminished storage area suggests less emphasis on social storage and related public ceremonies at Kato Zakro than elsewhere.

The pyramidal stone double-axe base, grape seeds, small branches, burned animal bones, and cups containing olives and pumice found in the Built Well, Fountain, and Spring Chambers are widely regarded as offerings to a deity (Gesell 1985: cat. 134, 136). Given the importance of water in promoting safe passage to visiting traders, the uniqueness of these features, and the deposition of offerings, I have proposed that these installations served as receptacles for offerings to a water deity.

Similar sorts of offerings are known from earlier hydraulic installations in the Near East (Woolley 1954; Delougaz et al. 1967). In addition, the performance of rituals connected with these installations need not exclude practical use related to the industrial activities carried out in the "Palace." For example, at Ur, Woolley (1954:108-109) excavated a series of vertical terra-cotta drains dating to the Early Dynastic Period, which extended deep into the soil. They were pierced by percolation holes on the sides and served to facilitate drainage. Small, votive offering vessels and model terra-cotta boats found at the bottom were interpreted by Woolley as

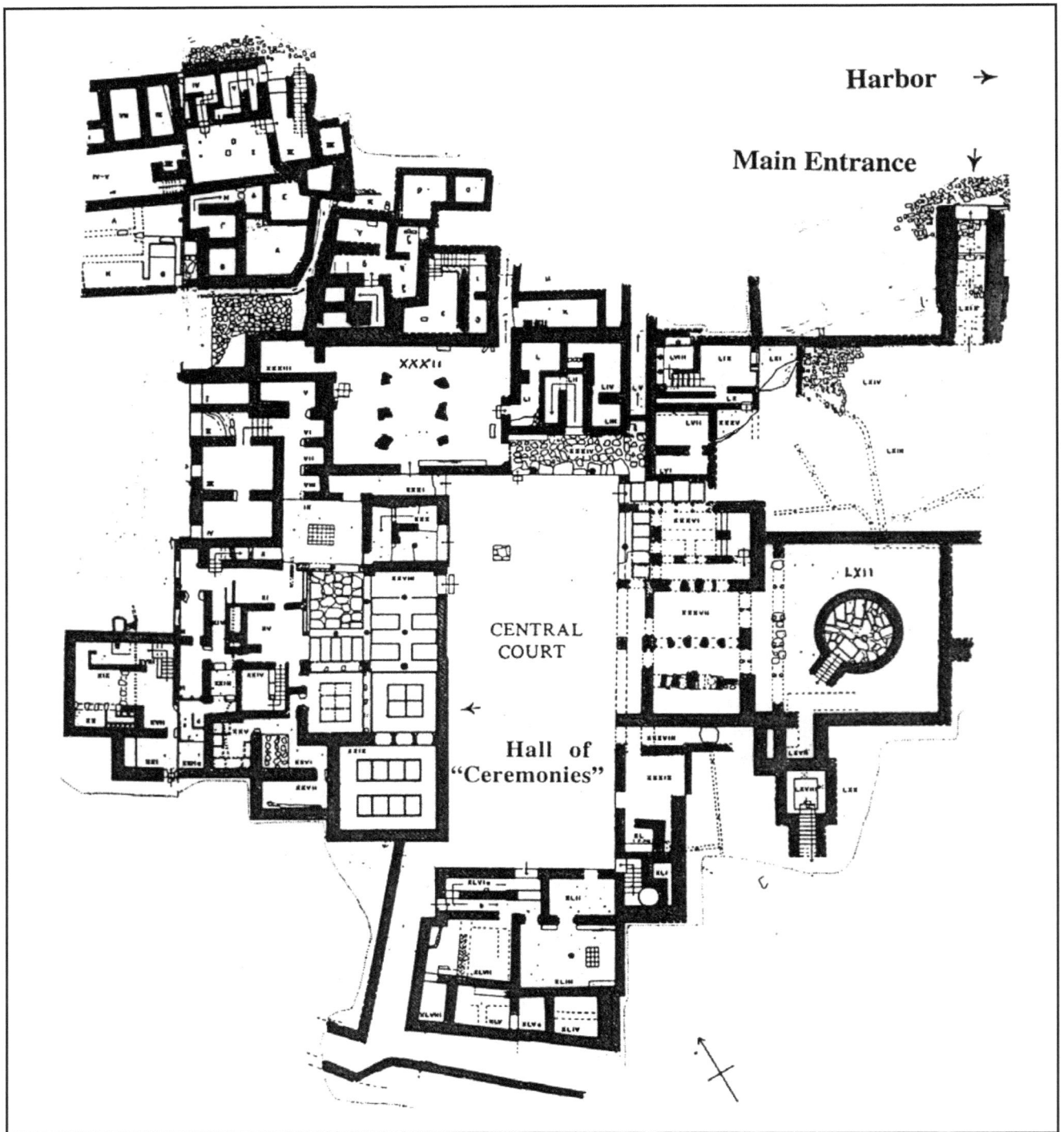

Fig. 7 Kato Zakro, "Palace" (after Platon 1985)

offerings to the god Ea (Sumerian En.Ki), lord of the waters under the earth. The character of the finds would seem to indicate their ritualistic nature.

Walter Burkert (1992) has tried to demonstrate that East-West connections went beyond accidental borrowings or contacts, but instead operated on the level of basic anthropological ideas as illustrated in more complex structures common to both Greek and Mesopotamian myths. His belief is that once the fact of transmission has been established, then further connections become more likely. Cook (1965:583-585) believed that the name 'Poseidon' was a another form of

Zeus, and later translated the name as Lord of the Earth (Potei-Dâs, dâ being the Doric for ge) which is equivalent in meaning to the name of the Sumerian god En.ki (lord of the earth). Interestingly, and perhaps not uncoincidentally, another Enki (Akk. Ea) was the god of the underground sea or fresh waters.

Later Linear B texts from both Pylos and Knossos mention Poseidon (Ventris and Chadwick 1956:126). As Burkert (1992:90) observes both Greek Poseidon and Sumerian Enki shared realms that were similar — if not the same. These commonalties in the meaning of the names and the functions of the deities and the similarities in the cult of Enki in terms of leaving offerings in hydraulic systems make it reasonable to suggest that the Minoans had a water deity as well. One might imagine offerings left in anticipation of arriving traders being received into the ceremonial halls of the "Palace" as the end point of a procession from the harbor. Such scenarios introduce the notion of agency and lived experience into the Minoan past.

CHANGE OVER TIME

Temporal changes in the architecture are seldom dealt with (cf. Driessen 1990; MacGillivray 1994; esp. Driessen and MacDonald 1997). Most chronological studies focus on pottery styles and others treat the Minoan past as idealized and fixed in an eternal spring. The "Palaces" literally float in a period that spans hundreds of years (e.g. Klynne 1998), from roughly 1900 BCE to 1450 BCE. This lengthy period is punctuated only by earthquake damage and rebuilding, the volcanic destruction of nearby Thera, and the destruction of Minoan civilization at the end of the Second Palace Period (ca. 1450 BCE).

Triangular causeways and round, stone lined receptacles were features of the West Courts at Mallia, Phaistos, and Knossos (Fig. 5) during the First Palace Period (ca. 1900-1700 BCE). As noted earlier, these courts have been interpreted as the sites of harvest festivals based on fresco evidence depicting a public celebration and their ease of accessibility (Marinatos 1987; also Davis 1987). The pits suggest granaries to some and the causeways are regarded as processional walkways (for full discussion and references, see Strasser 1998). Strasser has shown that the pits at Knossos and Phaistos lacked the sealant required to keep grain dry for long term storage. He favors a return to the rubbish pit interpretation favored by Evans (1935: 61ff) or the tree planter interpretation favored by Immerwahr (1983) and Preziosi (1983), and illustrated in a fresco from Knossos.

By the beginning of the Second Palace Period (ca. 1700-1450 BCE) these pit features remain unchanged at Mallia where the causeway continued to serve as the behavioral focus for a series of six roofed granaries (Marinatos 1987). The Mallia structures are quite different in actual appearance from the sunken pits at Knossos and Phaistos, although they look deceptively similar in plan. We might imagine scenarios where a procession of townspeople left offerings in gratitude for, or in hope of a fruitful harvest, or alternatively, we might imagine "Palace" dependants receiving a ration.

The pits and causeway were covered over at Phaistos, which was also rebuilt, while just the pits appear to have been filled in at Knossos. These changes indicate a transformation of the public rituals carried out in the West Courts at Knossos and Phaistos. The prevalence of bull imagery that now occurs at Knossos, but is absent elsewhere has been interpreted as a symbol of Knossian power (Hallager and Hallager 1995). I have suggested (Hitchcock 2000: 88-94) that such imagery might be connected to the worship of a male storm or weather god. The bull is a symbol of the contemporary Near Eastern storm god Adad (Collon 1987; 1994) as well as later, Greek Zeus. In turn, Zeus' birthplace and tomb are purported to be on Crete (Evans 1921:151-163; Watrous 1996) and he is first mentioned in a Linear B text from Knossos in which oil is being offered to di-ka-ta-jo di-we [Diktaian Zeus] (Ventris and Chadwick 1956:305-307, Fp 1).

Other categories of evidence such as the petrographic analysis that show particular shapes of coarse ware pottery originating in particular areas (Day 1991) and the identification of trade routes for *giali* obsidian (e.g. Betancourt 1997) indicate intra-island trade patterns with regional foci on the trade or redistribution of particular commodities. These economic foci may be tentatively connected to the performance of different rituals as best illustrated in the relationship between trade and water-related offerings at Kato Zakro.

STRUCTURED DISTRIBUTION

Several examples of recurring associations of certain types of architectural features, artifacts, and artifact assemblages, what I defined earlier as 'structured distribution' (Hitchcock 1994) have also been determined. These patterns are not rigid, but constitute what Yiannouli (1992:156) calls "a more general pattern of spatial affinity"... "cross-cutting the many diversities of Minoan architecture:" The most prominent example of this patterning is the recurring association of storage activities, pillars, and the double-axe.

The terms "Pillar Crypt" and "Pillar Cult" were coined by Arthur Evans (1899-1900: 32-34) in reference to small, dark rooms located near the storage magazines at Knossos (Fig. 8). The fact that many of these pillars do not seem to serve a structural purpose re-enforces their symbolic character. These rooms contained a central pillar with incised double-axe markings that suggested their sanctity to Evans. They occur in most palatial structures in close proximity to storage magazines. At some sites they also served as storerooms. Many carry incised markings, contain pyramid shaped stands for holding cult emblems, and some have cists cut into the floor that have been interpreted as places for the deposition of liquid offerings. Some also contain or are associated with rooms containing bronze figurines.

These small, dark pillar rooms or "Crypts" might be seen as an architectural representation of an aniconic deity worshipped as stalactites and stalagmites by the Minoans in sacred caves (cf. Evans 1901; Gesell 1985; Begg 1987; Marinatos 1987). Similar patterns of association are known from caves on Crete where double-axes and dagger blades were found embedded in stalactites (Tyree pers.comm.; Hogarth 1899-1900). Fresco fragments from Knossos also show double-axes embedded in column capitals (Evans 1930: figs. 319, 321).

I have suggested elsewhere (Hitchcock and Preziosi 1997) that there are social, cultural, and symbolic implications related to the Minoan preference for the pillar over other types of support, what J. Sackett (1990) calls isochrestic

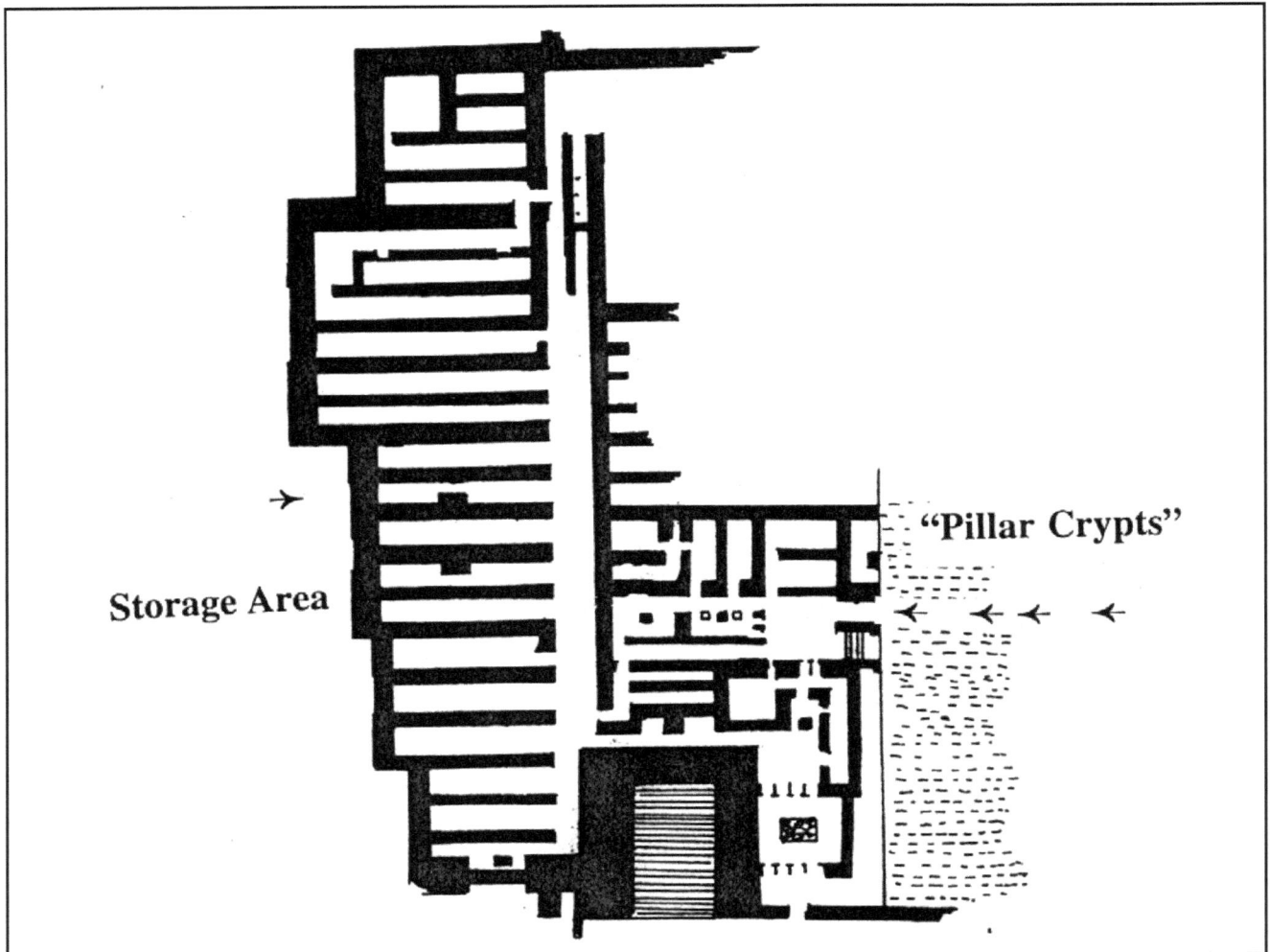

Fig. 8 Knossos, "Palace," West Wing, detail

variation. Isochrestism refers to the marked preference for a particular form or style when several options will serve the same function. The suggestion that "Pillar Crypts" were significant is based on the tendency of Minoan architects to locate pillar rooms or "Crypts" in a close spatial relationship to storage areas. By the Late Bronze Age at least thirteen Neo-Palatial buildings including "Palaces" and "Villas" (cf. Gesell 1985: 148, chart VII; also Hitchcock 1991a) incorporate a recurring pattern of architectural and spatial associations in the placement of pillar rooms, the double-axe as object or incised mark, and storage areas.

Based on this concept, we might choose to see a connection in the form of sanctification or perpetual liturgy and storage as indicated by the re-occurring association between pillars or "Pillar Crypts" and storerooms (Fig. 9). What I want to stress is the recurring relationship in the association of the pillar room with storage activities. In many Minoan buildings, these rooms had to be passed if not through, then at least beside in order to reach the storage area. In some of the "palaces," these routes were also twisted, narrow, and circuitous (Hallager 1987; also Begg 1987).

The recurring association of the pillar with storage areas in Minoan buildings might be seen as serving to protect or

sanctify the storage area while the stored goods could have been periodically released for expressions of communal celebration or solidarity (also Strasser 1998). It can be suggested that by the Late Bronze Age (ca. 1700-1450 BCE), the symbolic and social practices of village settlement in the Neolithic and Early Bronze Age were gradually monumentalized, transformed, politicized and brought under control of the central authorit(y)/(ies) of the Minoan "palace" system(s). I believe that ritual symbolism connected to the divine protection of stored goods had become a strategy and an ideology for social domination in the emergence, expansion, and continued existence of the Minoan "palaces." This continuity might be traced to an earlier practice of placing female figurines in the storage areas of dwellings, which was a widespread phenomenon as seen at EBA Myrtos, Fournou Korifi on Crete (cf. Warren 1972) and in Neolithic Europe (cf. Hodder 1990).

Continuity in terms of religious symbolism associated with the female on Crete was established in the form of the pillar as an architectonic representation of the stalagmites and stalactites that were venerated as aniconic (non-representational) images. Change occurred in terms of the politicization of that symbolism through its appropriation by the "palaces" and other "palatial" style "Villas." This was

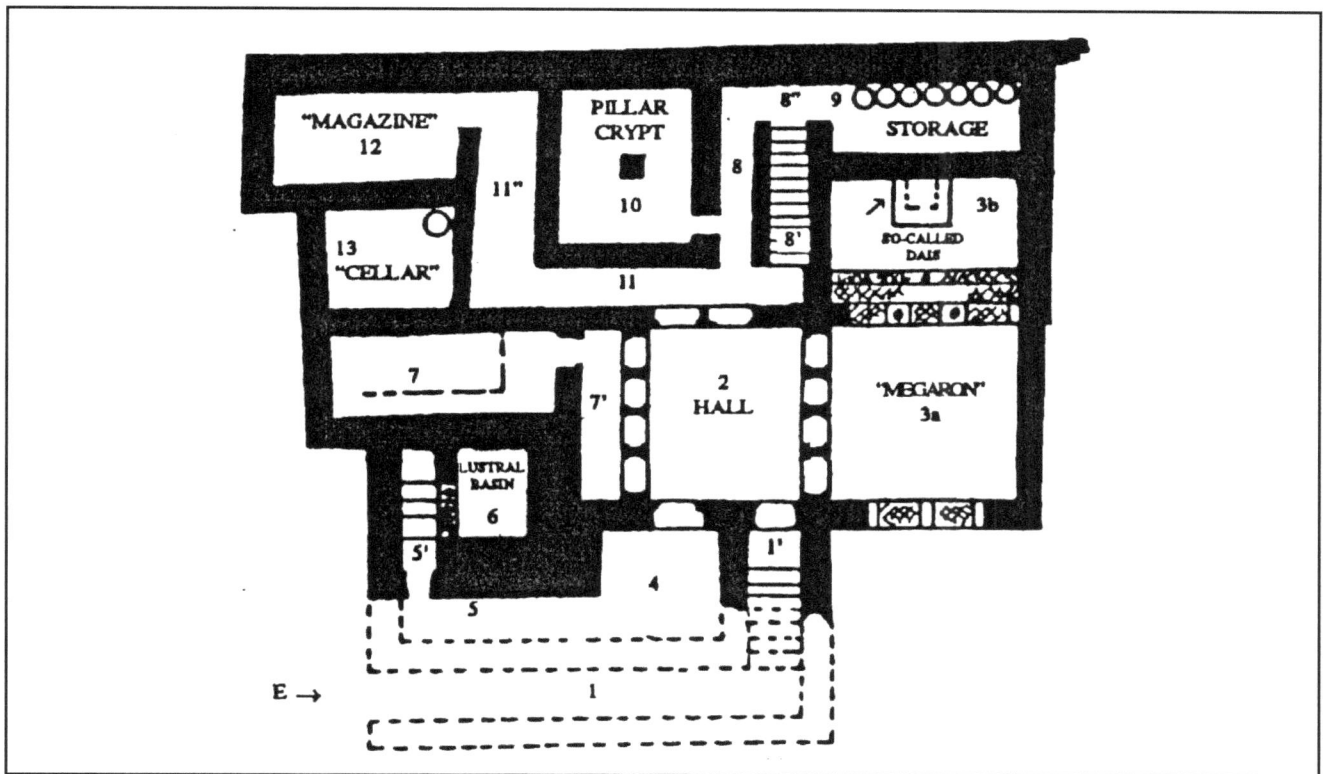

Fig. 9 Knossos, "House of the Chancel Screen" (after Evans 1928)

brought about through the active manipulation of visual and architectural symbols in a process that was dialectical and transformative (cf. Hodder 1987).

Other examples of patterning that I simply list here include the recurring association of basins with entry ways, the association of "Horns of Consecration" with entry ways and with "Tripartite Shrines," the recurring association of "Tripartite Shrines" and courts, and the association of archive rooms with the Minoan pier and door partition hall at Knossos, Haghia Triada, Mallia, and Kato Zakro (cf. Hitchcock 2000). That this last mentioned pattern occurs only at four sites re-enforces the notion that such halls were multivalent and given over to a variety of purposes: administrative, ceremonial, display, and religious rather than simply the residential quarters of Kings and Queens as assumed by Evans, Graham, and others. A pattern of ritual symbolism can be particularly connected with the West Wing as a locus of storage activities and "sacred economy" as illustrated by various associated small chambers with limited accessibility including "Pillar Crypts," "Tripartite Shrines," and "Bench Shrines."

CONCLUSIONS

To conclude, Umberto Eco (1994: 27) has stated that the process of deferral that has emerged out of Deconstruction results in a situation where every text means more, and the final meaning is an empty secret. However, "meaning more" is neither as empty nor devoid of communicative power as

the essentializing categories of similar forms, with their assumed, identical, simplistic, and static functions. With multiple entry ways, multiple passageways, and varying degrees of accessibility, Minoan buildings were simultaneously experienced by different living and breathing people in different ways. These range from the scribes who kept administrative records in Linear A, to the laborer who showed up to work the kiln at Phaistos, to the visiting trader who was welcomed in the so-called "Hall of Ceremonies" at Kato Zakro. In analyzing these buildings using approaches that might be termed 'contextual,' it is possible to interpret meaning as dispersed throughout a broad network of relationships. These relationships may be understood through a reconstruction of movement and experience, a careful examination of contextual evidence, relational differences, and structured distribution.

The worship of different deities or different aspects of a particular deity might be read from the performance of different rituals as orchestrated by architectural differences in the Minoan "Palaces," which may be best understood as administrative and cult centers. In some instances, specific suggestions were made based on analogous practices in the Near East that turn up again in later, Greece. A tentative attempt was made to relate distinct ritual practices to the socio-economic role the "Palaces" played in an intra-island trading network. It is possible that these architectural and social changes began in the "Neopalatial" Period in concert with the development of a more complex economic system.

These conclusions are not based on new evidence, but on new ways of *looking* at old evidence: emphasizing context over category, use over design, agency and experience over a passive and synoptic view, and structuration over semiotics. By taking into account context, particularly the role of space in establishing relationships among various components of the built environment, and rejecting many of the universalizing assumptions underlying the accepted understanding of Minoan architecture and society, it is possible to bring the past into a more active relationship with the present.

In stressing context and the phenomenology of lived experience in the past, I have tried to account for the use of Minoan buildings in the past. Part of the purpose of this investigation was to examine the relation or rupture (cf. de Certeau 1988), which sometimes unites and sometimes holds apart the past and the present: to open up this imperfect past that is always subject to completion by human agency in the present and in the future (see Shanks and Tilley 1987: 20ff.). In trying to return Minoan architecture to its past context, I have tried to emphasize the 'Otherness' of the Minoan past. In this way, the past might be treated as an active agent for change in the present rather than what Julian Thomas calls "History-As-Analogue or History as Same" (for example Thomas 1992) or what Timothy Yates (1990b) calls history as "Mirror Image."

Opening the study of the Minoan past to a plurality of approaches will necessarily result in a plurality of interpretations. Such an approach resists closure. Looking at entire buildings rather than at different clusters of rooms as I have done here might result in a different reading. In any event, the ironic status of such categories becomes apparent when, in looking at a room in its context, it becomes necessary to break out of my own constructed categories in order to understand how a particular space functioned in relationship to a series of connected spaces.

In opening out the field of meanings for Minoan Crete, I am attempting to keep the buildings, their spaces, and their contents "in play." Rather than closing with a totalizing narrative, we might begin a genuine project of writing a past and future history. Donald Preziosi (1995:15) has observed that "the modern invention of art (and I would include archaeology) and its 'history' - and of museology and museography - have not only been central to the fabrication and maintenance of modernity, but have also been ceaselessly enabling of all of modernity's various modernisms, including its periodically heralded aftermaths." While the invention of these disciplines to insure the (re)production of the past is modern, the practice of reproducing the past in the present to become the future is not.

From the earliest of written records, the present has been conceived as contingent on the past. It is no accident that some of our earliest words for future: IGIR.UD [Sumerian]; warkat ummi [Akkadian]; and appa siwatt [Hittite] mean the "back of the day" or "that which is behind you" (also discussed in Puhvel 1984:97-98; Schnapp 1996:30-31). By writing histories that are open-ended, plural, polyphonic, and 'Other' it will be possible to construct sets of new and diverse co-mingling historical traditions representative of a multi-cultural society. To paraphrase Derrida (1968:18), such a project should attempt to exhaust all the heuristic and critical resources of the sign in all domains and contexts with everything that such a strategy would imply.

Louise A. Hitchcock,
Research Associate,
Cotsen Institute of Archaeology, UCLA

Abbreviation used

Function Palaces Hägg, R. and Marinatos, N. (eds) (1987) *The Function of the Minoan Palaces*. Stockholm: Svenska Institutet i Athen.

Bibliography

Begg, D.J.I. (1987) "Continuity In the West Wing at Knossos," *Function Palaces*: 179-184.

Betancourt, P.P. (1997) "The Trade Route for Ghyali Obsidian," *Aegaeum* 16: 171-176.

Boyd-Hawes, H.A. (1904) "Gournia, Report of the American Exploration Society's Excavations at Gournia, Crete, 1901-1903," *Transactions, Department of Archaeology, University of Pennsylvania*. I.1: 37-41.

Branigan, K. (1987) "The Economic Role of the First Palaces," *Function Palaces*:245-249.

Burkert, W. (1992) *The Orientalizing Revolution: Near Eastern influence on Greek Culture in the Early Archaic Age*. trans. by W. Burkert and M.E. Pinder. Cambridge, Ma.: Harvard University Press.

de Certeau, M. (1988) *The Writing of History*. trans. by T. Conley. New York: Columbia University Press.

Collon, D. (1987) *First Impressions: Cylinder Seals in the Ancient Near East*. Chicago: University of Chicago Press.

Collon, D. (1994) "Bull-Leaping in Syria," *Ägypten und Levante: Internationale Zeitschrift für ägyptische Archäologie und deren Nachbargebiete* 4:81-85.

Cook, A.B. (1965) *Zeus: A Study in Ancient Religion*. Vol. II.1 New York: Biblo and Tannen.

Davis, E.N. (1987) "The Knossos miniature frescoes and the function of the central courts," *Function Palaces*: 157-161.

Day, P.M. (1991) *A Petrographic Approach to the Study of Pottery In Neopalatial East Crete*. Unpublished Ph.D. Dissertation, University of Cambridge.

Delougaz, P., H. Hill, and S. Lloyd (1967) "Private Houses and Graves in the Diyala Region," *Oriental Institute Publications* 88.

Derrida, J. (1968) "Semiology and Grammatology: Interview with Julia Kristeva," rpt. In J. Derrida, (1981 [1972]) *Positions*. trans. by A. Bass. Chicago: UCP, 15-36.

Driessen, J. (1990) "An Early Destruction In the Mycenaean Palace at Knossos," *AAL Monographiae 2* Leuven.

Driessen, J. and MacDonald, C. (1997) "The Troubled Island. Minoan Crete before and after the Santorini Eruption," *Aegaeum* 17.

Eco, U. (1994 [1990]) *The Limits of Interpretation*. Bloomington and Indianapolis: Indiana University Press.

Evans, A.J. (1900-1901) "The Palace of Knossos: Provisional Report of the Excavations for the year 1901," *Annual of the British School at Athens* 7:1-120.

Evans, A.J. (1901) "Mycenaean Tree and Pillar Cult," *Journal of Hellenic Studies* 21: 99-204.

Evans, A.J. (1921) *The Palace of Minos at Knossos*. Vol. I London: Macmillan and Co.

Evans, A.J. (1928) *The Palace of Minos at Knossos*. Vol. II London: Macmillan and Co.

Evans, A.J. (1930) *The Palace of Minos at Knossos*. Vol. III London: Macmillan and Co.

Evans, A.J. (1935) *The Palace of Minos at Knossos*. Vol. IV London: Macmillan and Co.

Gesell, G.C. (1985) "Town, Palace, and House Cult In Minoan Crete," *Studies in Mediterranean Archaeology* 67 Göteborg: Paul Åströms Förlag.

Giddens, A. (1993 [1984]) *The Constitution of Society: Outline of the Theory of Structuration*. Cambridge: Polity Press.

Graham, J.W. (1957) "The Central Court as the Minoan Bull-Ring," *American Journal of Archaeology* 61: 255-262.

Graham, J.W. (1987 [1962]) *Palaces of Crete*. Princeton: PUP.

Hallager, E. (1987) "A 'Harvest Festival Room' In the Minoan palaces? An architectural study of the Pillar Crypt Area at Knossos," *Function Palaces*: 169-177.

Hallager, B.P. and Hallager, E. (1995) "The Knossian Bull - Political Propaganda In Neo-Palatial Crete?," *Aegaeum* 12: 547-556.

Hitchcock, L.A. (1994) "The Minoan Hall System: Writing the Present Out of the Past," in M. Locock (ed) *Meaningful Architecture: Social Interpretations of Buildings. Worldwide Archaeology Series*. Aldershot, Hampshire: Avebury, 14-43.

Hitchcock, L.A. (1997) "Space, the Final Frontier: Chaos, Meaning, and Grammatology In Minoan Archi(text)ure," *Archaeological News* Vol. 22: 46-53, 134-142.

Hitchcock, L.A. (2000) *Minoan Architecture: A Contextual Analysis. Studies in Mediterranean Archaeology Pocket-Book 155*. Jonsered: Paul Åströms Förlag.

Hitchcock, L.A. (2001) "Naturalizing the Cultural: Architectonicized Landscape as Ideology in Minoan Crete," Unpublished Paper presented at Building Communities: House, Settlement and Society in the Aegean and Beyond, Cardiff University, April 17-21, 2001. (Typrewritten)

Hodder, I. (1982) "Theoretical Archaeology: A Reactionary View," in I. Hodder, (ed) *Symbolic and Structural Archaeology*. Cambridge: CUP, 1-16.

Hodder, I. (1987a) "The Contextual Analysis of Symbolic Meanings." In I. Hodder (ed) *The Archaeology of Contextual Meanings*. Cambridge: CUP, 1-10.

Hodder, I. (1990b) *The Domestication of Europe*. Oxford: Basil Blackwell.

Hogarth, D.G. (1899-1901) "The Dictaean Cave," *Annual of the British School at Athens* 6: 94-116.

S.A. Immerwahr, (1983) "The people in the frescoes," in O. Krzyszkowska and L. Nixon, eds., *Cambridge Colloquiem on Minoan Society* Bristol: Bristol Classical Press, 143-153.

Jameson, F. (1992; 1991) *Postmodernism, or, The Cultural Logic of Late Capitalism*. Durham: Duke University Press.

Johnson, M. (1993) *Housing Culture: Traditional architecture in an English landscape*. London: UCL Press Limited.

Klynne, A. (1998) "Reconstructions of Knossos: Artists' Impressions, Archaeological Evidence and Wishful Thinking," *Journal of Mediterranean Archaeology* 11: 206-29.

Levi, D. (1981) "Festos E La Civilta Minoica," *Incunabula Graeca* 66 Rome: 1981. I.1 Plates; I.2 Plans.

MacGillivray, J.A. (1994) "The Early History of the Palace at Knossos (MM I-II)," in D. Evely, H. Hughes-Brock; and N. Momigliano (eds) *Knossos: A Labyrinth of History. Papers presented in honour of Sinclair Hood*. Oxford and Bloomington, In.: Oxbow Books and The David Brown Book Company, 45-55.

Marinatos, N. (1984) *Art and Religion In Thera*. Athens: Mathioulakis.

Marinatos, N. (1987) "Public Festivals In the West Courts of the Palaces," *Function Palaces*:135-143.

Marinatos, N. (1993) *Minoan Religion*. Columbia, South Carolina: University of South Carolina Press.

Marinatos, N. and Hägg, R. (1986) "On the Ceremonial Function of the Minoan Polythyron," *Opuscula Atheniensia* 16: 58-73.

Moore, H.L. (1985) *Space, text and gender: An anthropological study of the Marakwet of Kenya*. Cambridge: CUP.

Moore, H. L. (1990) "Paul Ricoeur: Action, Meaning and Text," in C. Tilley (ed) (1990) *Reading Material Culture*. Oxford: Basil Blackwell, 85-120.

Pernier, L. and Banti, L. (1951) *Il Palazzo Minoico di Festòs, II*. Rome: La Libreria Dello Stato.

Platon, N. (1985 [1971]) *Zakros: The Discovery of a Lost Palace of Ancient Crete*. Amsterdam: Adolf M. Hakkert.

Preziosi, D. (1983) *Minoan Architectural Design*. Berlin: Mouton.

Preziosi, D. (1995) "Museology and Museography," *Art Bulletin*. 13-15.

Puhvel, J. (1984) *Hittite Etymological Dictionary*. Berlin: Mouton.

Richards, C.C. and Thomas, J.S. (1984) "Ritual activity and structured deposition In later Neolithic Wessex," in R.J. Bradley and J. Gardiner (eds) *Neolithic Studies*. Oxford: *British Archaeological Reports* 133, 189-218.

Sackett, J. (1990) "Style and ethnicity in archaeology: the case for isochrestism," in M. Conkey and C.A. Hastorf (eds) *The Uses of Style in Archaeology*, Cambridge: CUP, 32-43.

Samovar, L.A. and Porter, R.E. (1997) *Intercultural Communication: A Reader*. Belmont, Ca. Wadsworth Publishing Co.

Schnaap, A. (1996) *The Discovery of the Past*. London: British Museum Press.

Shanks, M. and Tilley, C. (1987) *Reconstructing Archaeology*. Cambridge: CUP.

Shanks, M. and Tilley, C. (1989) "Archaeology into the 1990's," *Norwegian Archaeology Review* 1-54.

Shaw, J.W. (1971) "Minoan Architecture: Materials and Techniques" *Annuario* 49.

Strasser, T. (1998) "Storage and States on Prehistoric Crete: The Function of the Koulouas in the First Minoan Palaces," *JMA* 10: 73-100.

Thomas, J. (1992) *Rethinking the Neolithic*. Cambridge: CUP.

Tilley, C. (1994) *A Phenomenology of Landscape: Places, Paths and Monuments*. Oxford: Berg Publishers.

Ventris, M. and Chadwick, J. (1956) *Documents In Mycenaean Greek*. Cambridge: CUP.

Warren, P. (1972) *Myrtos: An Early Bronze Age Settlement in Crete. Annual of the British School at Athens Supplement* 7 Oxford: Thames and Hudson.

Watrous, L.V. (1996) "The Cave Sanctuary of Zeus at Psychro: A Study of Extra-Urban Sanctuaries in Minoan and Early Iron Age Crete," *Aegaeum* 15.

Wiener, M.H. (1987) "Trade and rule in palatial Crete," *Function Palaces*: 261-267.

Woolley, C.L. (1954) *Excavations at Ur: a record of twelve years' work*. London: E. Benn.

Yates, T. (1990a) "Jaques Derrida: 'There is Nothing Outside of the Text,'" in C. Tilley (ed) Reading Material Culture. Oxford: Basil Blackwell: 206-280.

Yates, T. (1990b) "Archaeology Through the Looking Glass," In I. Bapty and T. Yates (eds) *Archaeology After Structuralism*. London: Routledge, 154-202.

Yiannouli, E. (1992) *Reason in Architecture: the Component of Space. A Study of Domestic and Palatial Buildings In Bronze Age Greece*. Unpublished Ph.D. Dissertation, University of Cambridge.List of Illustrations.

THE RHETORIC OF BUILDING CONSTRUCTION

Barbro SANTILLO FRIZELL

Si monumentum requiris, circumspice
Sir Christopher Wren

Abstract: At Mycenae during the Late Bronze Age, walls and buildings were constructed on a monumental scale previously unknown in Greece and never surpassed again in its history. Due to its grandeur and abundant use of enormous conglomerate blocks, the masonry style was named Cyclopean by the ancients. The article focuses on the role of monuments in the landscape, showing how during a period of no more than a hundreds years the surrounding territory of Mycenae was transformed into a huge building site. Here the high technology, advanced logistics and organisation required to erect these monuments were displayed in public, thus functioning as a far-reaching vehicle for royal propaganda.

In the display of the building operations the surrounding landscape with its particular morphological and geological characteristics played an important role. The procedure of building monuments formed an integrated part of the visual images that the ruling elite at Mycenae aimed at in their political propaganda. Through an anlysis of the building procedure I will show that the constructive choises was an intentional message focussing more attention on the buildings during construction than on the finished product.

CONSTRUCTING A LANDSCAPE OF POWER

The citadel of Mycenae is situated on a low knoll protected by Mt Ayios Elias (750 m) to the north and Mt Zara (666 m) to the south (Fig. 1). Its difensive and offensive strategic position has been important for its dominating role in the history of Late Bronze Age Greece. In addition to the favourable topographical setting a highly developed infrastructure was constructed. Without this organisatorial ability its leading position in the political history would have been impossible to keep. Fresh water supply to the citadel and the settlement outside the walls was secured through pipe-lines, cisterns and fountains. Communication was secured through a developed system of well-built roads, which also speeded the movements of soldiers. These were protected by defensive systems, such as watch-towers and walls. Through military high ways it controlled the three major pass routes connecting the Gulf of Corinth with the Gulf of the

Argolid. On the three-dimensional rendering, which has been produced for this article to illustrate the topographical situation at Mycenae, the roads surveyed by Lieutenant Steffen during 1881-82 are marked (Fig.1). Steffen's *Hochstrasse 1* is the road which runs directly below the northern wall of the citadel going east following the hill slopes of Kondovouni (Agrilo Vunaki on Steffen's map) and Koutzoyianni - further north it runs thorough the middle of the three valleys, which connect the Argive plain with Corinth. *Hochstrasse 2* runs north following the foot of Mt Ayios Elias. At a lower level, west of this road were identified traces of a road, which probably connected Mycenae with the *Hochstrasse 3*, which run through the pass of Dervenaki, Nemea and further north. (Steffen (1884: 8-9). *Hochstrasse 4* lead from Mycenae to the Heraion, a focal place of religious activties in the Argolid from prehistoric times and onwards. It further connected Mycenae with the centres in the coastal area. There are further several roads which passes through the inhabited area and from the plain west of Mycenae leading to the citadel. I will turn to a discussion of these below.

The well conceived network of roads was constructed for a variety of functions: communication, transport, consolidation and control of the territory, religious, military manifestations and other ceremonial purposes. The roads and the bridges spanning the ravines are remarkbly well-built and substantial parts of them can, after more than three thousands years, be identified in the landscape and can be walked.

From the top of Mt Ayios Elias (750 m) is free sight to Corinth to the north and the sea with the harbours of Nauplion and Tiryns. Its role as watching post and place for beacon signalling is evident and logical considering its height and position which permits such visibility. Traces of structures

GREECE

MYCENAE

Map

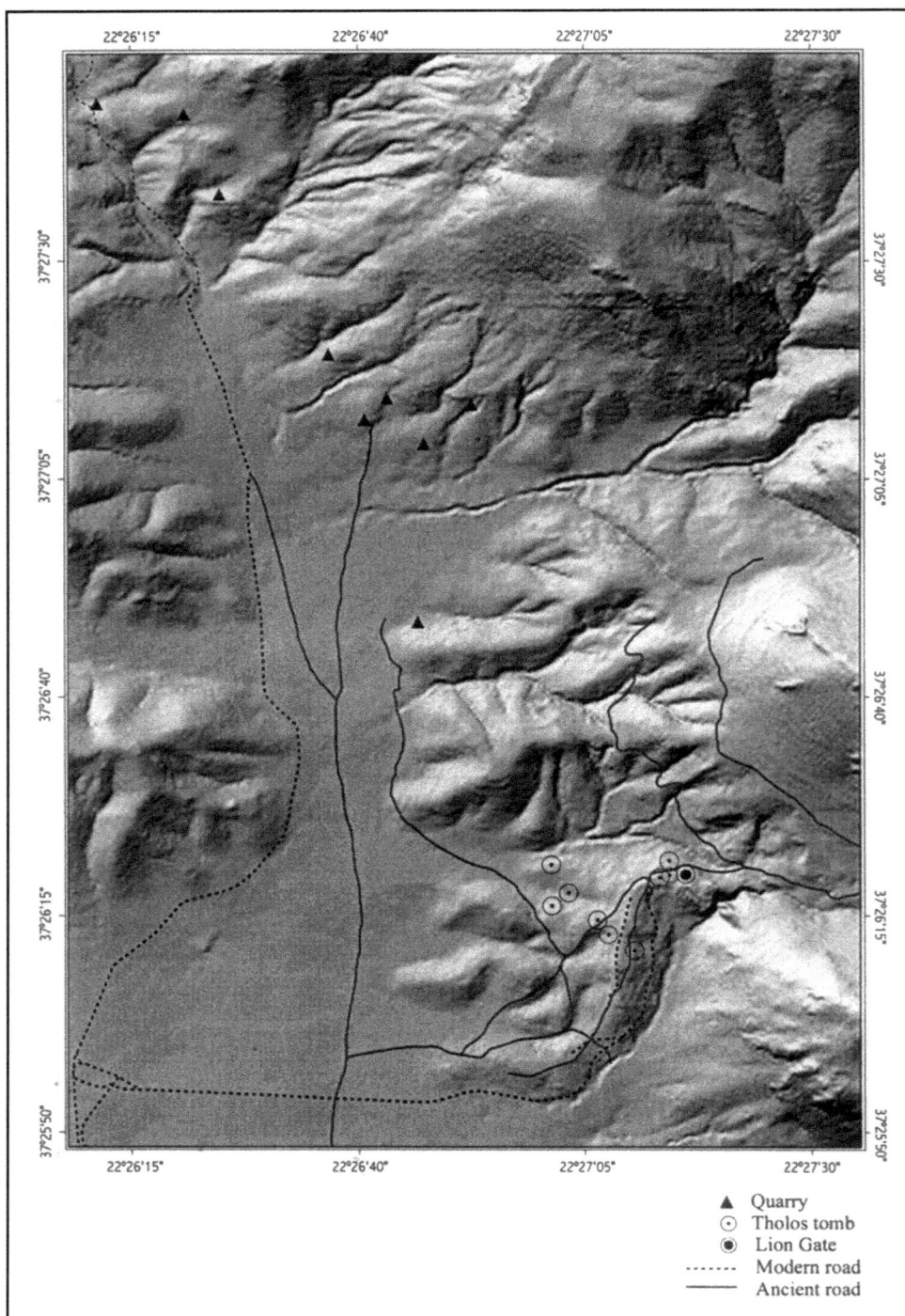

Fig. 1. Shaded relief model of the project area. The model was created by scanning the four Greek military maps in scale 1:5000, Korinthos-Nauplion, Sheet 6375, 1,3,5,7. The pictures were thereafter manually digitalized with the program R2V from Able Software Co. The software programs Surfer and Arc View were used to do the modelling. By Sölve Eriksson, Söderhamn 2000.

of Cyclopean masonry on its top bear witness of permanent structures and how it functioned during the night with fire signal is reflected in the beautiful lines of the classical drama Agamemnon of Aischylos (280-315) "Kindling high with unstinted force a mighty beard of flame, they sped it forward that, as it blazed, it o'erpassed even the headland that looks upon the Saronic gulf; until it swooped down when it reached the look-out, nigh unto our city, upon the peak of Arachnaeus; and next upon this roof of the Atreaidae it leapt, yon fire not undescended from the Idaean flame."

Mycenae became the leading city of the Argolid during the Late Bronze Age (1600 -1100 BC). The Homeric epithet "rich in gold" is a suitable epithet for the Early Mycenaean period, from which belong the rich shaft graves excavated by Schliemann. The "well-built" and "broad-paved" city belong to the Late Mycenaen period. This is the time of its greatest political expansion and the era of the "tholos tombs dynasty". The socio-political context had then radically changed. Mycenae held a leading position, not only in Mainland Greece but also in the Aegean and beyond. The display of power through building which is manifest during this period had far-reaching targets.

Contrary to many other famous Bronze Age places, Mycenae was never completely buried over time and its monumental ruins have always constituted a visible past in the landscape. The memory of its glorious past lived on throughout the history of ancient Greece, kept alive through the myths which were a common cultural property for all Greeks independently of where they lived. During the eighth century BC, the Homeric myths were reactivated, probably through the spreading of the epics, and a cult to the Homeric hero Agamemnon was introduced at Mycenae. In classical times when the great Attic dramas echoed its legendary history, Mycenae was destroyed by its enemy city, Argos, and lost its former importance. During the Hellenistic period when the old city was turned into an Argive *kôme*, a revitalisation can be noticed. There is a renewed interest for the old Bronze Age monuments, such as the tholos tombs, which could be interpreted as the remains of cultic activities (Alcock, 1997, 24). The old prehistoric city walls were restored and reused and a substantial enlargment of the wall was built. A most fascinating way chosen by the inhabitants to display the links with their glorious past was the building of a theatre upon the monumental tholos tomb of Clytemnestra. The cavea of the Hellenistic theatre was centrally placed directly upon the dromos of the monument with the enormous mound of the tomb, attributed to Atreus, to the right and a splendid view of the Argive plain down to the coast. In this dramatic setting one can only imagine what feelings a performance of the drama Agamemnon would evoke.

The memories were kept in the local traditions but took on a more mythical flavour as times passed on. During the Graeco-Roman period, local traditions and folklore finally ascribed Mycenae's prehistory to a mythical past and attributed its monumental buildings to the cyclops, giants of Greek mythology (Pausanias II, 16.5-7). The Bronze Age monuments could thus live on and be charged with new and different symbolic values according to their role and cognitive function for the people living and visiting the place.

BUILDING MONUMENTS

In a rhetorical context the role of the citadel would be of primary importance being the centre for elite manifestations. Here foreign embassies were received, religious processions and military ceremonials performed, activies which can be more easily imgained through reflections in artefactual remains from the Mycenaean period, such as wall paintings, vases, seals and similar art objects. I will here focus on the role of building construction in such a context and I will concentrate on the tholos tombs. At Mycenae the tholoi reached a level of artistic refinement, technological advancement and rhetorical expression as in no other site, only at Orchomenos in Boetia there is a single tholos of this standard. In the following discussion I will focus on the propagandistic role of the monument during construction, aspects that in previous research have been ignored.

The tholos tomb as grave type was widely spread in Late Bronze Age Greece; more than a hundred such tombs of varying sizes and degrees of refinement have been found, dating from the Early to the Late Mycenaean Period. Most of them are quite modest in size and architectural refinement. At Mycenae nine tholoi, more than at any other site, were built. Here the largest and most monumental dry masonry domes were constructed. This shows the importance of the place but also explains why the development towards the monumentalisation of this particular building type took place here, where the building tradition was firmly rooted. They were lavishly decorated on the facade with stone columns and other decorative sculptured elements, and were meant to be visible - at least for some time. The concept was an underground chamber modelled after the more frequent rock-cut chamber tomb. After the burial the tombs were closed; the doorways and corridors were covered with earth and hidden in the landscape.

All the tombs at Mycenae had been opened and emptied during antiquity and some were already then shown to tourists and visitors. When the ancient traveller Pausanias visited Mycenae towards the middle of the 2nd century A.D., the local guides indicated three of the most monumental tombs. Two of these are situated close to the entrance gate of the citadel, the so called Tomb of Clytemnestra, the wife of Agamemnon, and the Tomb of Aigisthos, her lover. These names, transmitted to us through Pausanias' work are the conventional names used also today. The so called "Treasury of Atreus" is here called the Atreus Tomb. It is built in the ridge south west of the citadel and is the largest and most monumental of all tombs. To the north of the road leading to the citadel lies the Lion Tomb, which is only slightly smaller than the Atreus Tomb. Due to its ruined state - the whole upper part of the dome has fallen in - it has been given less attention.

Three of the tombs are outstanding in their size, monumentality and architectural refinement: the Lion Tomb, Atreus Tomb and Clytemnestra Tomb. The cupola of the Atreus Tomb has a diameter of 14.60 m and 13.20 m in height. The Lion Tomb has a slightly smaller diameter, 14.38 m, and have probably been more or less the same in height. The tomb of Clytemnestra is 13.40 m in diameter. These are built in the dry masonry technique with well-dressed, ashlar blocks of local limestone and conglomerate.

Geology gave the architects and builders the material necessary to ideate buildings of a monumentality hitherto unknown in Greece and which was never surpassed again in its history. The geological basement of the area around Mycenae is dominated by rocks from two isopic zones (Higgins & Higgins 1996: 45-50). The knoll of Mycenae and the steep hills to its north and south is composed of Late Triassic to Middle Jurassic limestones. A part of the walls of the city, buildings and the tholos tombs were built of this limestone, which was quarried from the foot of the hills of Mt Ayios Elias. The lower hills west, north and south of Mycenae is made of a very different rock. It is composed of marls and conglomerates which were deposited here by rivers and streams that flowed into the graben during the Late

Pliocene to Pleistocene periods. This bed rock contains a very well cemented conglomerate which have different properties than the limestone and which the ancient people took advantage of in constructing their buildings and city walls. Since the conglomerate has much more widely spaced joints in its bedding it was available in much larger blocks than the limestone. These blocks, still visible in the surface, were quarried in several quarries along the lower edge of the mountain range leading north from Mycenae. These can still be seen today. The exploitation of this stone has given the character and style of the masonry at Mycenae. Due to its grandeur in style and the abundant use of enormous blocks the masonry style was named Cyclopean by the ancients (Pausanias II, 16. 6), attributing the construction of walls and buildings to giants.

Conglomerate was used extensively in the citadel, especially for lintels and door-posts, but also at other particular delicate points in the constructions where extra large blocks were needed. Thanks to the extensive use of very large blocks as building material, the prehistoric structures have been little disturbed in later times, in contrast to the Classical and Hellenistic buildings and walls, from which stone blocks have been removed to be reused in churches and other buildings.

The nine tholoi at Mycenae were classified and dated by Wace on the basis of his observations on the appearance of the material and masonry. His chronological model starts with the more primitive tombs, built of field-stones or roughly dressed blocks and ends with the most elaborated and costly tombs, which were built with well dressed ashlar blocks (Wace 1925: 284-386). The underlying concept of his classification and the evolutionary chain proposed by him does not take into account the structural content, ignoring for example that the ratio thickness/tholos diameter in the Lion Tomb (which he classifies as earlier than the Atreus Tomb), being 0,38/14,38m, is three times less than the Atreus Tomb. In terms of absolute values the Lion Tomb is a more daring and difficult enterprise and therefore required a higher skill and a deeper knowledge of structural matters. This fact has no chronological implications, but it shows that technological development can not be evaluated on the basis of the appearance of the masonry style. In the same publication Holland wrote an architectural note confirming the position taken by Wace, but he also writes: "It is a difference (in material and workmanship) which must be due either to a development in time or to a very considerable difference in the wealth of the constructors" (Wace 1925: 396). The economical aspect is not further developed and Wace's tripartite classification scheme based on what is commonly called stylistical criteria is still the commonly accepted and widely spread version.

The find material can not support his elaborated theory; it does indicate that a group of tombs are built earlier but it does not support the detailed classification scheme and cannot sustain the chronological implications in his two later groups. The detailed chronology suggested for the tombs at Mycenae has no bearing for the tholoi in the nearby Berbati (Santillo Frizell 1984a, 32) and Dendra (Persson 1931, 24) and I think that is more likely the situation also at Mycenae. My discussion on the tholoi will not focus on chronology and "style" but on technological, topographical, economical and socio-political parameters.

The nine tholoi are situated in the cemeteries and along the roads (Fig. 1). The two oldest tombs are situated closed to the old roads leading up to Mycenae from the southwest and northwest. The most monumental tombs are situated in close proximity to the citadel; these are the Lion Tomb, Clytemnestras' and Aigisthos'. The biggest of them all, the Atreus Tomb has a dominating position on the modern road leading up to the citadel (Fig. 2 a-b). Why it is placed here and not elsewhere is a crucial issue and I will turn to that below.

In order to understand the topographical setting of the monumental tholos tombs and to understand their propagandistic value in their socio-political context, the construction procedure must be understood. The construction and the statics of the Mycenaean tholos have been more fully described and analyzed in previous articles in this research project and will not be repeated here (Santillo Frizell & Santillo 1984b; Santillo 1986). The results of our previous research form the necessary background for my interpretation of the propagandistic function of the monuments.

We must assume that before the actual construction, a plan and a program had been prepared for the construction project on the basis of various parameters, such as economical, technical, logistical and individual preferences. The location of the site for the tomb was of outmost importance. From a technical point of view, a place must be chosen where it was possible to excavate a trench big enough to construct the lower part of the dome inside. The means of transport, roads and distance from the quarries had to be considered. Its physical relation to the citadel and palace in its role as a funerary and propagandistic monument had bearing on the reception of the monument. In this aspect the Atreus Tomb can be said to have fulfilled all requirements keeping its position as an outstanding monument throughout its history. The organisation of this building site required the highest level of logistic and technical expertise.

Large blocks of conglomerate were used abundantly in the tholoi. The reason for this was to produce ashlars of greater size which increased the strength of the wall. Since a wall is a composite structural element constituted of ashlars and "empty" joints, the greater the number of joints in a wall, the less is its strength and durability. The stomion and the flanking walls of the tholoi had to be particularly strong, because, apart from the concentration of stresses, they had to provide an efficient support for the scaffolding and struts for the manoeuvres. In the Lion Tomb, the junctions between the small limestone ashlars and the big conglomerate blocks are particularly significant and show how well the Mycenaean master-builders understood the stress distribution (Fig. 4). Particularly large blocks were needed to cover the stomion gap in the tholoi. Usually three or four blocks were used for this purpose. The solution chosen for the stomion in the Atreus Tomb was only two blocks. The inner block is a gigantic one which had been dressed according to double curves of the interior walls of the cupola. This block, which

Fig. 2a-b. The Atreus Tomb and the modern road leading up to the citadel. This follows the ancient route that should have been laid out for the transport of the large lintels blocks. Photo R. Santillo.

is almost 8 m in length and 5 m in breadth, weighs over 120 tons. Such a heavy block had never been placed or erected in Greece before, and it was never repeated again in Greek history (Fig. 5).

It does not require too much imagination to understand that the most difficult task and delicate operation in the whole building procedure was to handle this enormous block! First it had to be extracted from the quarry and the interior profile had to be dressed; then it had to be put on a sledge and transported to the building site, where it was positioned over an empty gap in the stomion walls, temporarily buttressed by a wooden frame-work. The placement of the enormous block in the Atreus Tomb goes beyond all practical building needs, and the reason for choosing such a solution must be sought elsewhere. Why did the architects at Mycenae choose an almost impossible constructive solution when building this funerary monument? The commissioners of the monumental tholos tombs were surely members of the ruling elite. Only at that level in society could a building enterprise

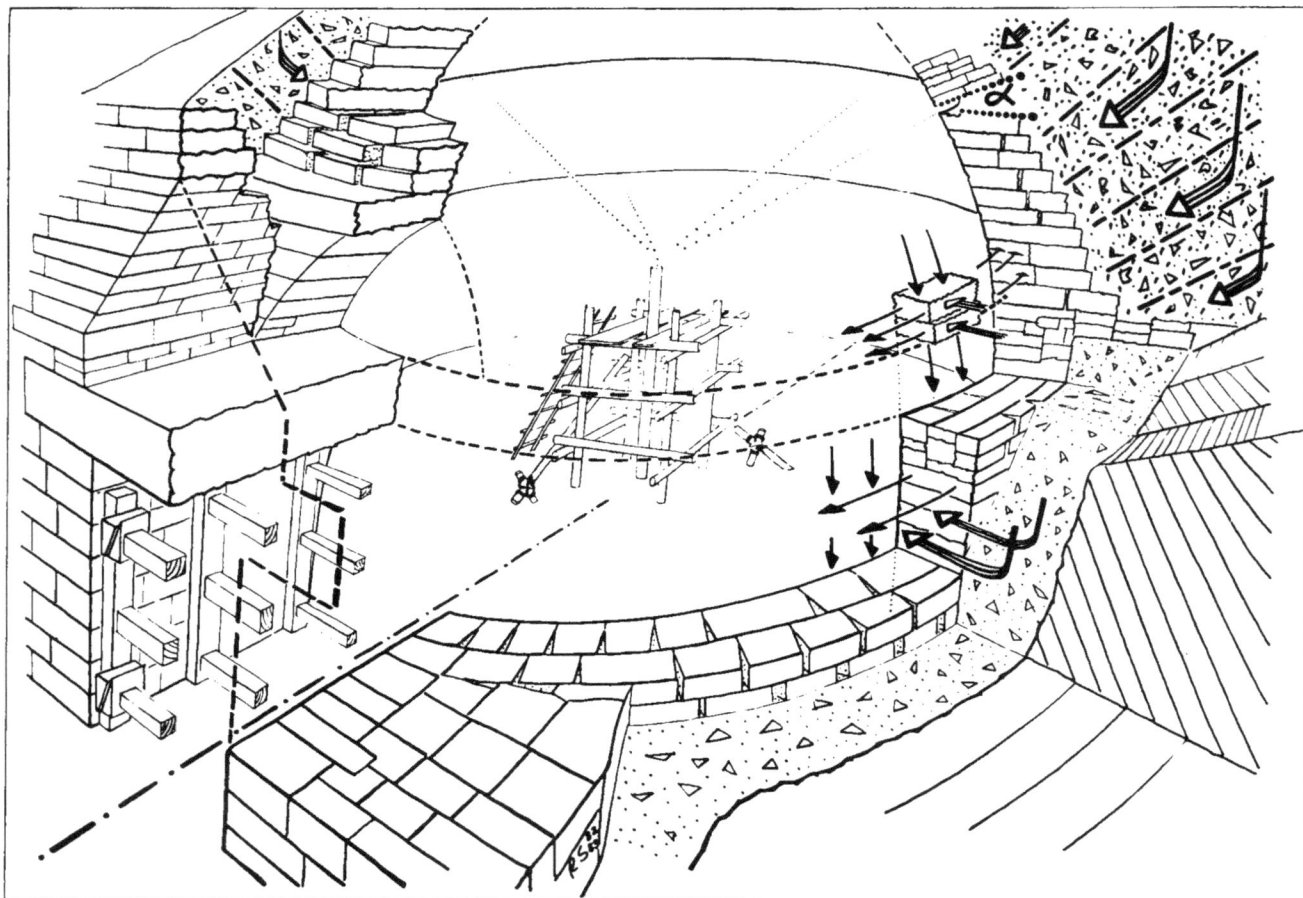

Fig. 3. Companion drawing to the description of the construction and structural behaviour of the Myceanaean tholos tholos tomb. Drawing by R. Santillo.

Fig. 4. The Lion Tomb. Th collapsed dome leaves the lintel blocks exposed. Photo R. Santillo.

Fig. 5. The interior of the Atreus Tomb rendered by the English traveller Edward Dodwell in 1834. The different inclinations of the left and right edge profiles of the great lintel block is clearly seen.

on this scale be projected. Without excluding the primary function to protect the corpse and other symbolic aspects linked to mortuary monuments, such as a dynastic claim and a projection for the afterworld, I will argue that the greatest aspect of propaganda in erecting this monument lies in the building procedure.

BUILDING OPERATIONS ON DISPLAY

To build these monuments required a concentration of wealth to provide the technological knowledge, craftmanship and manpower. Control over the territory and ownership of the quarries is a prerequisite for the building operations. The monuments thus became part of displaying the power over the territory.

With examples from other cultural spheres, such as ancient Egypt , the neo-Assyrian and Roman empire, I will illustrate the problems involved in the transport and placement of enormous blocks and how these achievements became an important part of the visual rhetoric. These cross-cultural analogies will complement the lack of written or pictorial sources of the Mycenaean culture, enlarge our referential framework and bring us into contexts of displaying technical achievements.

In Egypt, the tradition of quarrying, handling and positioning stone colossi had started already in the Old Kingdom with the construction of the pyramids and mortuary temples. During the 18th Dynasty, enormous obelisks and colossal statues were erected in the sanctuaries. One of the biggest statues (700 tons) ever erected in Egypt was commissioned by Amenhotep III, who was one of the greatest builder of ancient Egypt. This pharao manifested his energies in gigantic building projects, such as the temple of Ammon at Luxor. Several quarries at Aswan have been identified as dating from his reign (Klemm & Klemm 1993, 307-320).

The rulers of powerful neo-Assyrian empire (9th-7th centuries B.C.) adorned their capital cities and palaces on the upper Tigris with reliefs and sculptures of stone from the mountains in the north. The ornamental tradition in the palace architecture was to flank doorways of importance with sphinxes or bull colossi with human heads, sculpted from monoliths. The average weight of these sculptures was between 12 and 14 tons, but occasionally blocks of much greater size were used.

In the palace of the Assyrian ruler Sennacherib (704-681 B.C.) at Nineveh, Layard excavated in the last century a whole series of reliefs depicting the quarrying and transporting operations commissioned by the king. Together with the inscriptions, they constitute a completely unique, pictorial and epigraphical documentation dating from antiquity. Some of the slabs are preserved in the British Museum, but several are now lost and have only been preserved through the published drawings (Layard, 1849-53).

The stones for Sennacherib's palace were quarried in the Balatai, 35 km north of Nineveh.

In both Assyria and Egypt the main part of the transport was performed on the great rivers, presumably during the flooding periods, when the land transport could be minimized. In Egypt special ships were built for the transports of the enormous obelisks. The one commissioned by Queen Hatshepsut for the transport of her obelisk from Aswan to Thebes, was depicted at her mortuary temple together with other prestigious deeds (Clarke & Engelbach 1990, 37). The sledge which was used for the transport on land is very precisely rendered below the obelisk.

The removal of the Assyrian bull and lion colossi, which was effected in the 19th century by Botta at Khorsabad and by Layard at Nimrud gives a vivid picture of the difficulties involved in the transports (Larsen 1997: 175-166). Botta never ventured to transport the colossi in one piece but had them sawn into several parts. Layard decided to move his colossi from Nimrud in one piece. The difficulties he encountered were almost insuperable. That he nevertheless succeeded was due to the fact that the colossi he moved from Nimrud were about four times smaller in size than the colossi that were transported by Sennacherib. The transport on the river was not less complicated. Layard became aware of how important it was to master the River Tigris, with its marshes and its predictable and unpredictable floodings — not to speak

of the constant threat of pirates. Place, who excavated Khorsabad, lost almost all his find material in the marshland of the Tigris (Larsen 1997: 409-416).

The river Nile was a perfect arena for displaying all sorts of ceremonial events. It was the heart of Egypt and its main route of communication and the river banks from the quarries at Aswan all the way to the Delta were densely populated. Craftsmen, sailors, merchants and diplomatic envoys from the Aegean and Near Eastern countries were continually visiting Egypt, which at the time of the raising of the great obelisks had expanded its sphere of political dominance far up the Syro-Palestinian coast. The transport operations along the Nile had a large public. In Assyria the quarries are more peripherically situated in relation to the palaces and maybe that is the psychological reason why it was so important for Sennacherib to depict himself supervising the operations there.

At Mycenae the blocks were transported entirely by land. The quarries, providing the conglomerate were situated some kilometres north of Mycenae (Fig. 1). Huge blocks of conglomerate are still visible in the surface (Fig. 6). The route is not so long but difficult, since the slopes leading up to the citadel are heavily inclined. This creates other problems. For the transport of the biggest blocks and in particular the giant lintel block of 120 tons, which was used in the Atreus Tomb, a special road was required. A broad and well-paved road all the way from the quarry to the building site was indispensable. The roads west of the Atreus ridge leading up to the citadel were too steep to be used for this transport (Fig. 1). The inclination of the slope must not exceed 6 degrees (Santillo 1996). We know that the Mycenaean engineers were skilled

Fig. 6. In the area of the quarries, huge blocks of conglomerate (the material used at the citadel and in the tholos tombs) can still be seen exposed in the surface. Photo R. Santillo.

in building roads from the still existing high ways on the foot of Mt Ayios Elias. These have a standard width of c. 3.50 m, enough for marching soldiers and military or religious processions with two-wheeled light carts but not suitable for transports with wagons. For transport of goods, mules and other pack-animals were probably used. A broad well-built road, at least 5 m leading from the quarries on the plain and up to the of Mycenae was necessary for the giant block of 120 tons. In analogy with the state of preservation of the Mycenaean roads, which were surveyed by Steffen, this road should still be possible to identify. It must have been extremely well compacted, a circumstance that gives it more chances to be traced. In addition its unusual wideness should make it possible to identify the track. The only possible road that was identified during our survey of the plain was the road, already marked out by Steffen, as the ancient road from Argos to Corinth. Today it passes through cultivated fields and where the road has been cleared, it measures 6 m (Fig. 7). To have survived several millennia it must have been very well compacted from the beginning.

Fig. 7a. The ancient road from Argos to Corinth marked on the map of Steffen.Photo B.S. Frizell

Fig. 7b. View of the plain where the same road as in Fig. 7a passed with its deviations to the quarries. It is highly probable that this was the road used to transport the heavy stone masses. Photo R. Santillo.

The block was brought from the quarry on a sledge. This is the only possible solution for such heavy loads. The vehicle was used by the Egyptians, as can be seen on the renderings of the transports of obelisks and statues, and the for the Assyrian colossi. Sledges have been used since prehistorical times for all sorts of transports on shifting grounds, snow, ice and earth.

The Roman author Ammianus, was, if not a direct eyewitness, a contemporary of the event when the biggest obelisk ever brought from Egypt arrived in Rome. He describes vividly the difficulties and extreme efforts of the project: "A ship of a size hitherto unknown was constructed, to be rowed by three hundred oarsmen" (Amm. Marc. 17.4.6-23). It was brought to a place on the Tiber south of Rome. There it was put on a sledge and carefully drawn into the city. It was the same type of sledge, called *chamulcis*, Ammianus says, that was used when ships were launched or drawn up on the shore. Still today sledges are used in Mediterranean shipyards (and must be) when launching boats into the water.

The Assyrian reliefs are unique in their details. They show a group of men hanging on a pole which is connected to the sledge. This operation is crucial for the transport: it gives the impetus which moves the sledge forward and makes it possible for such a limited number of men to pull such a weight (Fig. 8). That the same mechanical device was used at Mycenae, can be deducted from the huge lintel block in the Atreus Tomb (Santillo 1990). From the inside of the tomb it can be seen that the block has inclined edge profiles (Fig. 9). The same can be seen on a huge block walled into the

dromos walls (Frizell Santillo 1998, 179). This means that the pole, that is the mover, was once moved on the block which was transported on a sledge. It should be noted that this device is not a lever, which is the usual explanation, but what with a technical term is called a 'cam mechanism' (Santillo 1990). Using this device, manpower can be considerably reduced and thus make possible the transport of a block of this size. In an arrangement of four rows of men, as on the Egyptian and Assyrian reliefs, the operation required only a total of four hundred men (Santillo 1990).

At a certain point the "triumphal" procession proceeding ahead on the plain, had to turn direction towards the heights of the citadel. The roads leading up to the citadel west of the ridge were to steep. The only possible road was the road which corresponds to the modern asphalt road leading up to the citadel (Fig. 2 a-b). It is the only one with an inclination which at no point exceeds the magic 6 degrees. When the block was moved uphill, it had to be turned around and the more sharply inclined profile was used for the mover. This difference in profile of left and right side can still be seen on the lintel block in situ since the builders intentionally left these signs behind (Santillo 1997).

We have to imagine a public event never seen before! The surrounding territory was densely populated. The visibility from the mountains and hilltops is particularly good around Mycenae. From the hills of Argos and the mountains behind Mycenae, it was possible to see the transport of the colossus on its way on the plain and then uphill to the citadel of Mycenae. Such an event must have attracted people from far and near.

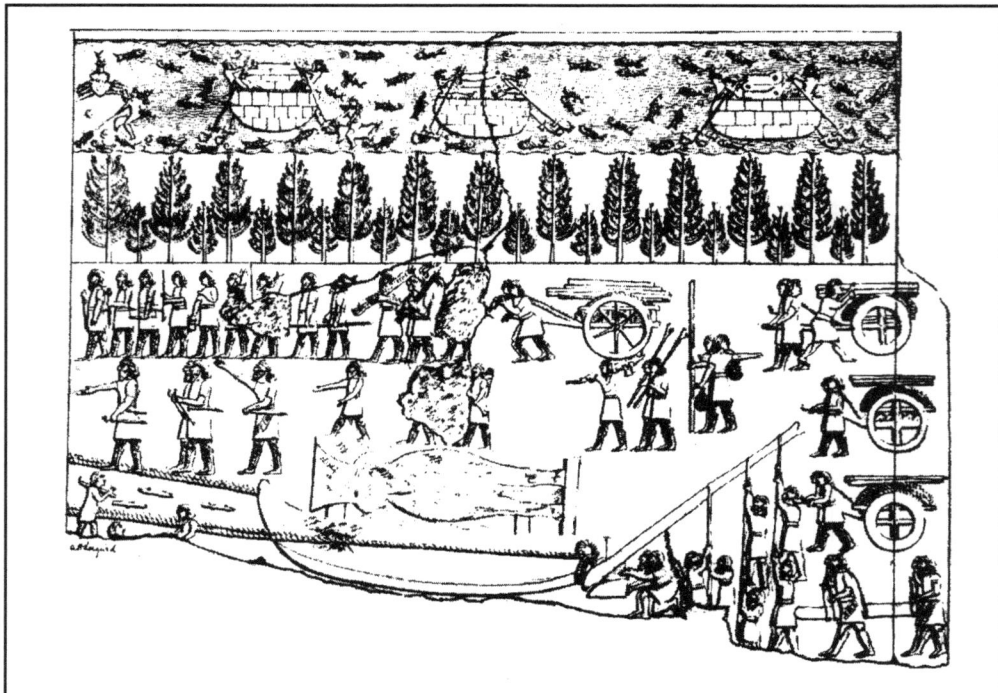

Fig. 8. Detail of Assyrian relief from the palace of Sennacherib. The bull colossus is placed on a sledge and dragged by four rows of men. Behind the sledge there is a pole on which three men are hanging. When the men let go of the pole (the mover), it acts upon the block (the follower) and gives the impetus which moves the block (or sledge) forward.

Fig. 9. The left edge profile of the huge lintel block in the Atreus Tomb (seen from the inside of the chamber). This side was used for the mover to act upon when the block was moved on the plain. Drawing R. Santillo.

The final and exalted moment of the operation was the positioning of the huge monoliths. The lintel block in the Atreus Tomb, which weighs three times Sennacherib´s greatest bull colossi, can be compared to the Egyptian obelisks, with the great difference that this block was used as an element in a building. The positioning consequently required particular operative solutions. A crucial part of the

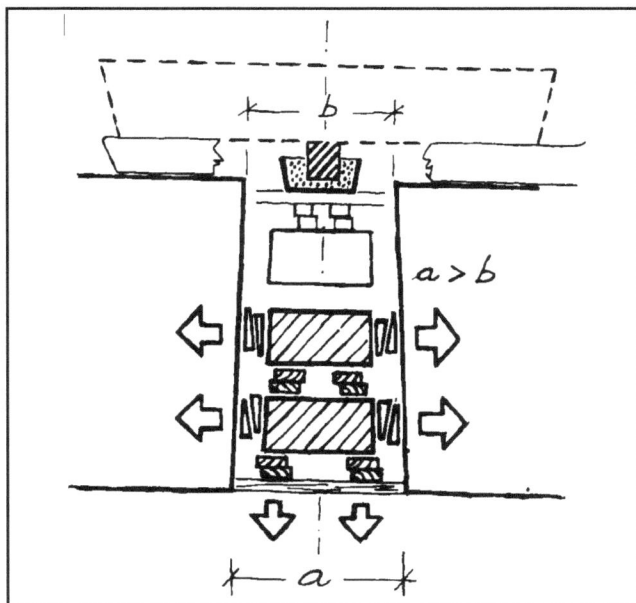

Fig.10. The huge lintel block was launched on a sledge over the stomion gap, which was blocked by wooden struts and shoring. The sledge was removed by means of wedges, a mechanical device still used today in Mediterranean shipyards (Santillo 1990, fig. 48).

operation was then the removal of the sledge and the lowering of the stone colossus onto the stomion wall by a gradual lowering of the scaffolding (Santillo 1990).

The progandistic value of these operations can be perceived through the visual images created by the commissioners. In his tomb, the governor Tehutihotep describes and depicts the event of the transport of his colossal as a magnificent manifestation (Fig. 11). The statue is dragged by 172 men all of the highest rank in the society, priests and officers (Newberry, 1894-95, 19-26). Queen Hatschepsut commemorates the event of the transport of her obelisks on her mortuary temple at Thebes together with other prestigious deeds, such as the expedition to Punt (Clarke & Engelbach, 36-37).

At his palace at Nineveh, Sennacherib gave the pictorial representations of the quarring and transports a most prominent position, placing them on the walls of the court which led into the throne room. The doors were flanked by the same bull colossi whose transport is described on the reliefs. The king himself is represented as supervising the work at the quarry and the transport along the Tigris to Nineveh. Whether he actually was present himself or is only symbolically represented on the reliefs does not really matter: the significance lies in his self-image, which shows how important he considered this enterprise in the royal propaganda.

By means of costume and captions, the labourers in the quarry and the men hauling the bull colossi are identified as "inhabitants of hidden mountain regions, conquest of my hand" (Russel 1991: 260).

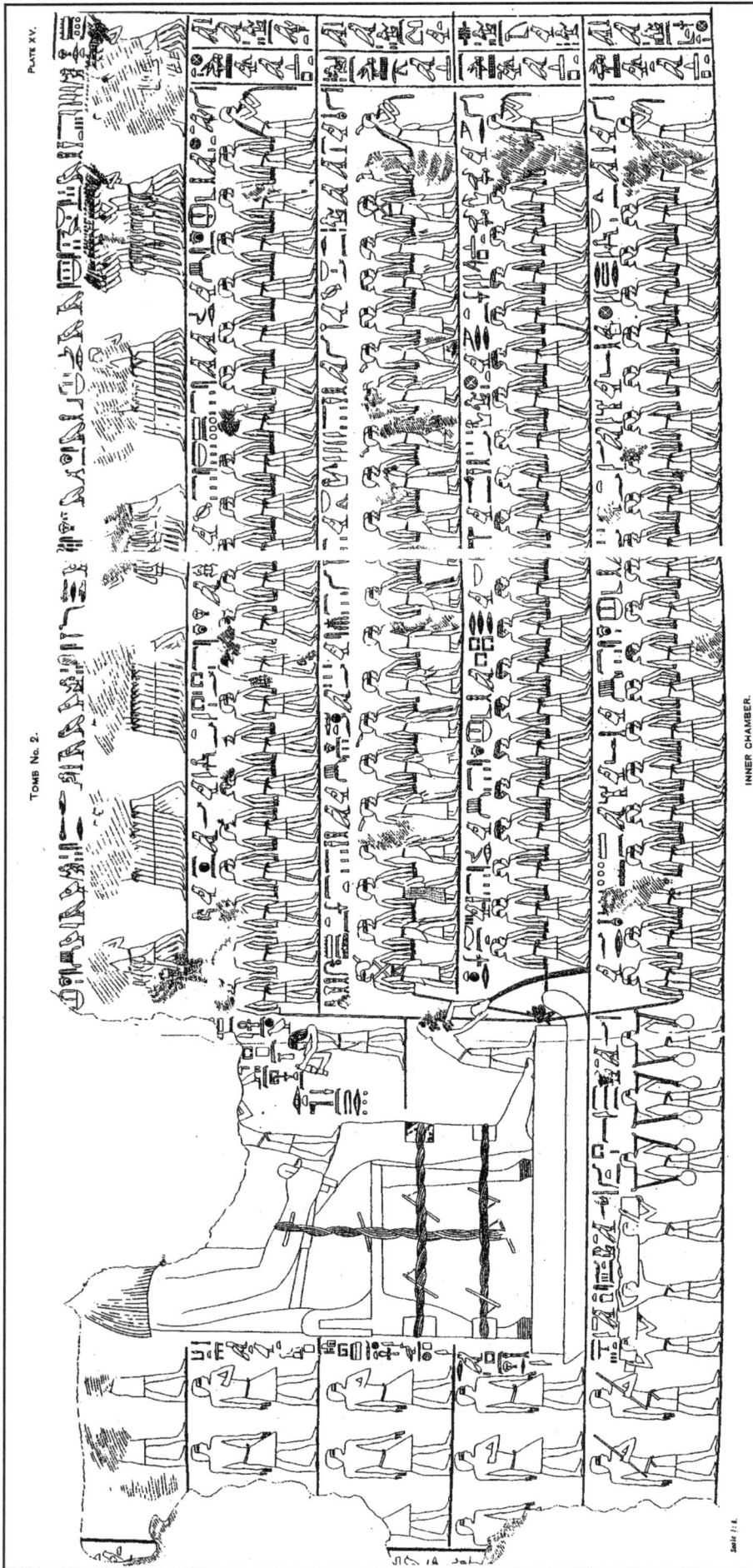

Fig. 11. The transport of the alabaster statue of district governor Tehutihotep depicted in his tomb (Newberry 1894-95).

Sennacherib used building in his propaganda more than any other ruler before him. He attributed the discovery of his primary source of sculptural alabaster to divine revelation (Russel 1991: 115). A very conscious building program was conceived, which exalted the difficulties involved in the building operations. He depicts himself as supervising the work in the quarry and accompanying the colossi on their journey to Nineveh. He provided his palace with the biggest colossi of all Assyrian rulers, allegedly weighing 40-50 tons (Russel 1991:115). The weight of his colossi illustrates the magnitude of this project and the great prestige it conferred to Sennacherib in relation to his predecessors. Therefore he could claim his palace building to be "without rival".

From the Roman period we have no pictorial sources, but the value of these events as public phenomena is occasionally mentioned by the authors. The Romans were probably the first people to venture a transport of such a heavy masse of stone on the open sea. Augustus was the first emperor to bring an obelisk to Rome as a symbol of the conquest of Egypt. The ship which was constructed for the purpose was, according to Pliny, greatly admired and became a tourist attraction. It was thereafter exhibited at Puteoli, the international harbour on the Gulf of Naples (Plin. Nat. 36.14.68-71).

In 1586 the first great obelisk of the Renaissance period was reerected in Rome. It was considered an almost impossible task which was given to Domenico Fontana. In his vivid description of the operation he comments on the public interest: "It was a beutiful performance in many ways, an infinite number of people had came to watch and in order not to loose their places they remained without eating from morning until the evening. Some built wooden platforms for the people who came and they earned a lot of money" (Fontana 1590, 28). Trumpet signals and bells were used to create rhythm and to facilitate the coordination of the movements. Music has in all times been an important accompaniment of labour and military operations and we can only conjecture that also at Mycenae trumpets were used at these occasions. From Homer, we know that the salpinx was used in battle to give signals. Similar instruments were used by the Assyrians during these operations (Fig. 8).

RHETORIC FOR WHOM?

Why did the Mycenaean Greeks choose to design and build a monument on such a high technical and constructional level and who were the people in the audience? The monumental building at Mycenae started in the fourteenth century B.C. during the LH III A1 period. This was a period of great expansion of the Mycenaeans in the Eastern Mediterranean. With the fall of Knossos, which occurred slightly earlier, they took over the role of the Minoans in the eastern trade. The chief destination of Egyptian imported objects now shifted from Crete to Mainland Greece. Mycenaean pottery occurs at several sites in Egypt. The nature of the relationship and contacts that these finds represent have been much discussed and I will not repeat that discussion here, only briefly

summarize the two basically opposite views regarding the degree of contact between the Aegean and Egypt during the Late Bronze Age. The "minimalist" view sees no direct contacts between the states, maintaining that the objects of trade were brought by Levantine or Cypriote middlemen (Merrillees 1998: 149-154). An opposite view is held by Bernal who advocates a kind of Egyptian hegemony over the Aegean (Bernal 1993: 446-494). A more balanced view is held by Cline who interprets the finds at Mycenae as evidence for direct contacts, such as trade and royal embassies arriving and visiting Mycenae. Most of the finds of Egyptian origin at Mycenae belong to the reign of Amenhotep III, whose reign, following his "modified revised chronology" should dated to 1390-1360 (Cline 1994: 5-8). At Mycenae it corresponds to LH III A. These finds are the "The topographical list" on the mortuary temple at Kom el Hetan, which also lists Mycenae among the Aegean place-names (Cline 1994:112-115, Pl. 3) and the finds at Mycenae bearing his cartouche, which are the best-dated Egyptian material from the tombs at Mycenae (Cline 1994: 215-216, 143, Pl. 3). No other site in the Aegean has so many inscribed objects of Amenhotep III and Queen Tiyi.

At Mycenae several objects were found; among those a number of faience plaques. These plaques were used in rituals related to foundation ceremonies. Mycenae is the only place in the Aegean where objects connected with building activity have been found. In Egypt foundations deposits are found below religious buildings, statues, obelisks and royal palaces. As to their presence at Mycenae, various explanations have been given; a dedication for the foundation of an Egyptian shrine at Mycenae (Hankey 1981: 46), or for a statue of Amenhotep III, which should have been set up at Mycenae (Cline 1987: 10-11). There are, however, no evidence of an Egyptian shrine nor any pharaonic statue at Mycenae, as we know so far. We cannot know where these plaques were placed originally since they were found in a secondary context, but it is logical to see their presence in connection with the inauguration of some important monument or building where Egyptians played a role. The result of diplomatic and/or military contacts or exchange which consisted in building expertise with experience to handle stone colossi, is a plausible explanation to the existence of these foundation plaques, dedicated by Egyptians collaborating in this extremely difficult and risky operation.

Contacts through military operations occurred and were probably much more frequent than the fragmentary evidence permits us to conjecture. Recently Mycenaean soldiers have been identified on some pictorial papyrus fragments from Tell-el-Amarna. It is in fact the only one known which depicts a battle (Schofield & Parkinson 1994: 157-170). These were found together with a Mycenaean vase in a chapel dedicated to the cult of the pharaoh, possibly Amenhotep III. The Mycenaean Greeks have been identified by their boar-tusk helmets and their short, oxhide, metal-edged tunics.

Homer gives a scenario of captive Mycenaean Greeks, who had to work per force in building operations (Od. 14.270). When Odysseus and his men became captives after a raid in Egypt, many men were then killed "and others they led up to their city alive, to work for them perforce." It is tempting to imagine that this reflects a Late Bronze Age setting, where Aegean merchants, mercenaries and pirates regularly frequented Egypt. A public phenomenon, such as a monumental building, which could not be hidden in a secret workshop, was particularly apt to stimulate the exchange of ideas. The question araises, do we really need this corroboratory, fragmentary evidence to support the hypothesis that an exchange of building technology took place? The evidence from the buildings in fact lends strong support to the hypothesis of more frequent and continuous contacts between Egypt and Mycenae than does the ceramic and textual evidence. It think it is time to let the monuments talk once for a while.

The monumental tholoi buildings at Mycenae should be interpreted in an Eastern Mediterranean context. Other great builders at this time were the Hittite rulers. They built powerful citadels, also using great blocks like those in the Lion gate, flanking the entrance gates at Hattusa. The many similarities between Hittite and Mycenaean monumental building suggest a reciprocial exchange of ideas and architectural concepts, which reflects a competion within the political and military spheres.

The mighty Hittite empire now competed politically with Egypt. Mycenae was only a small state on the fringes of the cosmopolitan Eastern Mediterranean world — but it was aggressive, expanding and competitive. That the ruling class had ambitions to political power beyond the local level and aimed at an international role is shown by their monumental building projects. These can only compete with those of the Egyptians and the Hittites. That the Mycenaean Greeks were not passive receivers of cultural influence but took an active part is demonstrated by the way they chose to display their propaganda. They did not simply copy or import a monument, as the Romans did; their achievement was much greater. As a piece of architecture, the tholos tomb is purely Greek in origin and concept: it has no Egyptian or Hittite counterparts. The Greeks used their own building tradition, monumentalised it and incorporated a new component, the huge lintel-blocks, to increase the efforts and their prestige. In this, they created a propaganda monument of international standards.

Without an analysis of the building procedure and its various operational phases and considering only the perception of the finished monuments, a locally or regionally defined audience becomes a logical conclusion: a Greek monument for a Greek audience. The reason for the size and splendour of some of the tombs at Mycenae has consequently been explained in terms of changing conceptions of territory and regional political interests. No doubt there was a clear message adressed to a local audience and even more so to a regional public. This display of building efforts taking into possession the whole landscape could escape nobody and was a demonstration of power of the ruling elite. The propagandistic aim of this enterprise was more far-reaching than the finished product and it was expressed and appreciated during the lifetime of the commissioner — during the process of construction.

This was an excellent occasion to display the military power of Mycenae. In analogy with other ancient societies I am suggesting that the manpower used for these extraordinary occasions were soldiers and the symbolic leader of the operation was of highest military rank, maybe the king himself as chief commander. It is usually assumed that the manpower in similar operations were slaves, who could be used as unqualified labour force when needed. There is no evidence from antiquity to suggest that except for the use of captured enemies, who usually were soldiers themselves. The governor Tehutihotep, describes the men dragging his colossal statue as officers of highest rank. When Herodotos visited Sais in Egypt he was amazed by the buildings of pharao Amasis and most of all a shrine made of one single block. This was brought from Elephantine, an island in the Nile opposite Aswan and taken all the way down to Sais; "three years it was in the bringing, and two thousand men were charged with the carriage of it, pilots all of them" (Herodotos, 2.175). On the basis of the accurate measurements given by Herodotos it has been calculated that this block weighed 580 tons (Arnold, 1991, 60). It is logical that naval officers were used for the transports on the river.

The vehicle used in this display of power at Mycenae shows that the propaganda was directed at a much wider audience than is usually assumed. It went far beyond Mycenae and its surrounding petty chiefdoms in the Argolid; its farthest target was the high civilisations of the Eastern Mediterranean and the Near East. It can in this respect be compared with the modern "star wars", projects that have little bearing on actual warfare, but which convey immense prestige to the military capacity of a state, demonstrating its top level of technology and military logistics.

The landscape surrounding Mycenae was the arena for this performance. A broad and well-compacted road all the way from the quarry to the building site was indispensable for the transport of the huge lintel-block (Fig. 2 a-b). It had to pass below the Atreus Tomb, leading up to a broad, open, paved area, approximately corresponding to where the modern bus-parking is situated today The block, still on its sledge, had then to be turned in order to manouvre it into its final direction for the positioning above the stomion gap. The big blocks for the citadel and the other two monumental tombs, the Tomb of Clytemnestra and the Lion Tomb also needed a broad and well-paved road, even if the blocks used here are lesser in size. The roads west of the Atreus ridge leading up to the citadel were not suitable for this kind of transport (Fig. 1). All monumental buildings, where big blocks of conglomerate are abundantly used, should have been constructed during a fairly short span of time. In analogy with Egypt and Assyria (and many other socities) a sort of internal competion between rulers is possible but is must be seen in the perspective of the technological level of the constructors. The standard of technological knowledge achieved in these cultures need overlapping generations of architects, master-builders and craftsmen. These are needed to build up such an operational force and to keep the tradition alive. Without this technological context it would have been impossible to commission such a monument as the Atreus Tomb. In the sphere of traditional building where external exchange and influences are less obvious the basic requirements are similar (Frizell Santillo 2001). It takes many generations to acquire the expertise even if it manifest only during a relatively short period of time.

The obelisks of Egypt are unthinkable without the granite and the monumental buildings at Mycenae are inconceivable without the conglomerate. The geology was a prerequisite for these monuments. Several scholars have pointed to the use of conglomerate as a symbolic representation of power and expression of royal propaganda but doing so without considering the choise of material in a constructional context (Wright 1997, 177-180; Kuepper 1996, 115-118). It is not the material itself which confers the symbolic value but the constructional implications which, I think, I have demonstrated above. At Tiryns, this stone is used for huge door-posts at the entrance gates at the citadel and big treshholds where there is obvious constructive needs. The quarries of the material has not been identified. Transporting these blocks from the quarries at Mycenae to Tiryns means well-built roads and is logical in a design of enlarged military control over the territory. In becomes part in the project of dominance over the coastal area of the Argolid Gulf and the harbour at Tiryns, and explains why the citadel and palace here is so clearly shaped on the same model as at Mycenae.

Compared with the scholarly interest focussed on other archaeological material of the Mycenaean civilization, relatively little attention has been paid to its most conspicuous remains, the monumental buildings. This reflects a general situation. The reason for this surely lies in academic traditions, which in different ways have fostered and maintained artificially defined disciplines with borders often arbitrarily and randomly set. A conspicuous part of our archaeological heritage is the remains of buildings, especially in classical archaeology. In spite of this, classical archaeologists have very little, if any, professional training in dealing with architecture. They are nevertheless expected to document, evaluate and interpret the remains of buildings. The lack of insight into building technology has led to the practice of handing over these matters to architectural historians, who, however, have often no technical university degree and no practical building experience. Their university training is traditionally focussed on aesthetics and form, with a preference for monumental and grand architecture as objects of study, and perception becomes thus a major concern in their approach. Acting upon the demands of the archaeologists, the architectural historians have been busy reconstructing the original appearance of the buildings, and more effort has been put into reconstructing the decoration of facades and stylistical elements than understanding the structure of the building and the construction procedures. The historical interpretations are left to the 'experts'. This has led to a lack of understanding of the socio-anthropological aspect of building, that is the relation between man and his construction work.

The cognitive context of building technology has been even more neglected. A contextual study of building technology requires a broad, scholarly approach, combining archaeological data, the history of architecture and the practical experience of building. Such an approach is necessary to open up the possibilities of interpreting these buildings in a wider geographical space and historical context.

Acknowledgments

My warm thanks to Åke Wibergs Stiftelse for the financial support to undertake field studies of roads and quarries at Mycenae during the summer of 1999 and to Sölve Eriksson who has produced the three-dimensional model of the landscape around Mycenae.

References

Alcock, S. (1997) 'The Heroic Past in a Hellenistic Present', in P. Cartledge, P. Garnsey & E. Gruen (eds), *Hellenistic constructs: essays in culture, history, and historiography*. Berkeley: Berkeley University of California Press.

Arnold, D. (1991) *Building in Egypt. Pharaonic stone masonry*. New York Oxford: Oxford University Press.

Bernal, M. (1993) *Black Athena. The afroasiatic roots of classical civilisation. Vol. 2. The archaeological and documentary evidence*, New Brunswick Rutgers university press.

Clarke, S. & Engelbach, R. (1990*) Ancient Egyptian construction and architecture*. New York Dover.

Cline, E. (1987) 'Amenhotep III and the Aegean: a reassessment of Egypto-Aegean relations in the 14th century BC', *Orientalia* N.S. 56:1-36.

Cline, E. (1994) *Sailing the Wine-dark Sea. International Trade and the Late Bronze Age Aegean* (= BAR International Series 591).

Fontana, D. (1590) *Della trasportatione dell'obelisco vaticano. Libro Primo*. Roma

Frizell Santillo, B. (1984a) 'The tholos tomb at Berbati', *Opuscula Atheniensia* 15, 25-44.

Frizell Santillo, B. & Santillo, R. (1984b) 'The construction and structural behaviour of the Mycenaean tholos tomb', *Opuscula Atheniensia* 15:45-52.

Frizell Santillo, B. (1987) 'The nuragic domes - why false?' in *Nuragic Sardinia and the Mycenaean World. Studies in Sardinian Archaeology III*. (=BAR International Series 387), 57-74.

Frizell Santillo, B. (1989) 'The autonomous development of dry masonry domes in the Mediterranean area', *Opusula Romana* 17:143-161.

Frizell Santillo, B. (1997-98) 'Monumental building at Mycenae: Its function and audience', *Opuscula Atheniensia* 22-23: 103-116.

Frizell Santillo, B. (1998) 'Giants or Geniuses? Monumental Building at Mycenae.' *Current Swedish Archaeology* 6: 167-184.

Frizell Santillo, B. (2001) ' The dynamics of development in traditional house-building: Ethnohistory and dry masonry domes.' *From huts to houses. Transformations of ancient societies. Rome, Sept. 22-25, 1997* (Acta Instituti Romani Regni Sueciae, series in 4:o), 117-136.

Hankey, W. (1981) 'The Aegean interest in El Amarna', *Journal of Mediterran Anthropology an Archaeology* 1, 45-6.

Higgins, M.D. & Higgins, R. (1996) *A Geological Companion to Greece and the Aegean*. London: Duckworth.

Klemm, R. & Klemm, D. (1993) *Steine und Stenbrueche im Alten Egypten*, Berlin Heidelberg.

Kuepper, M. (1996) *Mykenische Architektur. Material, Bearbeitungstechnik, Konstruktion und Erscheinungsbild* (=Internationale Archäologie. Band 25). Espelkamp.

Newberry, P. (1894-95) *El Bersheh I-II*. London.

Merrillees, R. (1998) 'Egypt and the Aegean'. *The Aegean and the Orient in the second millennium. Proceedings of the 50th Anniversary Symposium Cincinnarti, 18-20 April 1997 (Aegaeum* 18), 149-154.

Persson, A. W. (1931) *The Royal Tombs at Dendra near Midea.*

Russel, J. M. (1991) *Sennacherib's Palace without Rival at Nineveh*, Chicago & London: The University of Chicago Press.

Santillo, R. (1986) 'Le cupole a secco, un contributo per una diversa conoscenza delle tombe a tholos, dei trulli e dei nuraghi', *Edilizia Militare 17/18* (rivista tecnica della Direzione Generale Lavori, Demanio e Materiali del Genio, GenioDife), Roma.

Santillo, R. (1990) 'Il blocco da 120 tonnellate a Micene: problemi e soluzioni del trasporto a terra e posa in opera, con inlcuse quelle analoghe per gli altri massi dell'antichità, *Archeologia* 1-2:17-18.

Santillo, R. (1996) 'Il Saxum Ingentem a Ravenna a copertura del Mausoleo di Teoderico', *Opusula Romana* 20:105-133.

Santillo, R. (1997) 'Mycenaean Lessons of Descriptive Geometry showing cam mechanisms to move huge blocks', in *Ancient Greek Technology Conference, Thessaloniki, 4-7 September 1997*, 439-445.

Schofield, L. & Parkinson, R.B. (1994) 'Of helmets and heretics: A possible Egyptian representation of Mycenaean warriors on a papyrus from El-Amarna', *BSA* 89:157-170.

Steffen (1884) *Karten von Mykenai*, Berlin: Dietrich Reimer.

Trolle Larsen, M. (1997) *Sjunkna palats. Historien om upptäckten av Orienten*, Stockholm: Symposion.

Wace, A. (1925) 'The tholos tombs', *BSA* 25: 283-396.

Wright, J. C. (1987) 'Death and power at Mycenae: changing symbols in mortuary practice', in *Thanatos. Les coutumes funeraires en Egee a l'Age du Bronze. Acte du colloque de Liége (21-23 avril 1986), (=Aegaeum* 1), Liége.

Ancient sources

Ammianus Marcellinus, *Book 17.*

Herodotos, *Book 2.*

Homer, *The Odyssey.*

Pausanias, *Description of Greece. Book 2. Corinth.*

Pliny, *Natural History.* c. A.D. 23-70.

PUBLIC SPACE IN ROMAN POMPEII

Karin FRIDELL ANTER, Marina WEILGUNI

Abstract: This study[1] is part of a larger project, investigating how the spatial environment functioned in deploying the inhabitants' social identity in Pompeii. The basic analysis is done with the help of the statistical-topological method Space Syntax. Here we have focused on the analysis of the potential for movement through the streets and public spaces of the town.

The first problem was to find a reliable map as a foundation for the analysis. Such a map was established through field observations in Pompeii in comparison to printed maps available. From this map was made an axial analysis of Pompeii's public space. This showed a pattern that is similar to the *spoked wheel* pattern typical for a category of spontaneously grown, unplanned towns, both historically and today. The pattern was distorted, however, by the existence of a regular grid plan in the eastern part of the town. Further peculiarities in the pattern are discussed in the article.

The Space Syntax analysis of the town plan poses interesting questions and subjects for further investigation, and suggests hypotheses that would otherwise not come to mind. It is likely that more comprehensive research with this method will help to elucidate the problem of the gradual growth of Pompeii, as well as its sociospatial functioning in the final period.

To illustrate what an analysis of the interface between inhabitant and stranger can bring, we attempt to follow two travellers in through the Vesuvius gate and the Sarno gate respectively.

This final part of the article shows in "real life" what a Space Syntax analysis can add to the understanding of ancient Pompeii.[2]

INTRODUCTION

This study focuses on the public, open space of the small Campanian town of Pompeii, destroyed 79 AD by the volcanic eruption of Mount Vesuvius. It is part of a larger project, the aim of which is to investigate how the spatial environment functioned in deploying the inhabitants' social identity, both in the internal life of the town and in the interface with visitors from outside.

The study has served to investigate the analytical possibilities inherent in the Space Syntax method for spatial analysis. It has focused on the analysis of the potential for movement through the streets and public spaces of the town, concentrating on the final phase before the destruction.

The town of Pompeii has been much studied and researched upon, but the social aspects of space have not been the main target for this. Notable exceptions are the works of A. Wallace-Hadrill (1994), R. Laurence (1994) and P. Zanker (1995).

THE TOWN OF POMPEII

Pompeii was situated in the fertile landscape of Campania, south east of Mount Vesuvius. The town was strategically placed at the river mouth of the Sarno. In the surrounding country, intensive agriculture was possible, and the road net connected Pompeii to other nearby towns.

At the time of its destruction the estimated number of inhabitants was about 10.000 inhabitants (Wallace-Hadrill 1994, 98). Pompeii was a functionally diversified town, comprising houses of varying standards, through traffic, commerce, different crafts, civic centres for politics, administration , culture and religion and even some agricultural activity within the town walls.

The extension of the town was about 1.300 m in the east to west direction, and 700 m in the north to south direction.

Map

[1] The study has been made possible by the generous financial support from Helge Ax:son Johnson's foundation, which enabled us twice to visit Pompeii for our fieldwork. Thanks are also due to Prof. Anne-Marie Leander-Touati, head of the Swedish Institute in Rome for friendly and scholarly advise, and to Stefania Renzetti and Pia Letalick of the Institute for administrative help. We also wish to thank the Soprintendeza Archeologica di Pompei, for providing the authorization to visit the entire street net.

[2] This doesn't work without some measure of empathy as well – but then, archaeology is not only "dry bones".

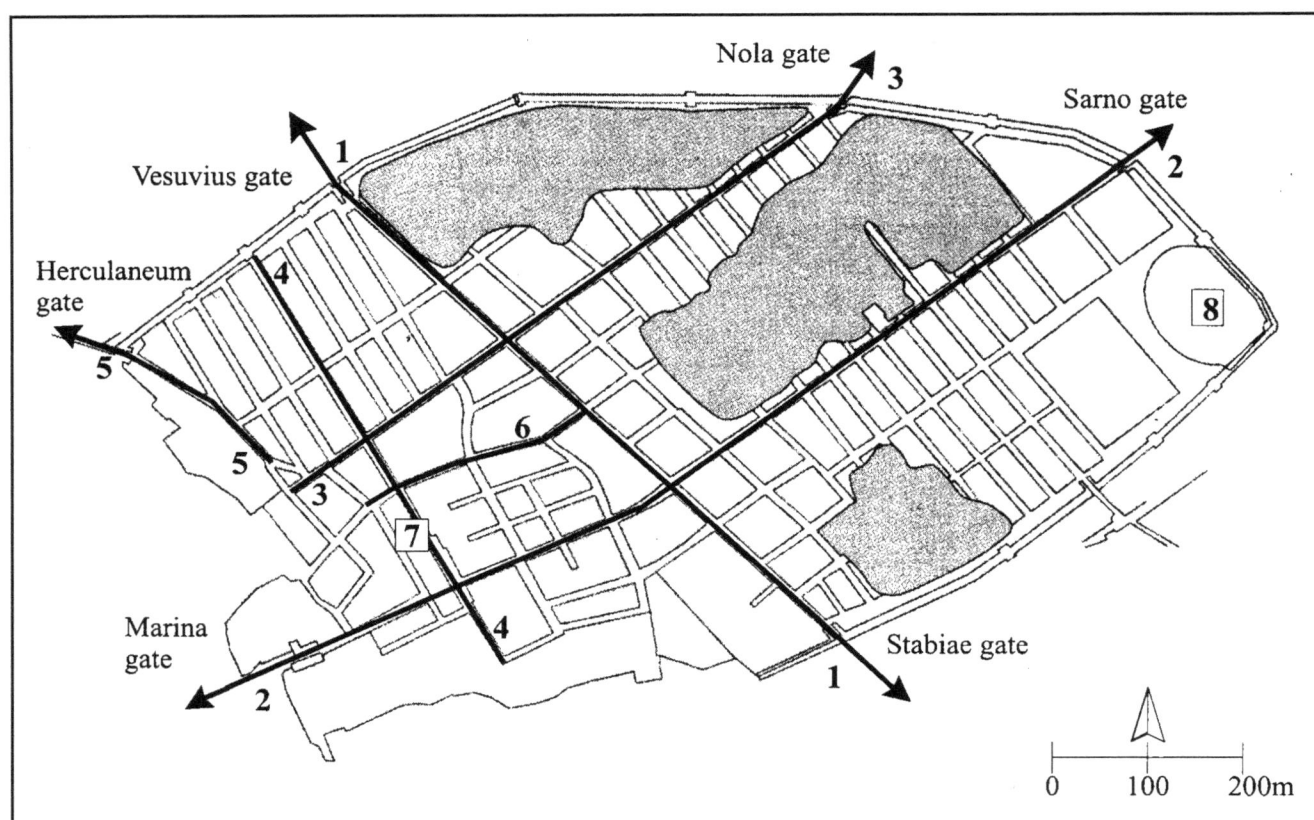

Figure 1. Map of Pompeii's principle outlines, after Geertman 1998, 17.
1=Via Stabiana/Vesuvio, 2=Via dell'Abbondanza/Marina, 3=Via di Nola/della Fortuna/delle Terme, 4=Via di Mercurio/del Foro/delle Scuole, 5=Via Consolare, 6= Via degli Augustali, 7=Forum, 8=amphitheatre. The street names are not ancient. Unexcavated areas marked in grey.

Inclination was primarily from north-west to south-east (average about 5%), but there were also obvious height differences in other directions. The south-west part of the town, where the Forum was placed, consisted of a marked hillock.

The town was confined within a town wall, which in the final phase was non-existent along several stretches, but nevertheless can be seen as the towns border. This wall had seven gates.[3] The street net was primarily ordered into grid like sections, with slight differences in orientation in different parts. The Forum hillock had, however, a completely different lay out. This has been interpreted as vestiges of an original, unplanned, town (Eschebach 1970, 17-40; Geertman 1998).

Buildings usually comprised more than one storey, and combined different functions under the same roof. There were also larger, official buildings such as baths, temples, theatres and an amphitheatre.

ESTABLISHING A USABLE MAP

A pre-condition for an analysis of the urban structure of any town or city is a correct map. Especially when using Space

Syntax as a method (see below under *Space Syntax method*), it is important to be as sure as possible about the actual layout of the street pattern. Regarding Pompeii, this posed some important problems, although a detailed and seemingly correct plan (CTP)[4] was published as recently as 1988.

First of all, only about 2/3 of the area is excavated. The street structure in the unexcavated area has been variously reconstructed on the maps available.[5] The logic of these reconstructions is not always evident when compared to observations made in Pompeii itself or to CTP 1988. Also, even the excavated parts of Pompeii are not consistently rendered, for instance when it comes to street width, the angles of street crossings and irregularities along the

---

[3] There are hypotheses about an eighth town gate to the north, investigated by, among others, Japanese scholars (*Opuscula Pompeiana*, different articles from 1991 onwards). As long as these hypotheses are not confirmed, we suppose only seven gates.

[4] Corpus Topographicum Pompeianum (CTP) is an extensive collection of plans, publication data and summaries of research agreements and diputes for about half of the excavated buildings, plus a large plan (scale 1:1000) for the whole excavated city.

[5] Such maps are found on the covers of CTP 1977-1987, in Richardson 1988 (cover), Laurence 1994, Geertman 1998, Zanker 1995 and other works on Pompeii. They appear to be based on different hypotheses about the angles of streets and house blocks in the unexcavated north-east area. The plans on the CTP covers show a hypothetical division of the eastern part into one southern and one northern grid, meeting in irregular street crossings over the hypothetical eastern continuation of Via degli Augustali. On the smaller scale plans of Laurence and Zanker the northern and southern grids seem to allow connections without such irregularities, although this is not shown on the plans. The big CTP map also gives evidence for the hypothesis that there was not – or at least need not have been – any systematic irregularity in the unexcavated part of the street net.

extensions of the streets.[6] Consequently, the widely spread "common plans" of Pompeii, are not compatible with each other, and in some cases certainly not with reality either. They could therefore not be used in our analysis.

The large and detailed CTP-map (CTP 1988, below called *CTP map*) could arguably have been used, but there were some problems. First, although its scale is larger than that of any other map, it is still too small for a detailed study based *only* on this map. For instance, it is not always possible to determine on the map if a sight line or a line of axiality *(see below under *Space Syntax method)* can or cannot pass a certain feature, such as a house corner. Second, the CTP map does not show any reconstruction of the unexcavated streets. Third, the smaller schematic plans reproduced inside the cover of the other volumes in the CTP series (CTP 1977-87) obviously do not tally with the detailed, large map. This meant that we could not be certain about the reconstructive intentions of the team behind the massive documentation presented in the CTP.

The upshot of all this was the necessity of a fairly detailed street pattern survey on the site itself, in order to determine a plan solution possible to use in an urban analysis. This was carried out in the summer 2000. The survey entailed establishing sight lines and axial lines possible to walk along, for all streets in the pattern. Where actual sighting and walking was not possible due to unexcavated terrain, we used compass to determine possible street directions starting from excavated street crossings. Our survey turned out to agree with the CTP map in all matters except those, where the scale of the plan made observations on the spot necessary. Therefore, we decided to base the Space Syntax analysis essentially on the detailed CTP map, augmented with the survey's observations of line continuity.

SPACE SYNTAX METHOD

The method used in this study is Space Syntax, which describes certain qualities of space in a quantifiable way. The method and the theory behind it were presented by two British architects, Bill Hillier and Julienne Hanson in *The Social Logic of Space* (1984) and further developed by Hillier in *Space is the Machine* (1996). The basis of the theory is that there is an interdependence between societal relationships and spatial configuration. Through representation, measurement and quantification Space Syntax describes certain aspects of spatiality within a society. These data offer a starting point for analysis of the social pattern as deployed in space, and may be combined with other, not predominantly spatial, data.

Analysing the archaeological remains of a society long since gone, poses problems inherent in the nature of these remains – there is no way in which to correlate the data obtained with a functioning reality. In Pompeii, as opposed to in living cities, there are no inhabitants and no visitors to ask for the uses and abuses of space, no people to be counted on certain places in the street pattern or to be observed in their daily tasks. Also, the spatial pattern itself is partially defunct due to the ravages of time, when it is excavated at all. Given these limitations, in a town as extensively excavated and preserved as Pompeii, there is still a lot Space Syntax can tell.

A Space Syntax analysis starts with identifying the convex and axial spaces within the spatial system.[7] When the spatial system has been defined, e.g. the town within the town wall as in Pompeii, the entire public space is broken up into its constituent convex parts. A convex space is a space without any concavity in its outline. The shortest path between any two points in the convex space thus never can pass outside the borders of this space (Hillier & Hanson 1984, 97-99). The convex dimension of the public space is primarily the stationary dimension, it reflects the spaces where the inhabitants live and work.

The axial dimension is expressed by drawing the longest and fewest lines that connect all the convex spaces of the system. Thus, the axial spaces pass through two or more convex spaces, stringing them up on the line representing the axial space (Hillier & Hanson 1984, 99-100).

The axial dimension of the public space is primarily the dimension of movement. It reflects the spaces as used by the visitor passing through the town.

By defining the convex and the axial structure of the spatial system, the prerequisites of an analysis are created. For analysing the public space of a town, the axial system often gives the most valuable information. It focuses on movement, which is natural for a system of thoroughfares and other streets. The convex dimension must not be forgotten, however, as the interface between the two dimensions mirrors the potential of contact between inhabitants and visitors. Also the relationship between the two dimensions of space can be studied: Are there many convex spaces threaded upon a few axial lines? Or can many of the convex spaces also be seen as separate axial entities? In the later case, the axial structure is broken up, and can be difficult to grasp for someone moving through it. The stationary dimension, rather than the dimension of movement, is stressed (Hillier et al. 1983, 50-55).

The relationship between different spaces in the system can be calculated and measured. For all Space Syntax calculations the notion of *distance* is important. Distance is seen as the number of spaces that must be traversed in order to move most economically from one space to another. A central measure based on distance is *integration*. The integration

---

[6] One example is the Via degli Augustali to the north east of the Forum. This is depicted as a wide and straight street, between the insulae 7.4 and 7.2 to the north, and 8.9 and 8.12 to the south, in for instance Richardson 1988, cover and CTP 1977-87, covers. In Laurence, 1994, and Zanker, 1995, the street is still too straight, although it seems a bit less wide than in the other maps. In reality this street is narrow and winding. The "common plans" of Pompeii abound in these kinds of errors. Note that Figure 1, based on Geertman 1998, also includes some distortions as compared to the real street pattern.

[7] *Axial space* is a term that will provoke many readers. We do however use it, as it is used in established Space Syntax terminology. The term *axial line* is sometimes used as a synonym.

value for a specific space expresses its total distance to all other spaces in the system (Hillier & Hanson 1984, 108-123).[8] A high integration value shows that a space is central to the spatial system and offers the possibility to conceive the spatial system as a totality. A low integration value instead points to a space that is in some sense also separate from the system of which it is part. Such a space is called *segregated*.

Apart from the ones discussed above, Space Syntax includes a variety of other measures and concepts. Our present study is, however, limited to the integration of axial space and some aspects of the interface between convex and axial configuration.[9]

THE ESTABLISHMENT OF THE PUBLIC SPACE IN POMPEII

The establishment of Pompeii's public space is based on some assumptions and decisions.

As public space we have defined streets and sidewalks, open spaces directly connected to streets, porticoes framing streets and open spaces or jutting out in front of various buildings. We have also included five large buildings around the Forum, whose functions are seen as extensions from the open public space. These are, on the east side: the Eumachia hall, the sanctuary for the imperial cult, the so-called Lararium (possibly also a temple of the imperial cult) and the Macellum (Zanker1995, 93-110). On the west is the covered market. In these cases we have treated the interior of the buildings as one single convex space, disregarding internal subdivisions. The same goes for three temple precincts, namely those of Apollo and of Venus on the Via Marina, and the so-called "Foro Triangolare" in the south of the town. All other structures are considered as non-public space.[10]

In the unexcavated parts of the town we have assumed that streets continue as straight lines, if there is no evidence contradicting this. The pattern of streets and blocks, *insulae*, in these areas has been assumed to be similar to that of the neighbouring areas. To create a working hypothesis, we have not assumed any unknown subdivisions of insulae, side streets or larger open spaces. This does not, however, mean that we exclude such possibilities.

A special problem is the existence or not of a street following the town wall, as this is only partly excavated. We have assumed such a street in areas where there is some evidence of a passage between town wall and house blocks - that is, in the north-east and in the south-east of Pompeii. The whole of the west and the south-west part of the town, as well as the area around the amphitheatre do not possess such a street.

In the north-west a town wall street seems to have existed in an epoch prior to the last, but to have been closed off at some time from the rest of the street system. This is indicated by antique walls blocking the north to south going streets[11] and by windows and possible walled up doors facing the now blocked area immediately inside the town wall. Thus, between the Herculaneum and the Vesuvius gates no town wall street is included in our analysis.

The space surrounding the town is considered as one single space, the *carrier*, comprising the spatial system of Pompeii.

POMPEII'S AXIAL PLAN

All the axial spaces of Pompeii, numbering 114, are shown in Fig.2. The most integretated axial spaces are shown in Fig 3. The axial plan shows the following important characteristics:

- The axially most integrated spaces come very close to the *spoked wheel* pattern discussed by Hillier. In this pattern the axially most integrated spaces surround and radiate from a less integrated town core. This pattern is typical for a category of spontaneously grown, unplanned towns, both historically and today.[12]

- The *spoked wheel* pattern is disturbed in the east part of the town, by several highly integrated axial spaces going north to south. Their high integration is in part caused by a repeated pattern of crossings with the most integrated east to west lines, an effect of the regular grid plan of eastern Pompeii.

- The streets leading to the town gates, have, with one exception, among the longest and most integrated axial lines. If these long lines do not actually pass the gates onto the carrier space, they are only one axial step from it. The exception to this pattern is the Via Consolare leading out through the Herculaneum gate in the north-west. Here the street is broken up into several axial spaces of medium integration.

- The axially most segregated spaces are mainly found in the areas close to the Forum and around the amphitheatre.

- The carrier space is one of the most integrated spaces of Pompeii, which indicates that interconnections with the countryside was an important aspect of the town's life.

Out of this axial plan there arise several interesting points for discussion.

---

8   The integration value is most often inverted, to give high integration the highest mathematical values. Here we use the term *integration value* in this sense.

9   This study forms the first part of a more comprehensive study on space and society in Pompeii. Further syntactical measures will be used together with other available information on function and form of the public space.

10   Many other, less important decisions, had to be made in order to define the public space of Pompeii. This is not the place to discuss them, but they will be enumerated in our forthcoming comprehensive study.

11   From the west Vicolo di Modesto, Vicolo della Fullonica, Via di Mercurio, Vicolo del Fauno, Vicolo del Labirinto and possibly Vicolo dei Vettii just west of the *castellum aquae*. The most western street, Vicolo di Narcisso, is at present subject to excavation in its northernmost part.

12   Hillier 1989 deals specifically with this pattern, also see Hillier 1985, 174-177. In Hillier & Hanson 1984, 115 such a wheel pattern is shown for the French village Gassin, although this specific terminology is not used. The same goes for the thorough description of integration patterns given in Hillier 1996, 149-181, cf. also 366.

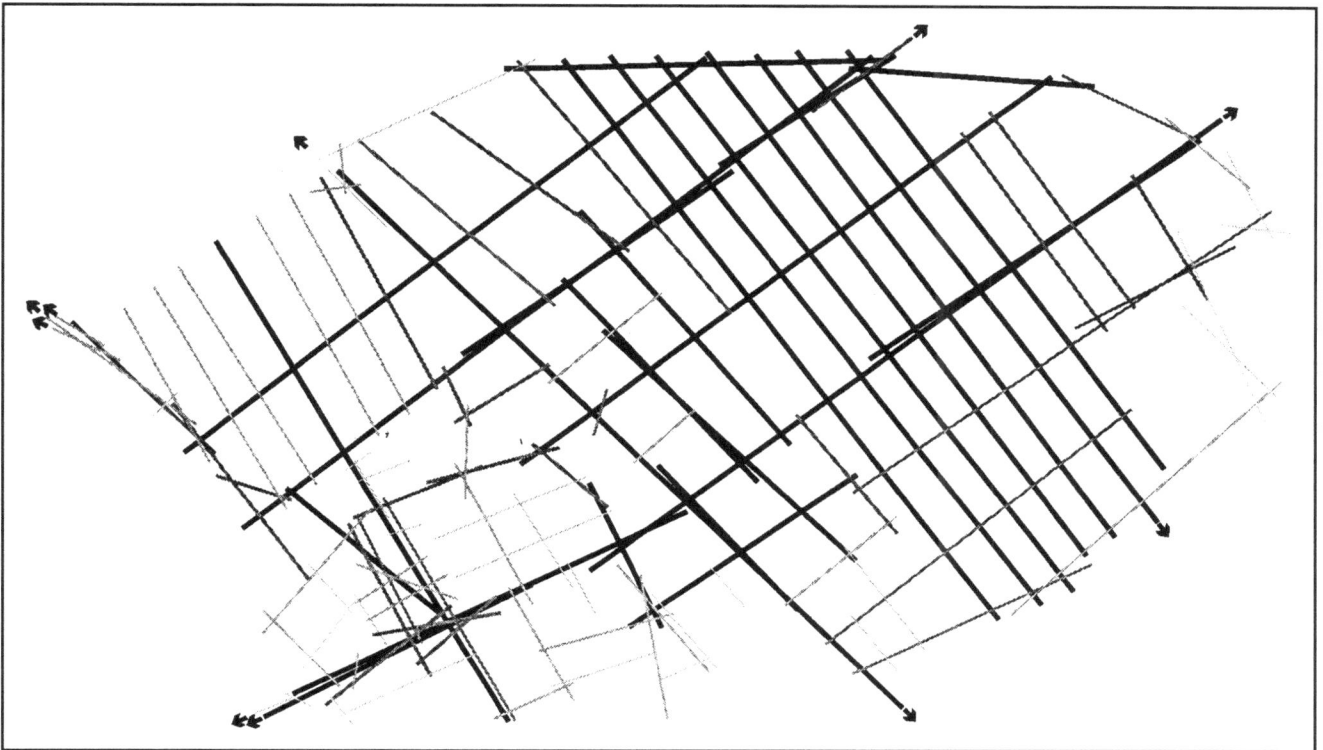

Figure 2. The axial plan of Pompeii. Fatter and darker lines indicate higher integration, in fractions of 25%.

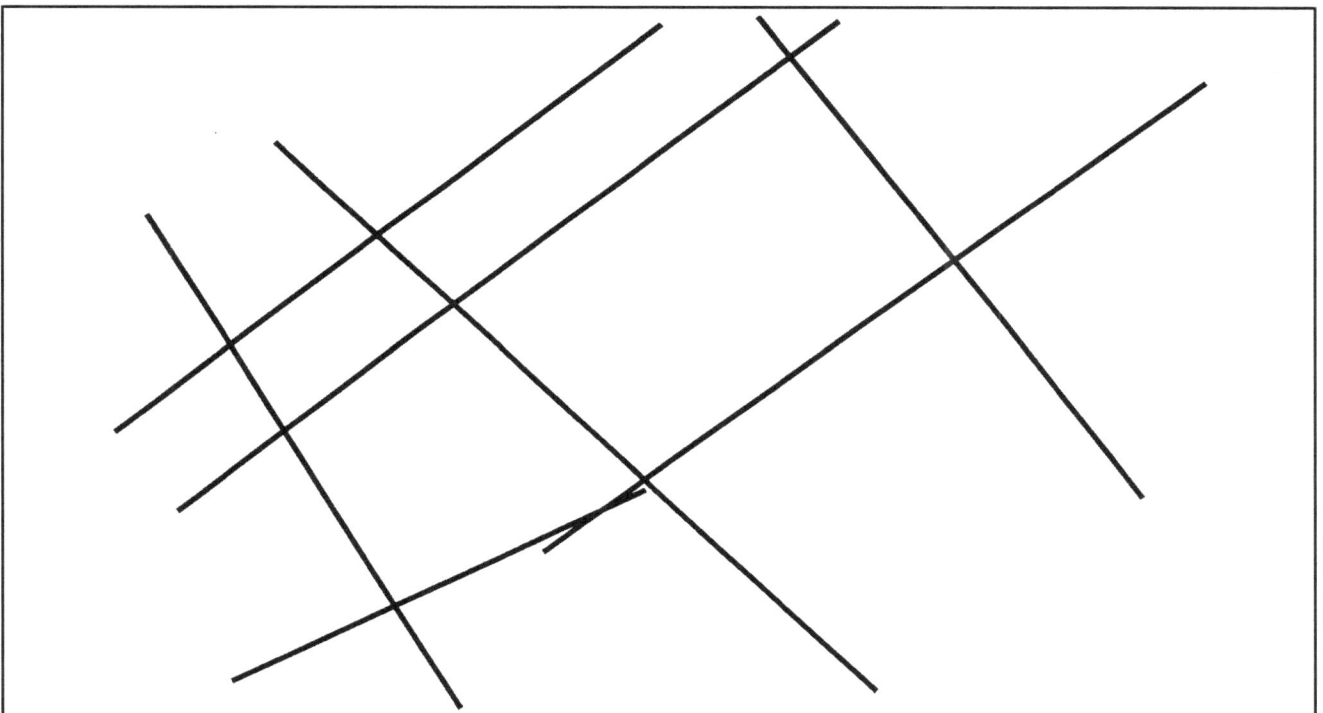

Figure 3. The most integrated axial spaces in Pompeii. These lines show the basic *spoked wheel* pattern.

1. Via di Mercurio

The streets necessary to the spoked wheel pattern are all among the very most integrated lines (See Figure 3) There are other slightly less integrated lines forming part of the pattern, but this persists even when these lines are removed. The necessary lines are in the east to west direction:

• The well known Via dell'Abbondanza/Via Marina in the south

• Via delle Terme/della Fortuna/di Nola in the north

In the north to south direction the streets are, from the east:

- Via Stabiana
- Via di Mercurio/del Foro/ delle Scuole (here called *Via di Mercurio*). This last line also comprises the eastern part of the Forum proper.

With one exception, all these streets and their axial spaces are connected to the carrier, either directly or by one axial step consising of a short line passing the city gate. The exception, Via di Mercurio, is an interesting anomaly as it does not lead to any gate. It crosses the Forum, but to the north traverses a segregated area, and ends up blindly against a tower in the town wall. In the south it again goes through a segregated neighbourhood and ends in the corner of a small alley. Along this axial line are placed two arches, one at the northern perimeter of the Forum and one in the crossing with Via delle Terme. In crossing the Forum, this line is flanked by the east Forum colonnade and its décor, as well as by the temple of Jupiter to the west. The view along the axial line is thus unique, giving the illusion of big city scape, masses of important architecture and likeness to imperial Rome itself (Zanker, 112-114).

Why has this street, leading from nowhere to nowhere, been invested with all these features, as well as with one of the highest integration values ? One possibility is a conceptual importance, partly to be derived from the fact that the street crosses the Forum. If this is so, it is strange that the street does not connect this civic centre to the town gates and the world outside. Could it be hypothesised that the Via di Mercurio once did have this connection? As has been suggested, the south-west part of the town may once have been the original ancient town core, later augmented by new districts. In this case the Via di Mercurio would be the old main street of an italic town, and its northward connection with the surrounding countryside. Thus, the Space Syntax analysis could support the view of a gradual development of Pompeii, and make Laurence's suggestion of a town simultaneously laid out less probable (Laurence 1994, 15-17).

2. Via Consolare and the Herculaneum gate

Via Consolare is the only street leading to a town gate, where the axial lines are not among the 25% most integrated. Further, the axiality of this street is much broken up, contradictory to the straight lines coming from other town gates. The Herculaneum gate is not a back gate, however, but an impressive structure with one carriage entrance and two walkways. The street also shows heavy traces of wheeled traffic, which suggests it was much used. Its fairly low integration in this analysis could be connected with the fact that the town clearly continues outside this gate, with shops, houses and colonnades – not only with a necropolis, as seems to be the case outside the other gates. An axial analysis including this "suburban" area would show higher integration values for Via Consolare.

Another reason could be defence purposes. The wall between the two northern gates, the Herculaneum gate and the Vesuvius gate, seems to have been additionally fortified at some point in the town's history. We have already mentioned the blocking of the streets going southwards, from what was once a street following the town wall. There are also indications for an added strengthening of structures in the area. The much broken up axiality leading from the gate to the Forum may have served the same defence purpose.

Obviously, defence was no longer needed once Pompeii became a Roman colony in 80 BC. The north-west part of the town should thus predate colonisation, as is the general opinion (e.g. Zanker 1995, 38, Abb. 2). Such strengthening of defence features have not been observed in other parts of the town. The relevance and the implications of this difference need further discussion.

3. The grid pattern neighbourhoods in the north-west and in the east

The two areas where a planned grid pattern is clearly evident, are the above mentioned north-west part of the town and the more extensive eastern area. The form of the insulae is similar in both areas, but there is a slight difference in street direction.

In spite of the superficial similarities, there are important differences between these two parts of the town. The integration pattern of the axial spaces shows much higher integration in the eastern part. Also the noticeable character, status and functions differ: In the west patrician town villas dominate the picture, and while the east also features fine houses, there is a more agricultural set-up. Vineyards and gardens are found in this district. This difference in pattern remains to be more thoroughly investigated.

4. The amphitheatre and its surroundings

Lastly, there is an interesting but rather uncomplicated feature to be mentioned: the amphitheatre's setting in a segregated area. This spot must have been popular and attractive for visitors from both within and outside the town, its attraction enhanced by the proximity of town vineyards with serving possibilities. But the amphitheatre could also be disruptive to the town's tranquillity, as is witnessed by the famous wall painting, depicting a brawl between pompeians and the visiting inhabitants of neighbouring Nocera (Ramage & Ramage 1995, 160). A segregated area minimised the risks of such a brawl spilling out into the town. For further good measure, the segregation could be made almost total: streets leading to the area from the integrated thoroughfares had portals possible to close with heavy doors!

THE INTERFACE BETWEEN CONVEX AND AXIAL CONFIGURATION – A PRELIMINARY DISCUSSION

In the introductory discussion on method, we mentioned the relationship between convex spaces and axiality. Here, the concept of *convex articulation* is an important one. A high degree of convex articulation means that many convex spaces are threaded upon one single axial line. This phenomenon means that a diversified and interesting environment is created

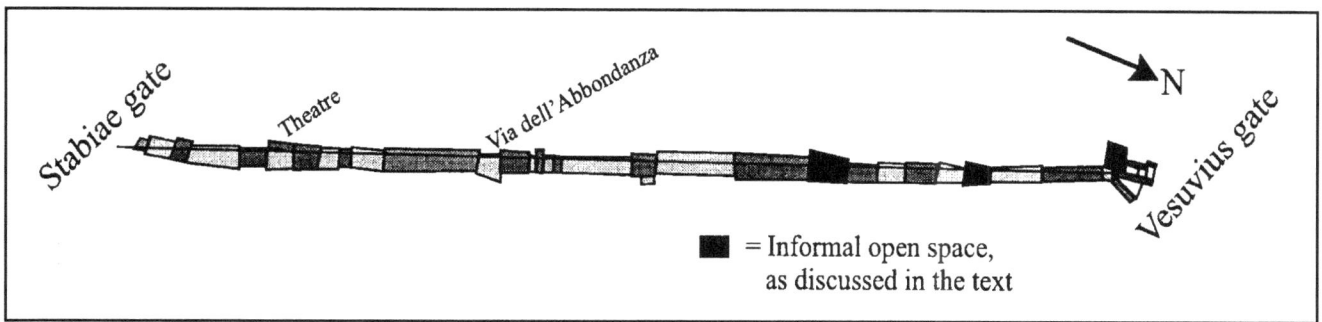

Figure 4. The series of convex spaces strung up along the axial space of the Via Stabiana, not to scale.

for the visitor passing through, an environment easy to remember because of its variation. This facilitates finding the way in the town (Hillier et alii, 1983, 48-64; Hillier & Hanson 1984, 100).

The degree of articulation possible to detect from a plan depends on the scale of the plan, and on the researchers decisions about the size of details to be considered as boundaries for convex spaces. These decisions in turn depend on the purpose of the study: a more overarching study of a large city need not include minor subdivisions of convexity, that would be interesting on the level of, say, a block. For Pompeii we have chosen a very high level of detailing, as the town would have been experienced primarily on foot, on a mule-cart or possibly on horseback. This means slow passage, which enables the traveller to notice minor boundaries and detailed articulation.[13] A further object for study is the non-spatial articulation of domains by such means as colour, façade decoration and changes in the pavement of streets and sidewalks – also important in a town of slow moving traffic.

We have hitherto not made a complete study of the convex articulation, but a few preliminary conclusions can already be drawn. One is, that axial spaces with low convex articulation occur predominantly in the grid plan areas. Otherwise, high articulation may be found both along integrated and segregated lines.

Non-spatial means of articulation are used very differently in different parts of the town. The Via dell'Abbondanza/Via Marina may serve as one example. Convex articulation is high along the whole street, with a slight falling off in the area closest to the Forum. The eastern part and the most western part are furthermore highly differentiated by such mean as the colour and form of the façades. The different modes of articulation can, but need not, single out the same domains. As a contrast to this, in the Forum part of the Via dell'Abbondanza/Via Marina the facades show a high degree of uniformity, which further enhances the lower convex articulation. This underlines the official and grandiose character of the Forum.

Another highly integrated street and strongly articulated street is the Via Stabiana, shown in Fig. 4.

Along this street there is no marked break in the convex articulation, although the theatre façade near the Stabiae gate offers uniformity of non-spatial articulation – in other words, the theatre is clearly made noticeable through a large façade differing from that of surrounding houses. Several small informal open places along this street created foci for encounters between inhabitants and strangers. Let us now visit some of these places together with a fictive stranger in Pompeii, to see how convex articulation worked out, bringing together stranger and inhabitant.

INHABITANT AND STRANGER – AN ILLUSTRATION OF THE INTERFACE

Our traveller is a woman, as Pompeii certainly was not only visited by men. She owns a small vineyard some miles out in the country, and travels together with her overseer. She reaches the Vesuvius gate, but before entering the town, she rests for a while in an *exedra* conveniently set up by a local benefactor. Here she chats with some of the local people going out to the necropolis to honour their dead, and so she is already drawn into the orbit of communication while still technically outside town. She passes the gate space which clearly marks the boundary, and after this sees the Via Stabiana sloping steeply to the south.

She has immediately entered into the first of the convex spaces forming an informal small square. This is the open area in front of the *Castellum aquae,* where the aqueduct of Augustan times arrives in town. This is a likely spot to fetch water for the houses nearby, if these are not directly connected to the aqueduct. An area in front of the castellum is outlined by large upright stone blocks, certainly meant to stop wheeled traffic, but possibly also delineating an area of some activity – water fetching or some work connected to water suggests itself. In addition too these water connected activities there is the existence of the grape gatherers post on the south side of the open place (Wallace-Hadrill, 1994, 215-216). This is a house with many entrances around a central space, suggesting communal activities and much comings and goings - it is plausible that the activities inside would spill out into the public space. So, there would be abundant

---

[13]   Our level of detailing in this preliminary study is based on the CTP map. Every shift in space boundaries, detectable by minute study of the map is included. For further investigations this has to be checked in reality. A few tests have been made in town, and the results were compatible with the CTP map.

opportunity to talk to people, ask for information, pass the time of day and perhaps even to hire labourers for the vineyard, or arrange for the dusty travelling clothes to be washed. A stable for travellers entering or leaving the town is also at hand to the west, there are shops and bars for food and drink, as well as a fine lararium on the east side of the space, should the traveller feel inclined to honour the gods of the place. A whole array of activities possible to observe, and to a greater or lesser extent to participate in, thus confront our visitor.

If she, however, goes on southwards the traveller will in time arrive at the next small open place, just before the Via Stabiana crosses the northernmost of the west to east axes, the Vicolo di Mercurio. Here a large private house opens up with its main entrance, providing benches for its visitors, or for those to the bar dependent on it. A shop entrance also opens onto the space, and stepping stones provide access to the east side of the street (Wallace-Hadrill 1994,214-216).This side is in our days largely inaccessible and overgrown, so where these stepping stones led cannot be determined. Just to the south of this, the convex articulation singles out the area of the street crossing. It is defined by a well and a tower for the distribution of aqueduct waters, but offers no other special incitement to stop for a longer while.

The next clearly marked open space, providing a place of temporary standstill, follows already at the next crossing to the south, with the Via di Nola. Here a workshop complex and a large shop are accessible (Wallace-Hadrill 1994, 211-212), as well as a small sanctuary to the *lares* and a well, decorated with a *silenus* head. Stepping stones for going southwards or crossing the street to the east – where in the same well-defined convex space there are several shops and a *caupona* for food and drink - are provided.

For the traveller, the street continues to unfold its various activities on her way south: informal places with mixed activities and convex spaces devoted mainly to commerce interchange. One of the commercial spaces is the stretch of the Via Stabiana following immediately to the south of the Via di Nola, where our traveller can shop according to her means. In a few spaces the street also features some spaces where the official Pompeii makes its impact: the *tetrapylon* of the Holconii at the crossing with the Via dell'Abbondanza does not only provide shade and a convenient overview of shops, bars and local altars, but also reminds the visitor of law and order and the possibility to take part in politics, if only by admiration.

Thus, meeting people going about their everyday work, participating in some sense in these activities by watching, talking, drawing water, resting and frequenting the same places to eat and drink, was eminently possible in the informal spaces provided along the entrance to town. The informal could certainly be combined with the economically profitable, as the shops, workshops, the stable and the bars show.

At the tetrapylon we leave our vineyard matron, contemplating the possibilities of encounters in town. In the stream of people passing by on the Via dell'Abbondanza,

she may notice an elderly farmer, with his mule packed with country produce. Let us now follow his way, and see him safely back after his errands are done.

ARTICULATION AS A MEANS OF FINDING YOUR WAY

The man with the mule is in Pompeii for the first time. How can he find his way in the town, safely reach his destination and dare to explore the city without fear of getting lost?

He reaches the town from the eastern countryside and enters through the Sarno gate. Once he has climbed the slope through the gate he can see the street, Via dell'Abbondanza, stretch out before him as a seemingly endless straight line. This in itself helps him to understand that he stands on an important thoroughfare. He can confidently continue to walk – or to ride his mule – knowing that this street will take him towards the core of the town. He can also observe that there are many other people doing precisely the same thing.

Soon, however, he will reach crossings with other streets. They are long and straight, just as the Via dell'Abbondanza, but their character is so different that he will hardly be tempted to turn into any of them. The main street is highly articulated, both spatially and by other means. Facades jut out into the street or are drawn in from it, forming a series of small convex spaces along the length of the street. Houses are differently coloured, and some of them have painted decorations, porticoes or sculptural architectural attributes. Also the activities demonstrate themselves with clear signals – broad openings to various shops, glittering marble counters for street side eating and drinking, and, for those who understand the signals, excluded premises for various types of recreation.

The crossing side streets have an altogether different character with undecorated facades, few openings and ever fewer shops, and a largely unarticulated convex space. Some of these alleys even seem semi-private, with doors that can seclude them totally from the hectic movement on the thoroughfare. It is obvious that entering these streets would be to venture into the local, private life of the inhabitants, and as our visitor is a stranger in town he does not hesitate to follow the main stream straight forward.

One of the crossing streets, Via di Nocera, is more similar to Via dell'Abbondanza, with shops appearing to sell local wine. But although this might call for a temporary deviation, our visitor can clearly see that this street would lead him out through another gate – and that is not where he is aiming.

After following the highly integrated Via dell'Abbondanza over a score of crossings, the visitor will eventually find himself in the very centre of the town. In the crossing with Via Stabiana he meets a street that is just as highly integrated as the one he has come on, and which shows similar abundance of articulation, commerce and people. To his left it slopes down towards a gate, and the steep rise to his right also seems to lead to a far off town gate. If he turns to the right here, he will continue through a highly integrated and articulated street.

He has now got an overview of an abundance of shops and open places where he could sell his produce.

But maybe the elderly farmer is not only interested in shops and entertainment, but would also like to see the more official parts of Pompeii. In that case, the very formation of the townscape can tell him to continue straight on along Via dell'Abbondanza. He passes under the imposing double arch of the Holconian *tetrapylon*, and finds himself in a street flanked by uniform stone facades. Although there are still shops and commerce, the scale is larger and the street not as articulated as in its eastern part. This is the neighbourhood of the Forum, the grandeur of which is influencing also the street leading up to it. Closer to the Forum the Via dell'Abbondanza is closed for vehicles, and those who want to enter the official town centre have to do it on foot.

After finishing his errands our visitor wants to return along the same way as he came. Finding this would hardly be a great problem, as the straight axial lines will lead him in the right direction and the articulated street with many convex spaces will make him recognise places were he has already been.

CONCLUSIONS

The Space Syntax analysis of the town plan poses interesting questions and subjects for further investigation, and suggests hypotheses that would otherwise not come to mind. It is likely that more comprehensive research with this method will help to elucidate the problem of the gradual growth of Pompeii, as well as the town's socio-spatial functioning in the final period.

Especially promising is the study of the convex and non-spatial articulation along the axially highly integrated thoroughfares. The high degree of articulation seems to indicate an active and important interface between inhabitants and strangers. Further understanding can be gained from the archaeologically detected functions of buildings opening up into convex spaces or other, differently articulated domains, as well as from the functions present in the public space itself.

Karin Fridell Anter, techn. dr. Department of Architecture, Royal Institute of Technology, Stockholm
karinfa@arch.kth.se

Marina Weilguni, Department of Archaeology and Ancient History, Uppsala University, Uppsala
marina.weilguni@antiken.uu.se

References

CTP, Corpus Topographicum Pompeianum, (1977-87) vol. 2-5. Ed. H.B van der Poel. Rome.

CTP, Corpus Topographicum Pompeianum, (1988) vol. 3, 'The RICA maps of Pompeii'. Ed. H.B van der Poel. Rome.

Eschebach, H (1970) *Die Städtebauliche Entwicklung des antiken Pompeji*. Heidelberg.

Geertman, Herman (1998) 'Lo sviluppo urbanistico della città e la sua storia. Il progetto olandese' , in *Sotto i lapilli*, ed. J. Berry. Milano.

Hillier, B (1985) 'The nature of the artificial: the contingent and the necessity in spatial form in architecture'. *Geoforum 16:2*, 163-178.

Hillier, B (1989) 'The architecture of the urban object' *Ekistics 334-335*, 5-21.

Hillier, B (1996) *Space is the machine*. London.

Hillier, B et. al. (1983) 'Space Syntax. A different urban perspective' *Architect's Journal 30*.

Hillier, B & Hanson, J (1984) *The social logic of space*. Cambridge.

Laurence, R (1994) *Roman Pompeii: Space and Society*. London.

Opuscula Pomeiana (1991-). Kyoto, Japan.

Ramage, N H & Ramage A (1995*) Roman Art*, second edition. London.

Richardson, L (1988) *Pompeii, an architectural history*. Baltimore & London.

Zanker, P (1995) *Pompeji: Stadtbild und Wohngeschmack*. Mainz.

THE GOLDEN HORDE MOSQUES

Emma ZILIVINSKAYA

Abstract: In the Golden Horde, the state which arose as a result of mongol conquests, Islam was accepted as the state religion in the 20-30th years of XIV century. The famous Arab traveller who visited many Golden Horde cities at that time mentioned 30 mosques at Sarai (the capital) only. By now 11 mosques only has been subjected to archaeological study over the whole Golden Horde area. However, this material allows to guess the basic principles of planning of such Golden Horde buildings.

Mostly, the Golden Horde mosques represent large square or rectangular (in plan) structures; their internal space was partitioned into naves by rows of columns. The main entrance in the north wall is opposite to mihrab and it is surrounded by portal which juts out of the wall. In the largest structures of this kind two additional entrances in the west and east walls may take place.

It seems to be probable that such type of planning arose in the Golden Horde owing to influence of Seljuk Asia Minor. It was this region where the mosques were built in the form of basilicas with flat overhead cover. In other parts of Muslim world the planning of mosques differs considerably from this style. Building technique and the decoration of mosques of the West regions of the Golden Horde area also are close to tradition of Seljuk architecture. Even in the central part of the Golden Horde territory, in the Lower Volga region, where the influence of Middle Asia and Iran dominated in building, both general planning and some details of mosques' interior correspond closely to analogous structures of Asia Minor.

Owing to large-scale archaeological excavations at the Golden Horde sites a number of architectural structures have been investigated in the last 35 years. Those are houses of various strata of city dwellers and such communal and cult buildings as mosques, mausolea, madrassahs, and bathhouses. These buildings have usually been viewed as separate structures or as parts of an architectural ensemble. Presently the abundance of the data enables one to distinguish similar buildings, to examine characteristic traits of their planning, and to compare them with their counterparts in other countries. It it especially true of mosques, which were the most important communal buildings in every Moslem city.

Mosques as prayer places emerged almost together with Islam. Early Arabian mosques consisted of an open courtyard surrounded by a wall, along which porticos with a wooden roof, supported by wooden pillars, were constructed. According to the majority of scholars (Creswell, 1958, pp. 7, 8; Grabar, 1973, p. 53), the multipillar pattern appeared under the influence of the Old Persian Apadana in Persepolis and the hypostyle halls of Egypt. It was further evolved in such Umayyad mosques as the al-Walid mosque in Damascus (7th century) and the Great Mosque of Aleppo (early 8th century), both of which were converted Christian basilicas. Under the Abbasids (9th century) the magnificent al-Mutawakil mosque consisting of a big courtyard encirled with pillared porticos was built at Samarra. This mosque pattern spread over the Caliphate along with the Arabian conquests. The mosques of 'Amr (7th century) and ibn-Tulun (9th century), al-Azhar and al-Hakim (10th-11th centuries) were built in Egypt. The best buildings of this type in Maghreb are the Sidi 'qba mosque at Qairawan (7th-8th centuries), the Great Mosques of Susa (9th century), Sfax (10th century) and Algiers (11th century), the Qarawiyyin mosque at Fez (9th

century), and the Kutubiyya mosque at Marrakesh (12th century). The Great Mosque at Córdoba, at the western frontier of the Caliphate, became a masterpiece of Moorish architecture. The nucleus of this immense architectural complex centered around the inevitable courtyard (*sana*) was built in the 8th century after the al-Walid mosque in Damascus. The planning of mosques with a court as a compositional centre remained dominant in the western part of the Moslem world henceforth (Creswell, 1958; Grabar, 1973; Encyclopaedia, 1927).

In Iran and closely related Central Asia the relevant architectural patterns developed in a completely different way. Although Arab governors did build the court-pattern mosques in Iranian cities, the Persians followed pre-Islamic models. Thus, local types of mosques, i.e., chortak-kiosks in the west and iwans in the east of the Iranian area, emerged (Herzfeld, 1935; Godard, 1962). The combination of the Arabian and local patterns resulted in the four-iwan planning, which became predominant in the 12th century. The earliest monument of this type is the Great Mosque at Isfahan.

Central Asia also adopted the Arabian court pattern, the earliest specimen of the kind being the 9th-10th-century Dandakan mosque (Pribytkova, 1964). However, under the influence of local traditions centric mosques also emerged there. According to G. Pugachenkova, the kiosk-pattern mosque appeared in southern Turkmenistan even earlier than it did in Iran, namely, in the 9th-10th centuries (Pugachenkova, 1958, p. 185). Pillar compositions with a central dome surrounded by smaller domes or vaults are attested from the 10th century onwards (Pribytkova, 1958, pp. 131-134; eadem, 1973, pp. 38-58). The merging and further evolution of the Arabian and local traditions resulted in the variety of Central Asian mosque types (Mankovskaya, 1980, pp. 102-121).

Mosques in Asia Minor underwent an original evolution. Under the Seljuks the inner court in the Arab-pattern mosques became roofed, first by a flat beam ceiling supported by wooden pillars, like in the 11th-century court-patterned Mahmud-bey mosque at Qasaba near Kastamoni and the Ulu Cami mosque at Afiyon (Benset, 1973, p. 16, fig. 39; L'art, 1981, p. 102, ill. 56). However, in the 11th century the erection of arcades resting on stone pillars began, although the ceiling remained flat. A small dome was erected over the ante-mihrab part of the building, while a sky-light as a survival of the court was made in the roof either at the centre of the hall or nearer to the entrance. A small fountain was often made under the sky-light. Varieties of this planning can be seen in the eleventh-century Ulu Cami mosques at Sivas and at Kayseri, the 13th-century Alaeddin Cami mosque at Konya, and the 13th-century Great Mosque at Zivrihissar (Benset, 1973, p. 17, fig. 31; L'art, 1983, p. 87, fig. 21, 22, p. 100, ill. 52).

The first mosques were probably built in the Golden Horde, the borderline nation of the Moslem world, under Berke, who was a Moslem and favoured city development. Yet, their large-scale erection is undoubtedly associated with the reign of Uzbek, under whom Islam was adopted as the official religion and cities flourished. Ibn-Battuta refers to this period while mentioning "thirty congregational mosques for solemn service... and a lot of other mosques" solely at Sarai (Tisenhausen, 1884, p. 306). Unfortunately, the number of mosques excavated all over the Golden Horde is lower than that mentioned by Ibn-Battuta. Nevertheless, the archaeological record gives an insight into their planning.

Given the wide distribution of the Golden Horde mosques, it seems advisable to describe them by the area.

THE VOLGA BULGARIA

The most famous monument of the Golden Horde Moslem cult architecture is the mosque of the Bulgar city, the capital of the Volga Bulgaria, known as the Tetragon and described in numerous publications (Smolin, 1926; Bashkirov, 1928; Smirnov, 1951; Voskresensky, 1966; Aidarov, 1970).

Before the site was abandoned in the 1330s, the building erected in the 1260s had undergone several reconstructions (Aidarov, 1970, p. 54).

The first period saw the erection of the walls of a rectangularoid structure, slightly widening southward (fig. 1). It was 32.6 m long, 28.2 m wide in the north, and 29.6 m wide in the south (all measurements taken from within). The walls, some 1.2-1.3 m thick, were laid of mortared blocks of untooled limestone. The west and east walls were reinforced with two rectangular buttresses each, while the south one had three. The northern entrance was framed with a portal, of which two rectangular pylons survived. A rectangular socle of the minaret was situated west of the portal. Four rows of columns divided the inner space of the mosque into five aisles. Each row had five columns, either rectangular (85 x 92 cm)

or square (92 x 92 cm) in section. The walls were plastered white both from within and on the outside. There was a wooden planking on the floor.

In the early 14th century the mosque was radically reconstructed (fig. 2). Its outlook was modified by the multifaceted towers on the corners. The two northern towers measured some eight meters in diameter, while the southern ones reached ten. Such a treatment of corners has not been attested for any other mosque, although similarly planned fortresses were built in Central Asia in the early Middle Ages. Later on tower-shaped cantilevered corner projections were characteristic of fortresses, caravanserais, and *khanqah*, i.e., pilgrim hostels. Huge round towers reinforced the walls of castles in Azerbaijan (Bretanitsky, 1966). The small decorative towers of the Kalyan mosque at Khiva must have the same origin, even though they are considerably reduced as compared with the corner buttresses of the Tetragon.

In the last period of the mosque functioning its interior was reconstructed. Doorways flanked by window openings were made in the east and west walls. Light tambours were annexed to all the three entrances from the inside. The pillars were replaced by six rows of columns resting on square bases. The bases and capitals were embellished with carved stylized palmettes characteristic of Azerbaijani architectural ornamentation (Bretanitsky, 1966, p. 378).

It is generally assumed that the Tetragon had a flat ceiling resting on arcades. The roof might have been gabled, which would have been consistent with weather conditions.

The Tetragon complex also included the Big Minaret, known from travellers' drawings. A cubic socle of the minaret was converted into an octahedron supporting a cylindrical tapering shaft. At the top there was a platform for the muezzin. Two sides of the minaret had three windows each. In the middle the minaret was encircled with an Arabic inscription. The minaret was 24 m high.

The surviving Lesser Minaret shows a similar design. Some five meters lower, it also has a cubic socle with cut off corners changing into an octahedron and a cylindrical shaft (Fig. 3). The shaft is surmounted by a platform supporting a superstructure with a gabled roof. The entrance to the minaret is situated on the north side. The upper part of the doorway, the arch inserted into the shaft and the bevelled corners of the socle are embellished with carving characteristic of Azerbaijani architecture. Moreover, the design showing three architectural volumes converting into each other as well as the somewhat squat proportions of the Bolgar minarets are reminescent of their Azerbaijani counterparts.

THE LOWER VOLGA AREA

Two congregational mosques have been discovered in the Lower Volga region, the core area of the Golden Horde. One of them was excavated at the Vodianskoe site in the Volgograd region (Yegorov, 1976). The mosque was rectangular in plan, measuring 26 by 35 m and oriented north-south (Fig. 4). The walls of the structure, laid of clay-mortared quarry stone, were 1.2-1.3 m thick. They were plastered white with lime mortar both from inside and on the outside. The doorway was situated in the north wall east of the central axis of the building and embellished with a portal.

A rectangular structure containing the mihrab niche formed a projection in the middle of the south wall on the outside. The plastered white hemispherical mihrab was flanked by

profiled pylons and decorated with a rectangular board. The latter had a red bordure and bore a stamped Arabic inscription standing out against a blue background.

Before the mihrab there was a rectangular ground (8.14 by 8.40 m) bounded on three sides by three-course high walls made of brick bat. Roughly dressed square flat stones supporting the wooden pillars on which the roof rested were inserted into all the three walls. A fluted marble column that supported a lauh, i.e. a stand for a copy of the Qur'an, was partly dug in at the centre of the ground. The downward-

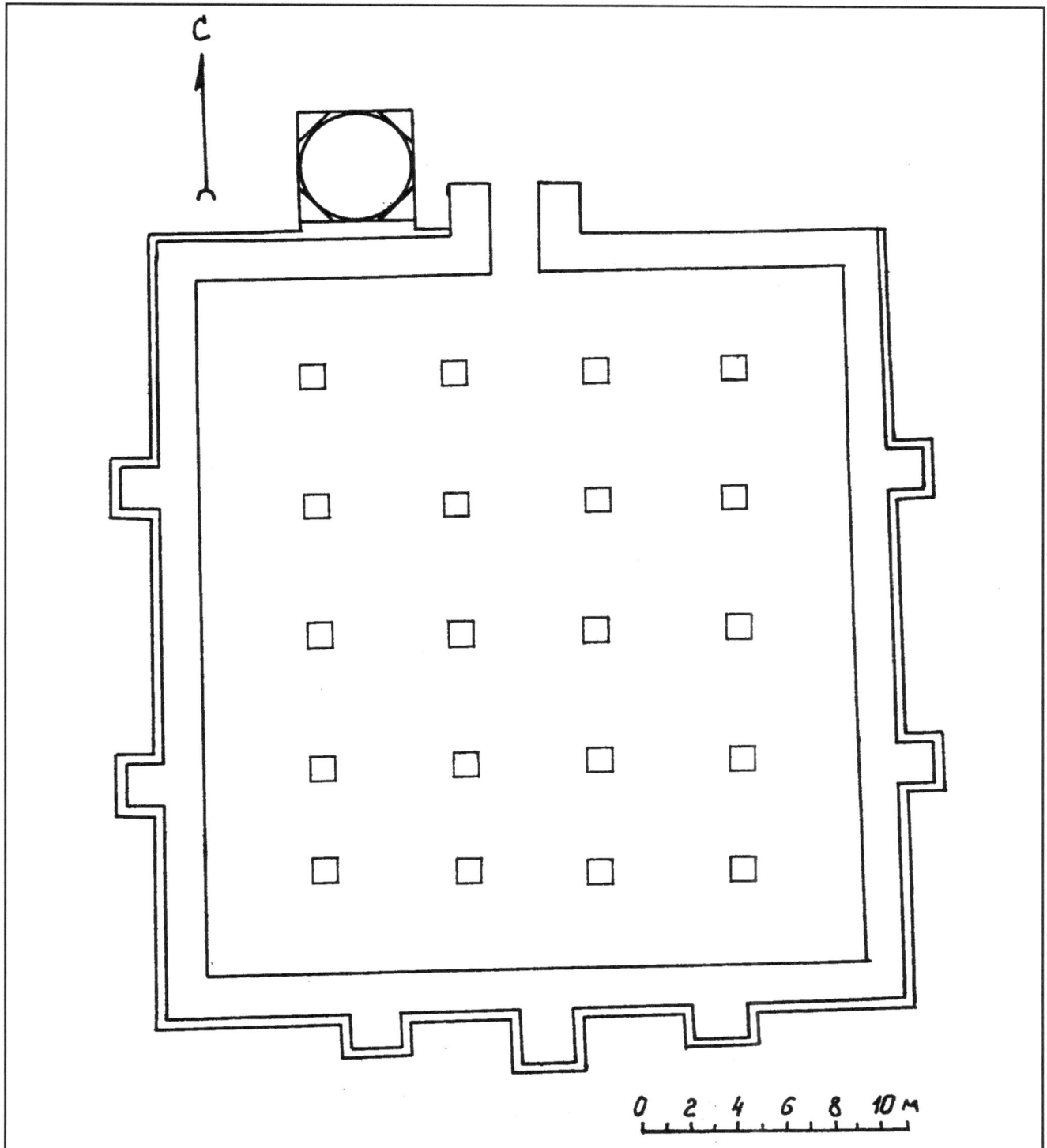

Fig. 1. The Tetragon in the first period.

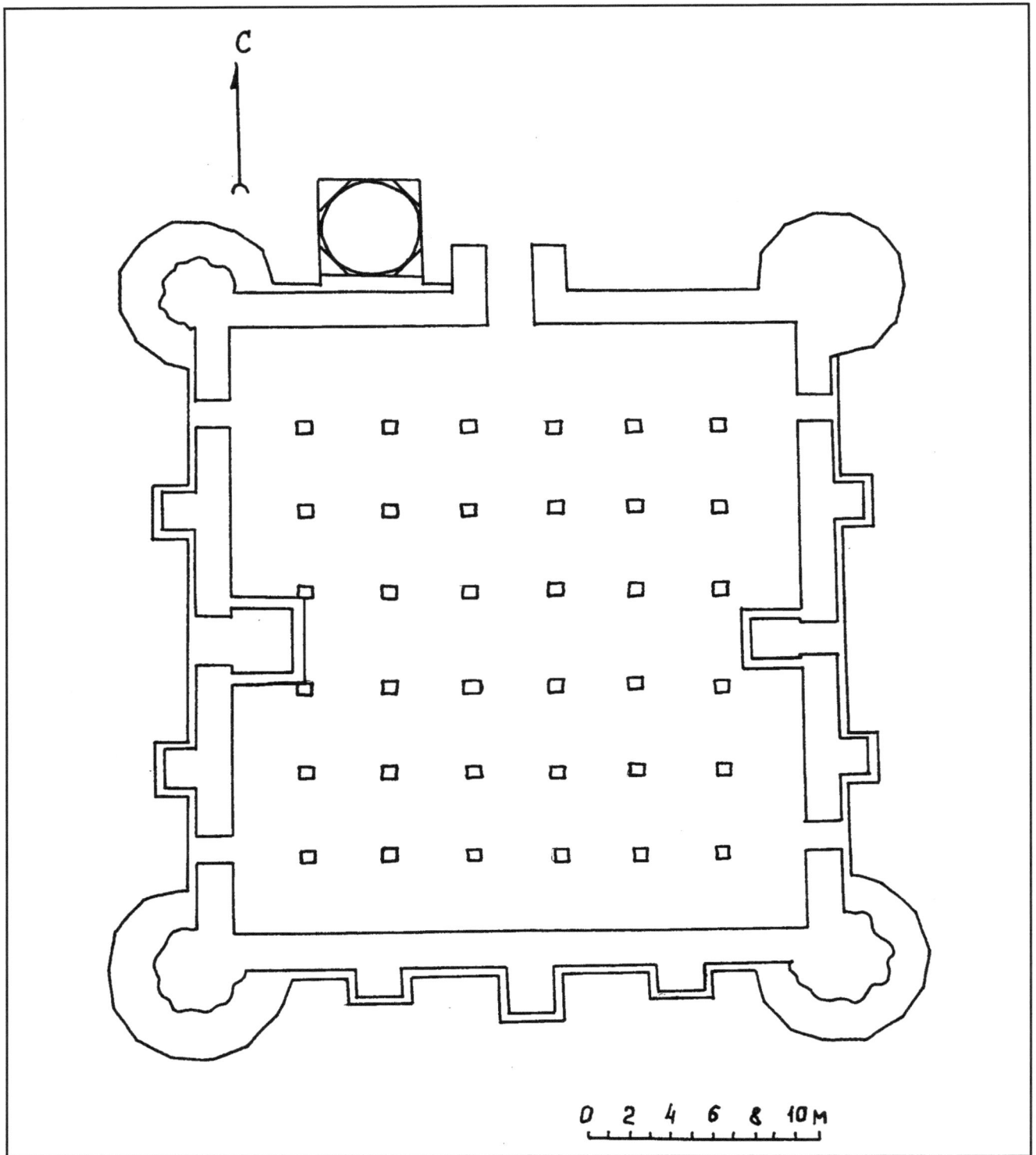

Fig. 2. The Tetragon in the second period.

tapering cylindrical column rested on an Early Byzantine marble capital placed at the bottom of the pit. Both the capital and the column probably had been brought for such an unorthodox use from the Crimea.

The remaining inner space of the mosque was divided by three rows of columns into six four-meter-wide aisles. During the excavations 24 grey granite 20-centimeter-high square column bases (30 by 30 cm) were encountered. Their corners were cut off to form an octagon and many of them had recess

patterns on the upper surface designed to facilitate the erection of wooden pillars. There was probably wooden flooring in the mosque.

A minaret was situated near the north-east corner of the mosque. Its socle, rectangular in plan (5.0 by 4.2 m), was attached to the east wall. The brick débris of the minaret shaft enables one to reconstruct its design. The shaft was built of semicircular in plan backed bricks and embellished with turquoise glazed brick and stucco insertions bearing Kufic inscriptions.

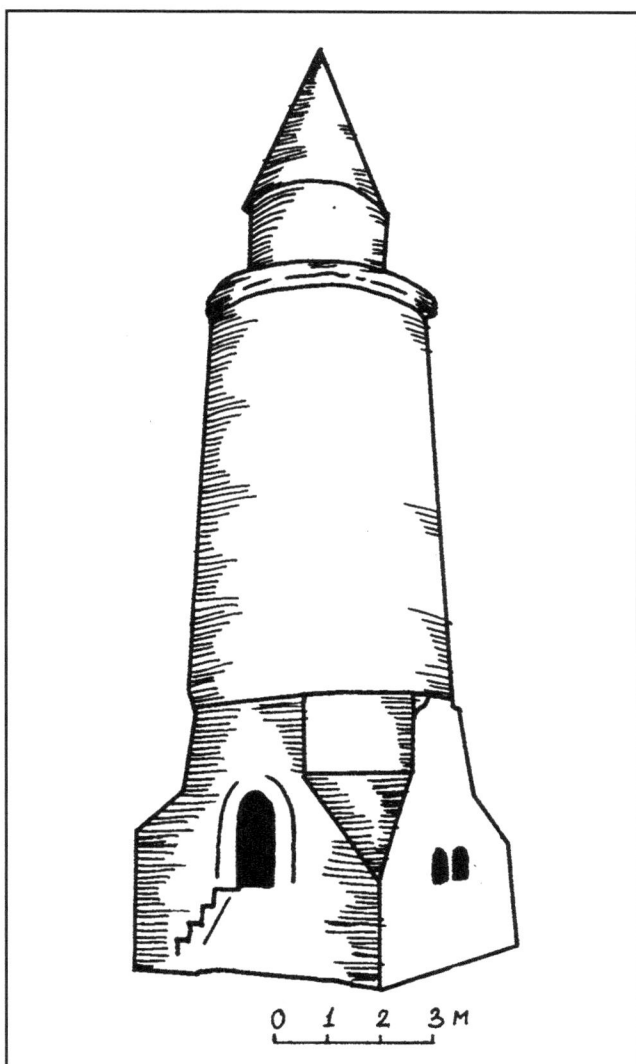

Fig. 3. The Lesser Minaret in Bulgar.

The Vodianskoe site mosque can be dated to the second half of the 14th century.

Yet another congregational mosque was excavated in the aristocratic ward of Sarai, the capital of the Golden Horde (Zilivinskaya, 1997). The mosque consisted of two compartments, i.e., the sanctuary and an annex in the north-west part of the building (Fig. 5). The burnt-brick clay-mortared walls of the mosque were almost completely dismantled at a later date. The excavators succeeded in tracing the plan almost completely from imprints of bricks and the wall bed sunk into virgin soil. The sanctuary was a room square in plan measuring 36.5 m by 35.5 m. The main entrance was marked with a huge portal in the north wall. There was another, smaller doorway in the middle of the east wall. It seems likely that there was yet another doorway in the west wall, but no traces of it have survived. The interior of the sanctuary was partitioned into nine aisles by eight rows of columns. Each row in its turn consisted of eight columns. Those were wooden pillars square in section, painted with white lime mortar and resting upon massive brick sub-floor foundations. The two columns flanking the mihrab were probably made of stone, since their foundations were

reinforced with wooden framework in order to make the shrinkage even. The rectangular mihrab was engaged into the south wall and had a *ganch*, i.e., carved plaster, frame. Before the mihrab there was a carved *ganch* lattice-work (the *maqsura*) the framework of which was composed of wooden sticks. An uncovered aula measuring 9.3 m x 9.0 m was situated at the centre of the sanctuary, near the main entrance. At the centre of the aula lay a large round water-tank faced with brick. The floor of the rest of the sanctuary was made of trampled down earth. The walls, like the columns, were probably plastered white.

An annex measuring 13.85 m x 9.8 m was attached to the exterior of the north wall, close to the western pylon of the doorway. The interior of the annex was richly adorned. The floor was paved with burnt brick, while the walls were decorated with mosaic panels composed of polychrome gilt tiles. A large heated adobe bunk, the *sofa*, was installed along the west wall. The ceiling rested on two columns, the stone foundations of which have survived. It seems likely that the room was not a cult one. This could have been a court-room or the premises of yet another institution attached to the mosque.

The Sarai mosque can be dated to the mid-14th century.

THE NORTH CAUCASUS

Three mosques have been investigated at the North Caucasian sites so far. Two of them were encountered at the Upper Julat site in the North Ossetia (Miloradovich, 1963).

The Lesser Mosque has survived mostly at the foundation level (Fig. 6). This small (9.8 by 6.6 m) building was meridionally oriented. Its foundation was made of mortared river cobble stone. The burnt-brick walls were almost completely destroyed. A mihrab in the shape of a square (1.15 by 1.15 m), slightly sticking out niche was set in the south wall. Within the mosque there were remnants of six square piers situated at the corners of the building and in the middle of the east and west walls. A cubic foundation of a minaret was attached to the mosque on the outside, near the north-east corner of the building.

Only two thirds of the Upper Julat Great Mosque area have been excavated so far (Fig. 7). The building was trapeziform in plan and latitudinally oriented. The west wall was not perpendicular to the north and south ones. According to our estimate, the structure was 11.8 m wide and some 22.8 m long. The wall foundations were built of mortared river cobble stone and the walls proper were made of face-tooled stone and burnt brick. The height of the walls can be estimated as six meters. In the south wall slightly west of its middle a rectangular (1.35 by 1.0 m) sticking out mihrab niche was encountered. The mihrab floor and probably its walls as well were embellished with turquoise-glaze tiles. The entrance was situated opposite the mihrab; a small outside pylon, probably being a remnant of a portal, was found there. An additional opening was made in the west wall opposite the minaret.

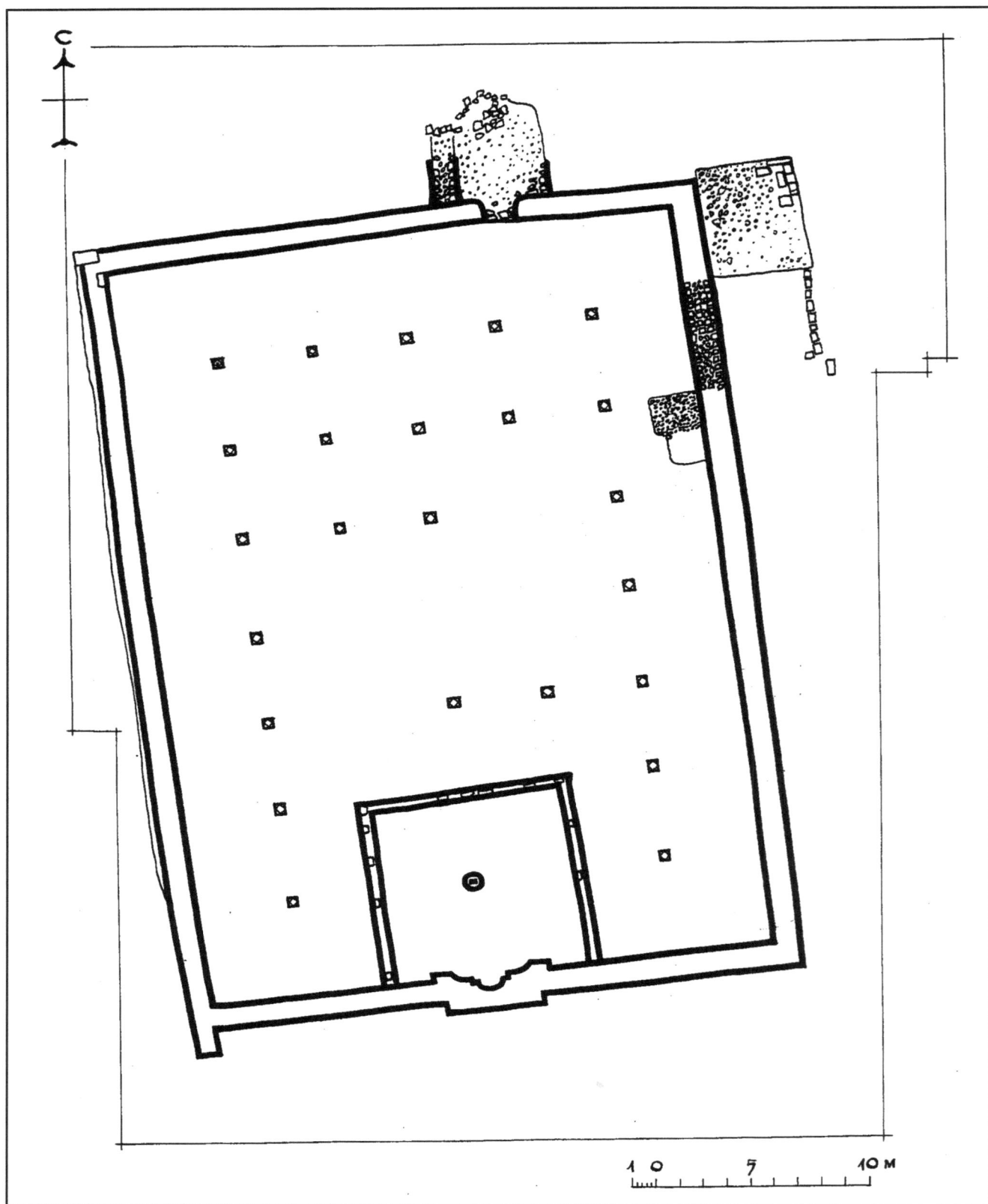

Fig. 4. The mosque of the Vodianskoe site.

The floor was paved with large brick slabs, part of which were glazed turquoise, ordinary brick and small cobble-stone. The walls were plastered and, probably, painted. No traces of either abutments or pillars were encountered in the mosque, so nothing definite can be said about its ceiling. The excavators held that a flat ceiling with a tiled gabled roof was supported by wooden pillars resting directly on the floor slabs (Miloradovich, 1963, p. 79).

The famous Tatartup minaret (Fig. 8) that survived up to 1985 also belonged to the Great Mosque. It was 20.8 m high with a rectangular socle (3.55 by 4.25 m) 2.35 m high. The socle

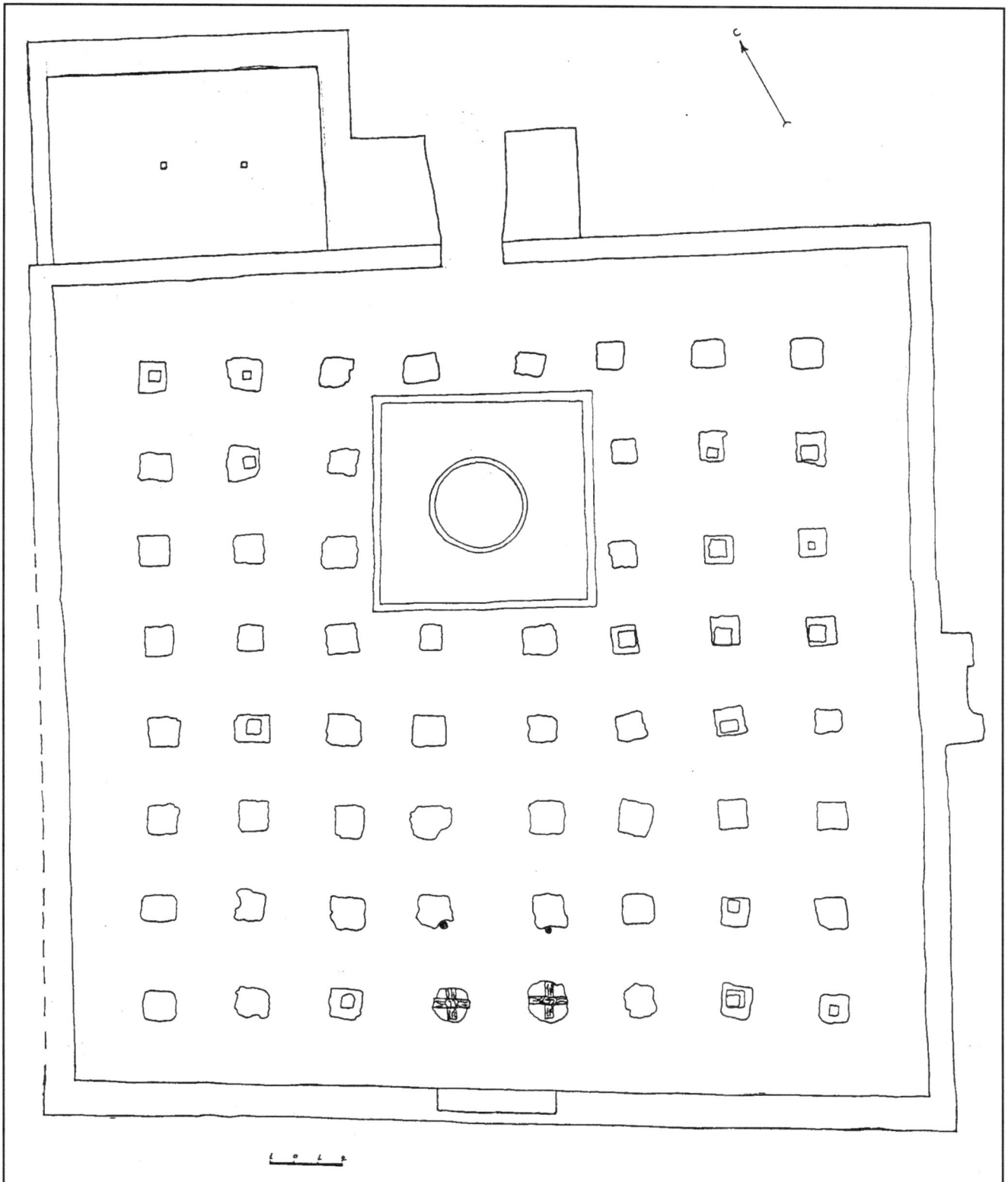

Fig. 5. The mosque of Sarai.

was made of brick and stone blocks. The shaft was conical and consisted of two parts, 13.1 m and 5.35 m high respectively. They were separated by a double stalactite zone that used to support the muezzin balcony. In the socle there was a horseshoe-arched doorway. A similar door led to the balcony. In the lower zone of the minaret there were two windows. Inside the shaft a brick spiral staircase wound around a pentagonal pillar.

The shaft was decorated with several ornametal zones, the main of which was the stalactite one. Right under it there were two bands of alternating glazed turquoise discs and brick lozenges. They were separated by an ornamental zone imitating a Kufic inscription. The upper part of the shaft was also embellished with geometric brickwork. The two mosques and the minaret of the Upper Julat date to the 14th century.

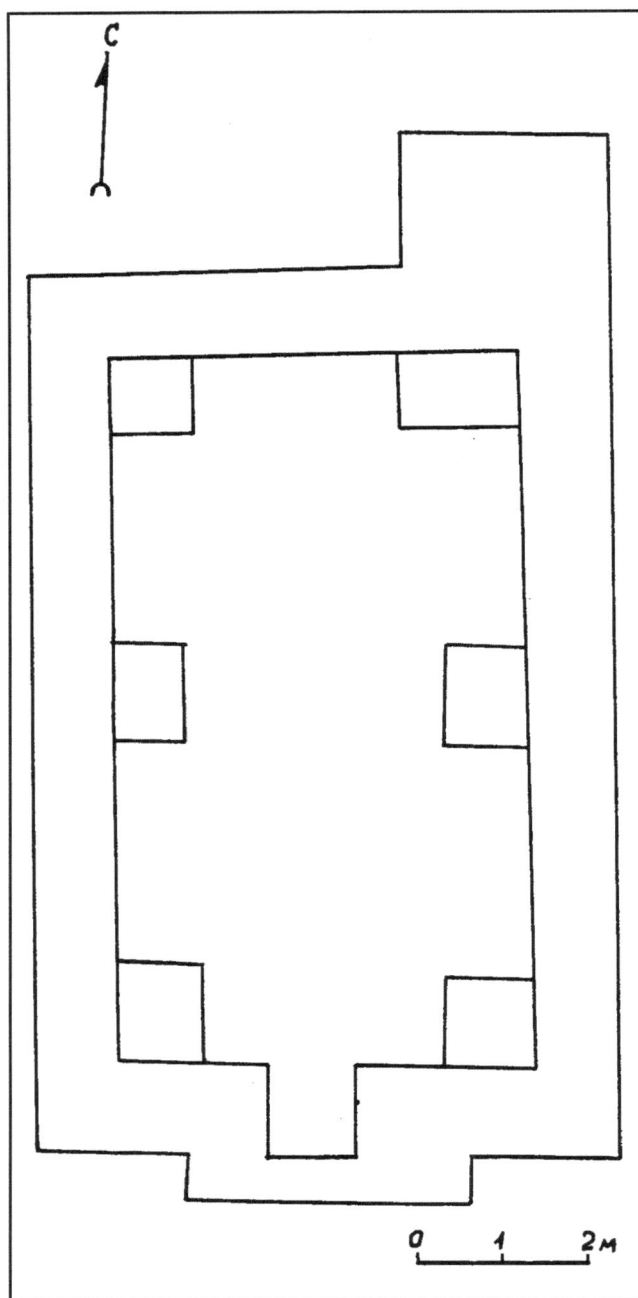

Fig. 6. The Lesser Mosque of the Upper Julat site.

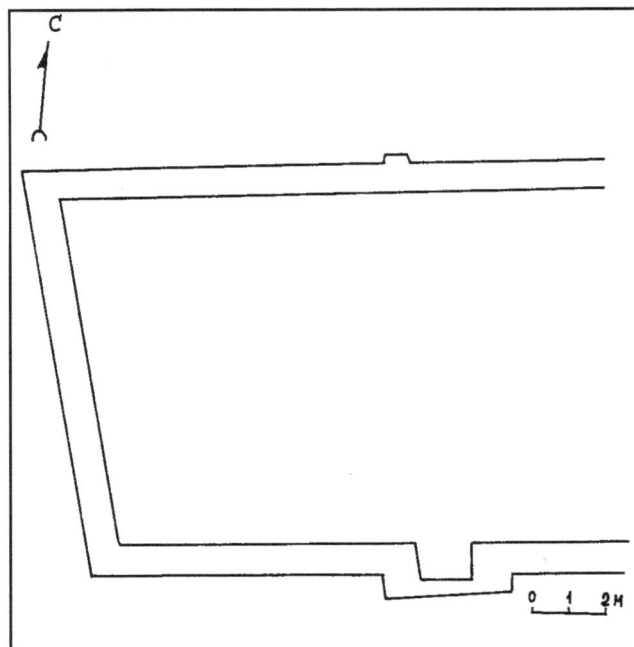

Fig. 7. The Great Mosque of the Upper Julat site.

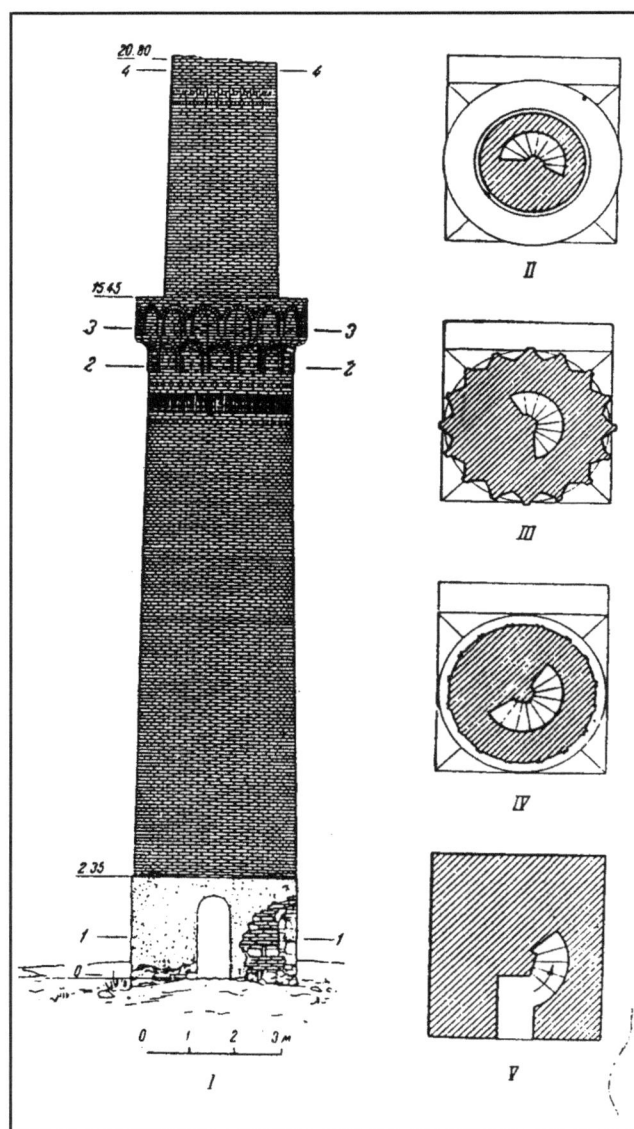

Fig. 8. The Tatartup minaret (by Miloradovich).

The largest congregational mosque in the Caucasus was excavated at the Lower Julat site in the Kabardian-Balkar Republic (Chechenov, 1999). The building was a rectangular, oriented north-south structure (Fig. 9). The south wall with the mihrab niche did not survive, therefore one can only estimate the dimensions of the building to be 17.65 by 25.7 m. The walls were made of mortared baked brick and were some 0.9-1.2 m thick. The brickwork rested on a base made of stone slabs and cobble stone. The entrance was situated on the north side. On the outside there was a portal, of which only the remains of rectangular pylons have survived. The interior was divided into five aisles by four rows of columns. Each row had 12 columns, of which only cylindrical stone bases have partially survived. The floor was paved with mortared baked brick.

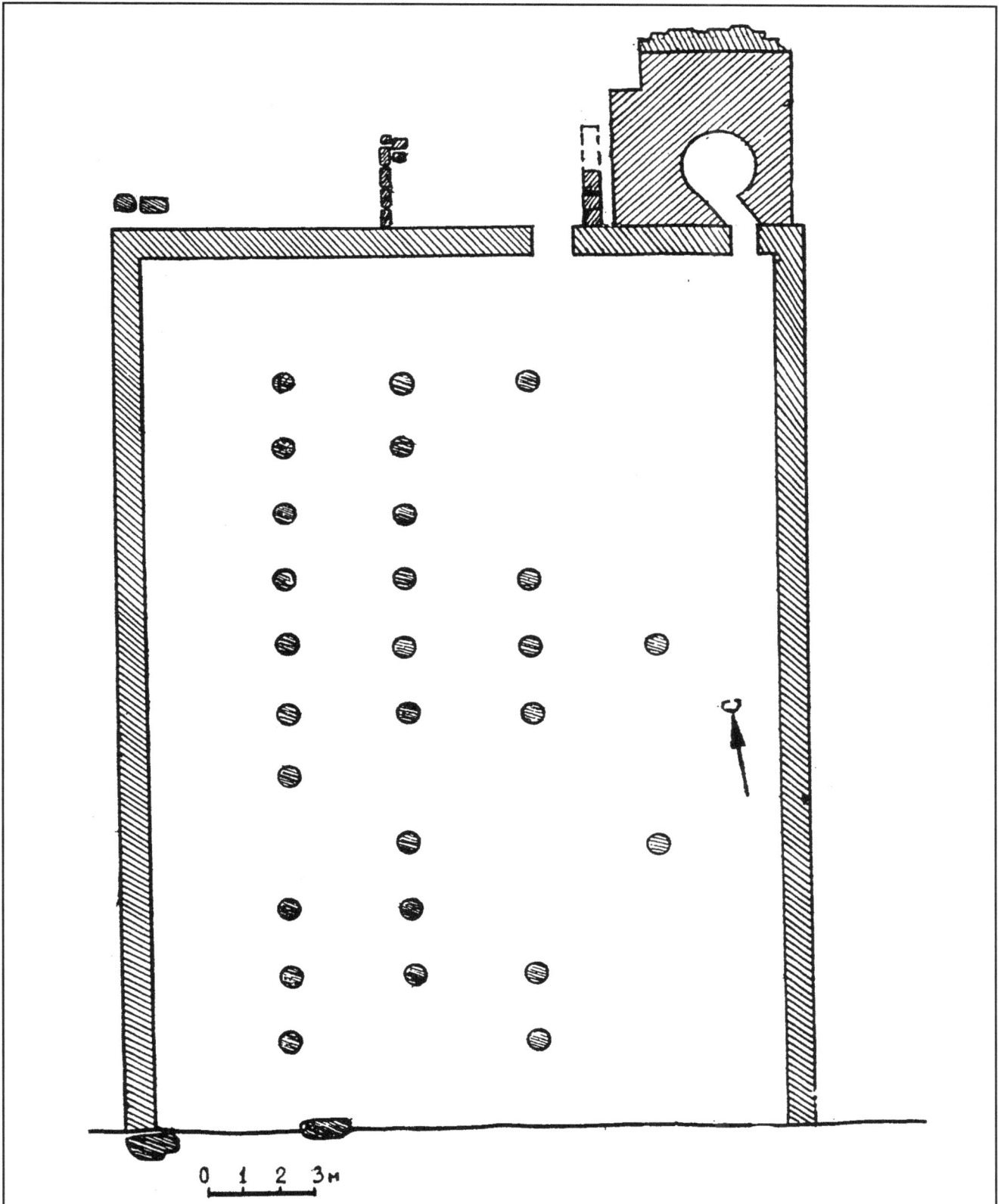

Fig. 9. The mosque of the Lover Julat site.

The minaret, of which a socle measuring 5.8 by 4.75 m has survived, was attached to the eastern part of the north wall. It was faced with large rectangular blocks alternating with geometric brickwork. The socle contained a round in plan room with traces of a wooden staircase. The minaret of the Lower Julat mosque was probably similar to the Tatartup minaret.

WESTERN REGIONS OF THE GOLDEN HORDE

A mosque-cum-madrassah of the Krym town in the Crimea is the most famous architectural monument of the western Golden Horde (See Bashkirov, 1926; Idem, 1927; Borozdin,

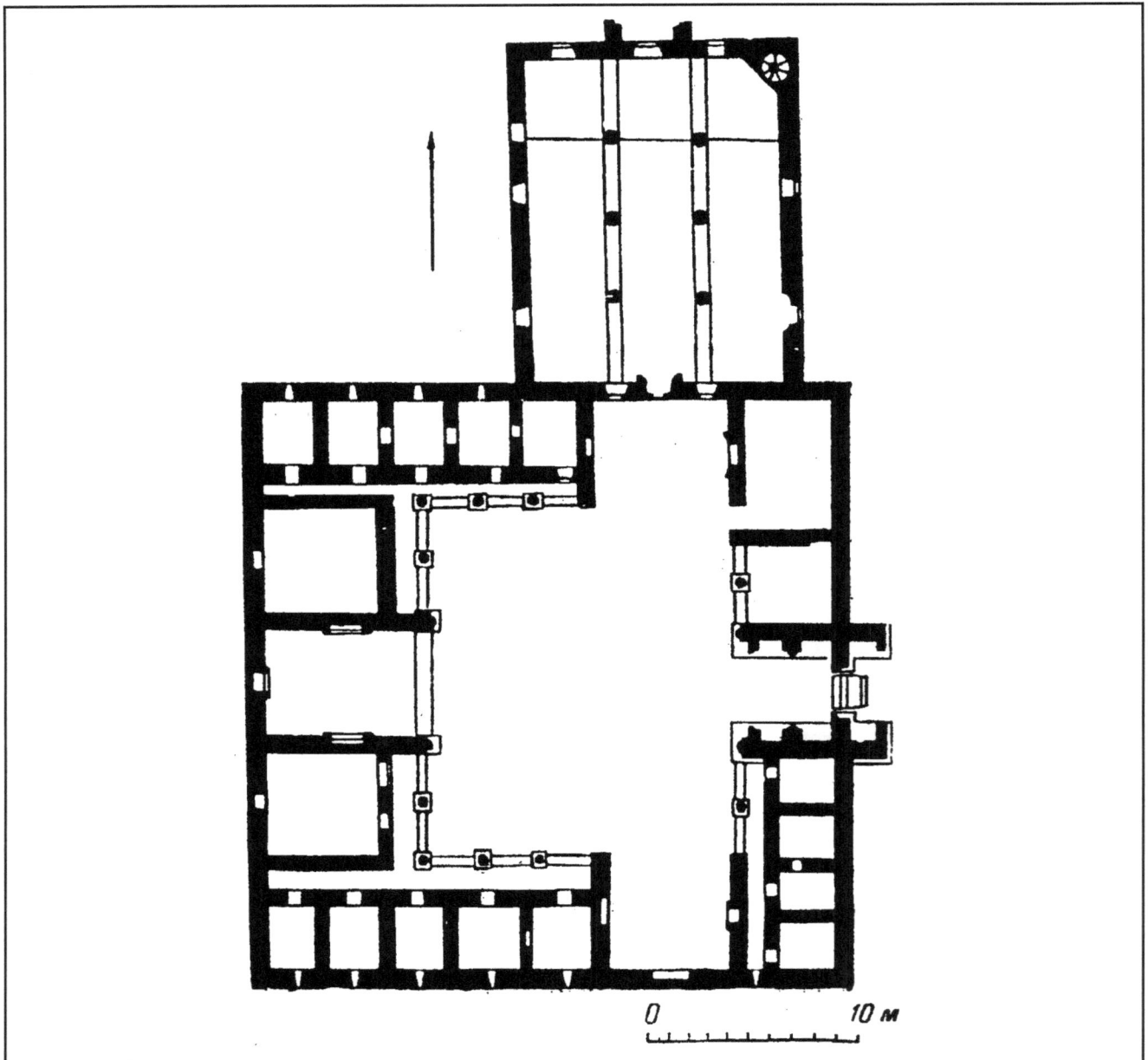

Fig. 10. The mosque-cum-madrassah of the Krym (by Jacobson).

1926; Idem, 1927; Zasypkin, 1927; Jacobson, 1964). The building that has fully survived is a basilica measuring 17.5 by 13.5 m with three pairs of octahedronal abutments linked by pointed arches (Fig. 10). The abutments support a rafter ceiling and a tile gabled roof. A cylindrical shaft of the minaret is built on the north-east corner of the building. A portal with a stalactite niche and carved stone friezes generally believed to be influenced by Seljuk art is attached to the south wall. The mihrab niche is similarly adorned.

The carved portal of the mosque bears an inscription recording a date in the Hijrah era corresponding to A.D. 1314, in the reign of Uzbek. A vast rectangular madrassah enclosing an open courtyard is attached to the mosque on the south side. It has been believed that the planning of the mosque-cum-madrassah can be traced to that caravanserais of the Seljuk Anatolia. Recent excavations of the State Hermitage expedition headed by M. Kramarovsky have shown, however,

that the mosque and the madrassah are not synchronous and cannot be regarded as a single complex.

M. Kramarovsky has investigated two more mosques at Krym that other researchers just mentioned in passing. The so-called 'Baybars Mosque' was situated not far from the madrassah. It was a three-aisle basilica 7.7 m long, 3.7 m wide in the mihrab part and 4.2 m. wide at the portal wall. The remains of an arcade have survived as three pairs of foundations for the column bases. A horseshoe mihrab niche was traced in the south wall while rectangular pylons were erected east and west of the entrance. From the numismatic record the mosque can be dated to the reign of Tokhtamysh.

The so-called 'Lead Mosque' or Kurshun-Jami was situated at the former estate of a renowned Russian painter, Ivan Aivazovsky. The rectangular structure (12.5 by 17.7 m) was built of mortared quarry stone (Fig. 11). The entrance was

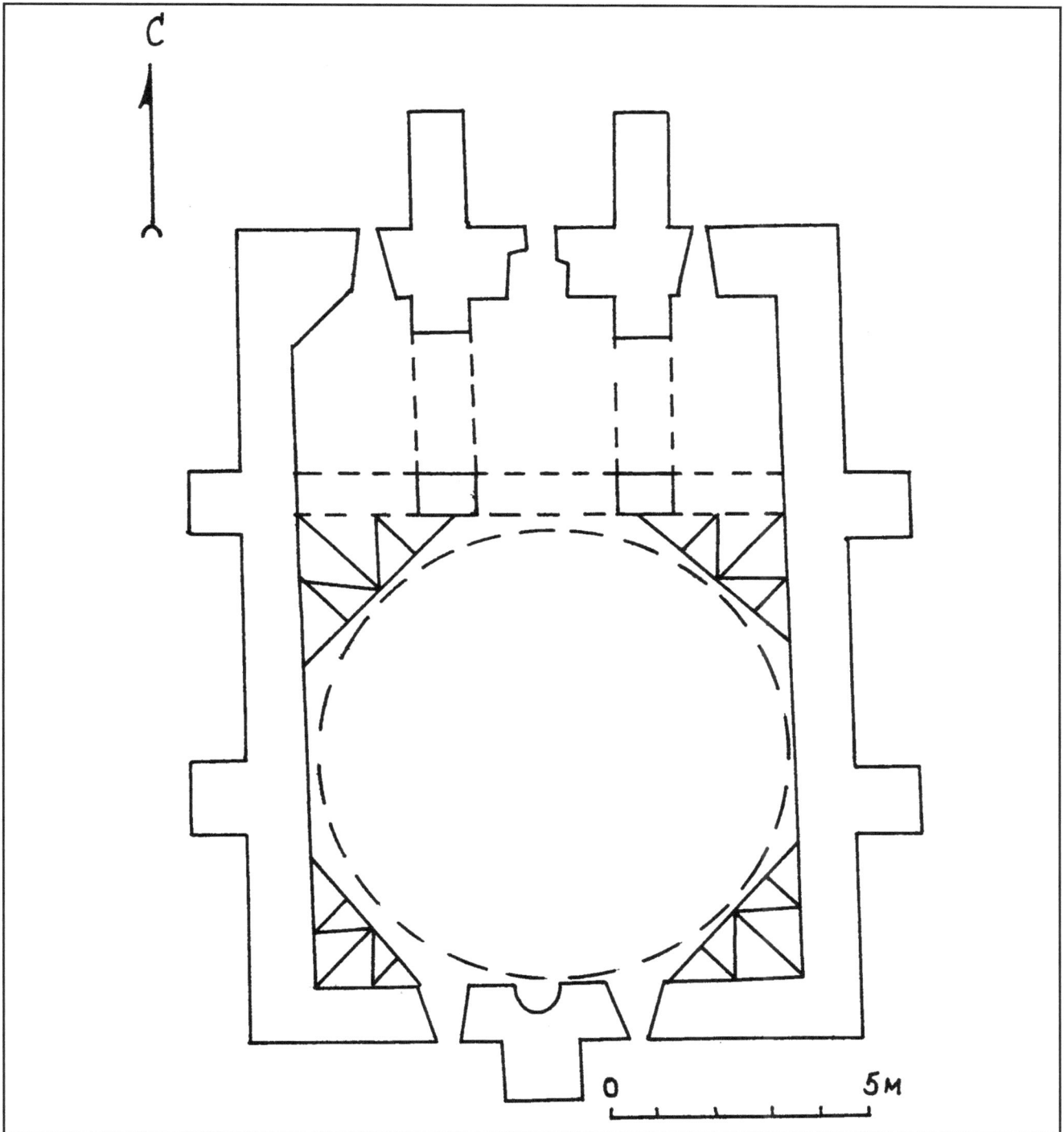

Fig. 11. The Kurshun-Jami.

flanked by portal pylons. The west and east walls were supported by twin buttresses, whilst the south wall was strengthened by a single buttress situated behind a deeply recessed rectangular mihrab niche. The remains of the minaret base have survived on the north-east corner. The building was partitioned into two uneven chambers. The square chamber (10.5 by 10.6 m) with a mihrab in the south wall was covered by a dome resting on pendentives. The rectangular (10.5 by 4.5 m) north chamber had three hemispherical domes (Bashkirov, 1927, p. 132). According to Evliya Çelebi, Kurshun-Jami was built by Bay Bugly Khatun, Kutlug Timur's granddaughter, as a tekke or a lodge

for dervishes and converted into a ward mosque in 1398 (Grigoriev, 1974, p. 27). Hence a somewhat unorthodox planning of the 'Lead Mosque'.

The remains of a large congregational mosque were excavated at the very centre of the Kuchugury site, in the vicinity of the Zaporozhye city in the Ukraine (Dovzhenok, 1961). The rectangular building (26.0 by 17.9 m) was oriented north-south (Fig. 12). On the north side there was a huge (8.5 by 6.5 m) brick-paved meridionally oriented tambour. The walls of the mosque were made of mortared baked brick and its interior was paved with burnt brick. The prayer hall was

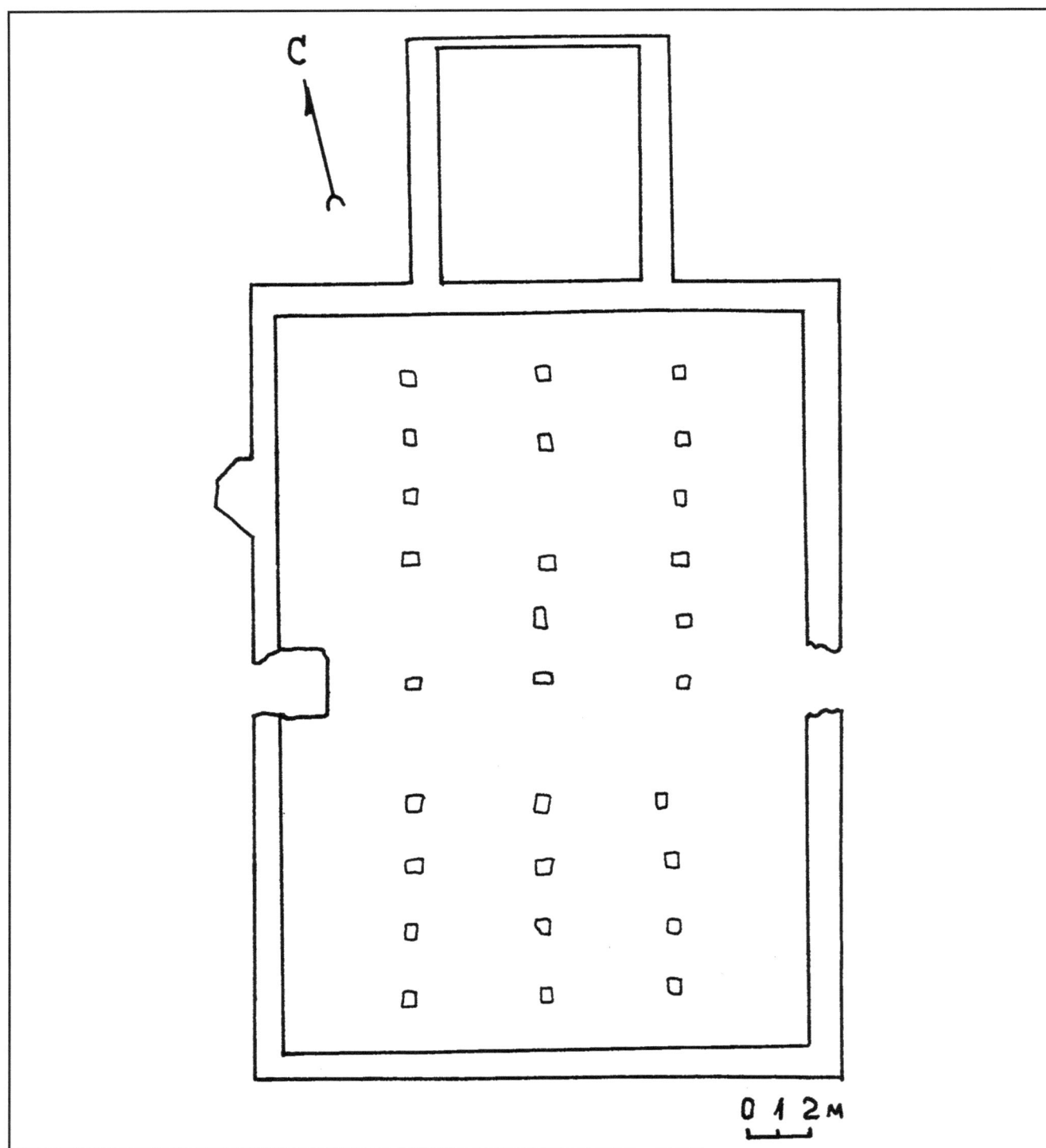

Fig. 12. The mosque of the Kuchugury site.

divided into four aisles by three rows of columns. The number of columns in a row varied from 9 to 11. Their bases, made of grey sandstone and measuring 50 by 50 cm, were discovered during the excavations. The upper corners of the bases were cut off to form an octagon. A horseshoe mihrab niche 80 cm wide and 35 cm deep was situated in the centre of the south wall.

The east and west walls of the tambour were lined with sofas or long benches. The remains of a wooden door were discovered at the entrance to the mosque. Moreover, two additional entrances were made in the middle of the east and west walls of the main chamber. A tambour was attached to the west entrance from the inside.

The minaret was built into the west wall at a six-meter distance from its northern end. Its socle was an octagon 2.5 m in diameter. Parts of a cylindrical shaft of the minaret with the remains of a wooden staircase inside were found in the débris.

The mosque, like the settlement itself, dates to the 14th century.

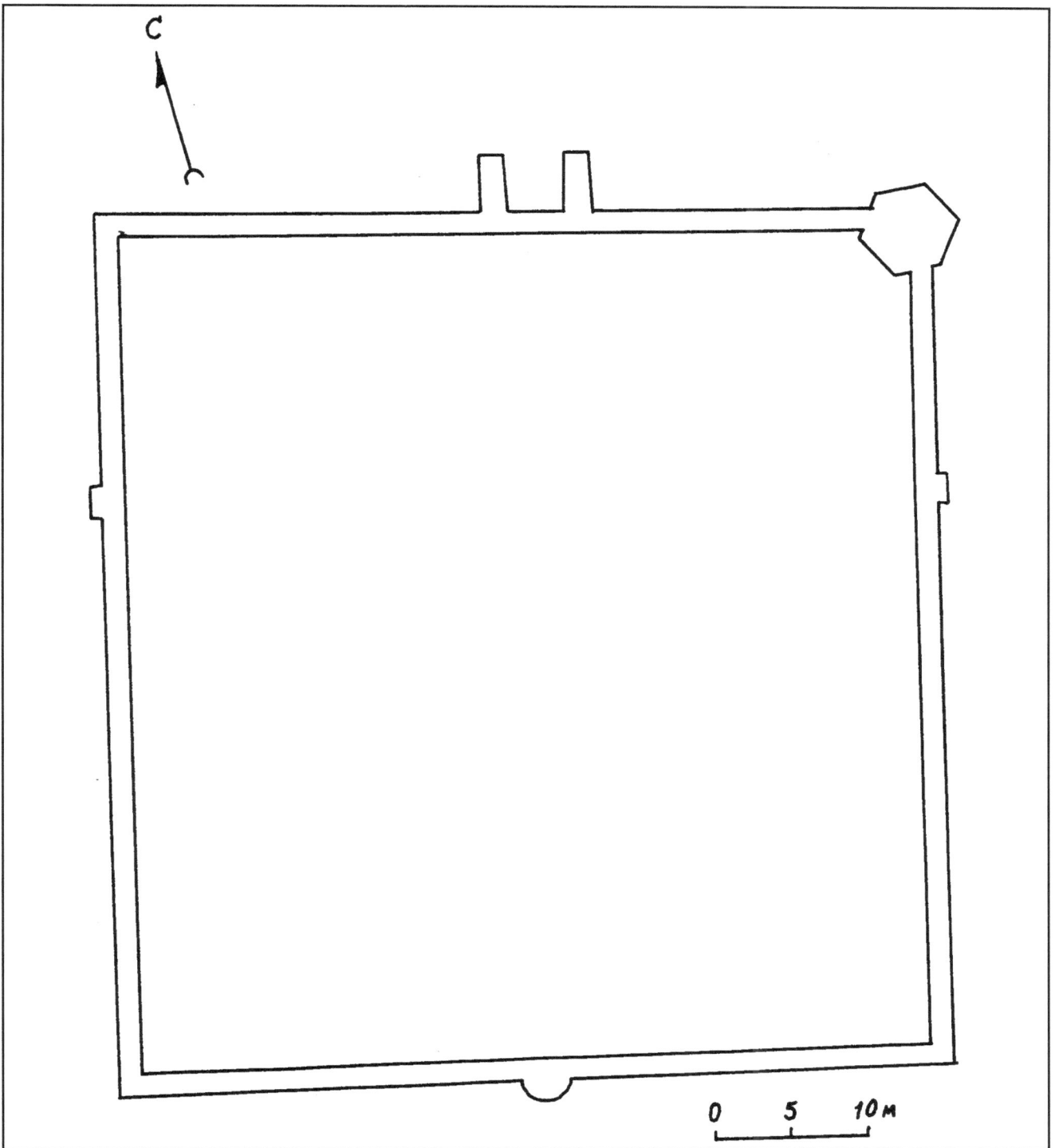

Fig. 13. The mosque of the Old Orkhey site.

The Old Orkhey site mosque in Moldavia is the westernmost mosque building in the Golden Horde (Bîrnea, 1985). This huge structure measured 57.7 by 51.5 m (Fig. 13). Its walls were solid masonry of slightly cut mortared limestone blocks. The walls are up to 1.3 m wide and the foundation reaches 1.7 m in width. In the north wall there was a doorway flanked on the outside by two rectangular pylons. P. Bîrnea holds that they supported a portal 7 m wide and some 10 m high (Bîrnea, 1985, p. 29). The portal arch was 3.8 m wide and 4 m deep. It was adorned with stone carving featuring altenating lozenges and hexagons. The blocks of a doorway that led

into the mosque have also survived. The doorway was 2.3 m high and 1.5 m wide.

The east and west walls had rectangular buttresses at a distance of 18 metres from the north end. Judging from their small dimensions, these were probably mere decorative elements. There was a horseshoe projection 2.6 m in diameter in the middle of the south wall corresponding to the mihrab niche. The north-east corner of the building was encompassed by the socle of the minaret. The socle was hexagonal in plan, with sides some 3.05-3.4 m long.

The mosque, like the other monumental buildings of the Old Orkhey, was unfinished. No traces of inner structures were encountered yet several stone column bases measuring 30 by 30 by 20 cm with corners cut off to form an octagon were among architectural details. Probably the building, like other Golden Horde mosques, should have been divided into aisles by rows of columns. A small diameter of the columns and the gigantic dimensions of the building enable one to assume that the mosque had a flat ceiling.

The Old Orkhey mosque can be dated to the mid-14th century.

x x x

Thus, the above survey has shown that the majority of the hitherto investigated Golden Horde mosques belong to a single type. They are either square or rectangular in plan and their interior is divided by rows of columns supporting a flat ceiling in the shape of either beams or columns. Rectangular mosques are usualy oriented meridionally, yet sometimes latitudinally. The main entrance is situated in the north wall, opposite the mihrab, and is framed by a portal. Huge buildings may have additional side entrances as it is the case at Bolgar, Sarai and at the Kuchugury site. Such a uniform, highly elaborated design simply could not have been developed in the Golden Horde. It should have been borrowed either from abroad or from the local sedentary population. The 'Uzbek Mosque' and the Tetragon were believed to have their origins in Seljuk architecture. A. Bashkirov, for instance, compared the mosque-cum-madrassah at Krym to the Ak-Khan and Sultan-Khan caravanserais at Konya (Bashkirov, 1926, p. 110; Idem, 1927, pp. 30-52). The comparison proved to be groundless when it had been shown that the mosque and the madrassah were built separately at different times. I think that one should turn for the relevant analogies not to Anatolian caravanserais but to mosques of the same region. As stated above, the mosques of Asia Minor consisted of rectangular halls divided into aisles by rows of pillars or columns supporting either beams or arcades, i.e. were basilicas with a flat ceiling. A sky-light under which a reduced inner courtyard with a fountain is situated is the most characteristic feature of Seljuk mosques. A small dome could have been erected over the ante-mihrab part. Thus, one of the simplest buildings of the Seljuk-Anatolian period, the Mahmud-bey Mosque near Kastamoni, is a three-aisle hall with two rows of wooden pillars, a beam ceiling and a gabled roof. The Ulu Cami mosques at Sivas and Afiyon are large multi-aisle halls with a transept leading to the mihrab and a flat ceiling resting on arcades (Benset, 1973, pp. 16-17; L'art..., 1981, pp. 100-102). Many similar examples can be cited.

It is worth noting that early basilica-like mosques can be occasionally encountered outside Asia Minor. Usually this is the case with Christian basilicas converted into mosques with the coming of the Arabs when urban expansion left no space for adding a courtyard, cf. the al-Aqsa Mosque in Jerusalem (Creswell, 1958, p. 211). However, this Umayyad mosque without inner courtyard could hardly have become a prototype for cult buildings of the Golden Horde.

The basilica mosques of the Seljuk tradition should be distinguished from such buildings as the Juma Mosques in Khiva (Voronina, 1985) and at Khazarasp (Mankovskaya, 1980, p. 109). The latter are huge halls with a flat ceiling resting on numerous columns. They belong to the type of pillar flat-ceiling structures (Mankovskaya, 1980, pp. 108-112). Although originally close to pillar-dome ones, they are simpler in execution. The area of such mosques is divided into standard squares with side length akin to that of a beam ceiling (3.5-4.5 m). Every square is covered not by a dome but by a flat ceiling. A large number of small mosques in Central Asia are so designed. If a building is greatly extended, a type called 'the forest of columns' by L. Mankovskaya emerges.

The hall of the Golden Horde mosques is divided into longitudinal aisles. This design can be seen in the early period of the Tetragon, in the mosques of the Kuchugury and the Lower Julat sites and, of course, in the 'Uzbek' and 'Baybars' mosques. In the structures of the Lower Volga the distance between the rows of columns and between the columns in a row is the same, yet the transept in the Sarai Mosque is indicative of its belonging to the basilica design. Moreover, this mosque has such an important detail of the interior as a small inner courtyard with a pond in the centre. Such courtyards, only with a fountain instead of a pond, are a characteristic feature of Seljuk mosques.

A dome covering the space before the mihrab in order to delineate it is equally typical of Anatolian mosques of the 11th -12th centuries. It seems likely that a square ground surrounded by pillars before the mihrab of the Vodianskoe site mosque served the same purpose. Of course, there was no hemisherical dome of brick or stone since it could not rest on wooden pillars. A beam ceiling over an eight-metre span also does not seem practical. It can be assumed that there was something like a wooden dome over this ground.

One should dwell upon such a detail of the Golden Horde mosques as a sticking out portal. Certain scholars (Aidarov, 1970, p. 41; Bîrnea, 1985, p. 31) hold that a huge portal of Central Asian type, the so-called *peshtak*, with a doorway shaped into a pointed-arch niche was erected in the Golden Horde mosques. This assumption, however, cannot be accepted. In the majority of Moslem buildings the *peshtak* niche is recessed into the exterior wall. If it sticks out from the wall, the outward thrust of the arch is counterpoised by buttresses in the shape of decorative minarets and side annexes. The presence of a portal with a pointed arch can be surmised only for the Sarai mosque, whose building technique shows many Central Asian traits. Its pylons are especially thick and the west one is strengthened by the wall of an annex. As to the other structures, the thickness of their pylons does not exceed that of the walls. Given their links with Anatolian architecture, one should rather expect there portals with a stalactite niche and stone carving akin to the surviving portal of the mosque-cum-madrassah at Krym.

The Kuchugury Mosque is especially worth noting in this respect. There the extension of the portal converted it into a large tambour-like room with benches along the walls.

Besides large mosques of the basilica plan there were other types of mosques in the Golden Horde. The Kurshun-Jami Mosque in the Crimea, generally believed to be a converted dervish lodge (Bashkirov, 1926, p. 124; Zasypkin, 1927, p. 132) was also built under the influence of Seljuk mosque architecture. The Lesser Mosque of Upper Julat is a pillar-dome building. Its design resembles that of such small pillar structures of Central Asia as the mosques attached to the eleventh-century mausolea of Hakim-al-Termezi and Khoja Isa (Borodina, 1974, p. 118).

To summarize, it should be stressed that the Golden Horde religious architecture emerged under a strong influence of Seljuk Anatolia. Seljuk building tradition was spread through Transcaucasia where such its examples as the Manuche mosque at Ani have survived (Arutiunian, 1951, Table 100). The existence of the Seljuk type mosques in Central Asia also cannot be excluded. Mosques with an aisled hall are recorded for pre-Mongolian Volga Bulgaria (Khalikov, 1979; Aidarov, 1979).

The Golden Horde cult architecture had its origins in the flat-ceiling basilica. Its planning, however, was modified and concessions were made to local conditions and taste. As a result, such original architectural designs as the tower-like buttresses of the Tetragon, the administrative annex of the Sarai Mosque and the extended tambour of the Kuchugury Mosque emerged.

References

Aidarov, S.G. Arkhitekturnoe issledovanie ruin sobornoi mecheti v Bolgarakh (Architectural examination of the congregational mosque ruins at Bolgary) // Povolzhye v srednie veka. Moscow, 1970.

Aidarov, S.S. and F.M. Zabirova. O rekonstruktsii i konservatsii ostatkov kompleksa mecheti (On the reconstruction and conservation of a mosque complex remains) // Novoe v arkheologii Povolzhya. Kazan, 1979.

Arutiunian, V.M, and Safarian S.A. Pamiatniki armianskogo zodchestva (Monuments of Armenian Architecture). Moscow, 1951.

Bashkirov, A.S. Sel'jukizm v drevnem tatarskom iskusstve (Seljuk traditions in early Tatar art) // Krym, 1926, no 2.

Bashkirov, A.S. Khudozhestvennye pamiatniki Solhata (Art monuments of Solhat) // Krym, 1927, no 1.

Bashkirov, A.S. Pamiatniki bulgaro-tatarskoi kul'tury na Volge (Monuments of Bulgarian-Tatar Culture on the Volga) // Kazan, 1928.

Benset Unsal. Turkish Islamic Architecture. Seljuk to Ottoman. New York, 1973.

Borodina, I.F. Osobennosti formirovaniia memorial'nykh sooruzhenii Srednei Azii (Characteristic features of the formation of Central Asian memorial structures) // Arkhitekturnoe nasledstvo, 1974, no. 22.

Borozdin, I.N. Solkhat // Novyi Vostok, 1926, nos 13-14.

Borozdin, I.N. Novye dannye o zolotoordynskoi kul'ture v Krymu (The new data on the Golden Horde culture in the Crimea // Novyi Vostok, 1927, nos 16-17.

Bretanitsky, L.S. Zodchestvo Azerbaijana XII-XV vv. i ego mesto v arkhitekture Perednego Vostoka (The Architecture of Azerbaijan

of the 12th -14th centuries and its Place in the Middle Eastern Architecture). Moscow, 1966

Bîrnea, P.P. Kamennoe sooruzhenie I v Starom Orkhee (Stone structure I in Old Orkhey) // Arkheologicheskie issledovaniia srednevekovykh pamiatnikov v Dneprovsko-Prutskom mezhdurechie. Kishinev, 1985.

Cresswell K.A.C. A Short Account of Early Muslim Architecture. Middlesex, 1958.

Dovzhenok, V.I. Tatarske misto na Nizhniom Dnipri chasiv Pizniogo serednievichcha (A Late Medieval Tatar site on the Lower Dnieper; in Ukranian) // Arkheologichni pam'atki USSR. Kiev, 1961, vol. 10.

Yegerev, V.V. Arkhitektura goroda Bolgara (The Bolgar site architecture) //

Materials and Investigations on Archaeology of USSR, 1958, no. 61.

Yegorov, V.L. and G.A. Fyodorov-Davydov. Issledovanie mecheti na Vodianskom gorodishche (The excavation of a mosque at the Vodianskoe site) // Srednevekovye pamiatniki Povolzhia. Moscow, 1976.

Encyclopaedia of Islam. London-Leiden, 1927, vol.2.

Godard A. L'art de l'Iran. Paris, 1962.

Grabar O. The Formation of Islamic Art. New haven and London, 1973.

Grigoriev, A.P. "Kniga puteshestvii" Evliya Çelebi - istochnik po istorii Kryma XII-XVII vv. (Evliya Çelebi's "Book of Travels" as a source for the study of Crimean history of the 12th -17th centuries // Istoriografiia i istochnikovedenie istorii stran Azii. Leningrad, 1974, no. III.

Khalikov, A.Kh, and R.F. Sharifullin. Issledovanie kompleksa mecheti (The excavations of a mosque complex) // Novoe v arkheologii Povolzhia. Kazan, 1979.

Herzfeld, E. Archaeological History of Iran. London, 1935.

Jacobson, A.L. Srednevekovyi Krym (The Medieval Crimea). Moscow-Leningrad, 1964.

L'art en Turquie. Fribourg, 1981.

Mankovskaya, L.Yu. Tipologicheskie osnovy zodchestva Srednei Azii (The Typological Traits of Central Asian Architecture). Tashkent, 1980.

Miloradovich, O.V. Srednevekovye mecheti gorodishcha Verkhnii Julat (Medieval mosques of the Upper Julat site) // Materials and Investigations on Archaeology of USSR , 1963, no. 114.

Pugachenkova, G.A. Puti razvitiia arkhitektury Yuzhnogo Turkmenistana pory rabovladeniia i feodalizma (The evolution of the South Turkmenistan architecture of the classical and feudal periods) // Materials of South-Turkmenistan Expedition, Moscow, 1958.

Pribytkova, A.M. O nekotorykh mestnykh traditsiiakh v zodchestve Srednei Azii v IX-X vv. (Some local traditions in Central Asian architecture in the 9th - 10th centuries) // Arkhitekturnoe nasledstvo, 1958, no. 11.

Pribytkova, A.M. O "krasivoi mecheti" Dandakana (On the "Beautiful Mosque" of Dandakan) // Arkhitekturnoe nasledstvo, 1964, no. 17.

Pribytkova, A.M. Stroitel'naya kul'tura Srednei Azii IX-X vv. (Central Asian Building Culture in the 9th - 10th centuries). Moscow, 1973.

Smirnov, A.P. Volzhskie Bulgary (The Volga Bulgarians). Moscow, 1951.

Smolin, V.F. Po razvalinam drevnego Bulgara (On the ruins of old Bulgar). Kazan, 1926.

Chechenov, I.M., and E.D. Zilivinskaya. Mechet' gorodishcha Nizhnii Julat (The mosque of the Lower Julat site) // Drevnosti Severnogo Kavkaza. M., 1999.

Tiesenhausen, V.G. Sbornik materialov, otnosiashchikhsia k istorii Zolotoi Ordy (A Collection of Materials Relating to the History of the Golden Horde), Vol. II, Moscow-Leningrad, 1941.

Voskresensky, A.S. and A.P. Smirnov. Arkheologicheskoe issledovanie sobornoi mecheti "Chetyrekhugol'nik" v Velikikh Bolgarakh (An archaeological examination of the congregational "Tetragon" Mosque at Velikie Bolgary) // Soviet Archaeology, 1966, no. 1.

Voronina, V.L. Kolonny sobornoi mecheti v Khive (The Columns of the congregational mosque in Khiva) // Arkhitekturnoe nasledstvo, 1985, no. 11.

Zasypkin, B.N. Pamiatniki arkhitektury krymskikh tatar (Monuments of the Crimean Tatar Architecture) // Krym, 1927, no. 2.

Zilivinskaya, E. The Golden Horde city pattern: evidence from excavations // Urbanism in Medieval Europe. Papers of the "Medieval Europe Brugge 1997" Conference, Vol. 1. Zellik, 1997.

THE INTERFACE BETWEEN ARCHAEOLOGICAL REMNANTS
AND HISTORICAL EVENTS
The Swedish Bishoprics during the Late Middle Ages

Antikvarie Ingvar MÅRALD

Abstract: This paper argues for the importance of not seeing the documentation of the building archaeological investigations as an isolated entity. By applying a dialectical approach with an interaction between archaeological and historical sources, already at the excavation stage, the basis of the interpretation can be deepened, and elements necessary to enter into details on, can be identified. An analysis of the development and historical importance of the Swedish bishoprics during the late Middle Ages demonstrate the advantages of the dialectical approach in the paper. Emphasis is placed on the necessity to separate ecclesiastical castles from those of other social groupings. Furthermore the importance of questioning the obsolete terms and concepts of building archaeology is underlined, since these terms lack connotations referring in depth to the purpose of a building.

Keywords: Late Middle Ages, bishoprics, dialectical approach, terminology, power political framework, the Archbishopric in Uppsala

INTRODUCTION

The purpose of this article is to give an overview of archaeology specialized in the research of buildings. The tendency in this field is to document a construction in a more precise way. Building archaeologists have become increasingly accurate, focusing on details in order to extract as much new information as possible from walls. The methodological evolution has taken up so much of interest that it partly has resulted in the depreciation of other sources of information. My intention is therefore to question the meaning of old concepts and foreground the advantage of working in an intensely dialectical relationship with other fields of study than is the case today. What I have in mind is the possibility of comparing the observations with other fields of study in order to obtain a more substantial basis for the interpretation when the study of building archaeology is carried out.

How then does my proposed method differ from that of a building archaeologist? Within building archaeology it is legitimate to study individual buildings, pointing out different

Map

stages of the construction of the building, relying on detailed investigations and plans. It has led to the circumstance that we account for complicated stratigraphic situations. This in its turn has a result that in building archaeological studies conclusions are drawn that are more wide-ranging than what can be confirmed by written historical sources. For the continuity of building archaeology a very important precondition is that we not only confirm what we already know. The frames of written historical sources should not delimit the purpose of an investigation. The development of methods has, however, advanced so far that scholars rely on the historical sources without questioning or investigating them. Although it is essential to use the potential of the historical sources during excavations, it is necessary to scrutinize their information and question results by established historians. I am convinced that it is necessary to use a more dialectical approach. This means that there must be an interaction between studying the historical context, situating the individual building in its historical framework, getting an overview of the archaeological situation to see within which fields it is necessary to delve deeper into details. What significance did it have during different periods of time and how is it possible to observe this in the analyses of building archaeology? Dialectical approach is especially rewarding when it is possible to examine a building with a long continuity.

During the last few years in Scandinavia there has been a discussion whether it is possible to distinguish between different kinds of buildings. It has been demonstrated that it is necessary to sort out ecclesiastical buildings as one specific type of buildings. The reason is that these buildings are meant to meet very different symbolic and functional purposes based on radically other needs than those of a secular building (Nordeide 1997). The purpose of this article is to demonstrate the importance of questioning the terminology on buildings used in previous research. It is of vital importance to distinguish between buildings of the same kind since its purpose with it might differ depending on who owned it; the king, the church, the nobility or farmers. This circumstance might explain why a reconstruction of a building has occurred at a specific time.

I have chosen to support my thesis by examining a period fraught with conflict in Sweden starting about the year 1450 and ending by the Lutheran Reformation in 1536, when Sweden passed from belonging to the Roman Catholic church to establishing a national state church based on Protestantism. Initially there will be a survey of Swedish ecclesiastical history in order to emphasizes what was important to the church leaders during this period and as a consequence what was of importance for the reconstruction of their official seats.

THE POWER POLITICAL FRAMEWORK

From the middle of the 15th century to the Reformation the Church was very much involved in the Swedish power politics. This owed more to political antagonism between fractions of the nobility, where the archbishops played an important role than to theological and juridical ideals and traditions. The Church intervened actively in the struggle leading to the participation of the archbishops and other bishops in the actual warfare.

The fact that the Church was involved in the political struggle for power has to do with antagonisms between a whole series of institutions, power blocs and ideals. The late Middle Ages were characterized by a struggle for power that was fought with theological, ideological and political means.

Political Complications with Ecclesiastical Participants

In 1397 a Union, The Kalmarunionen, was established between Denmark, Sweden and Norway. The union marked the beginning of an unruly time characterized by struggles for power between the kings of the union, the national councils of the realm and the Church, which among other things resulted in several rebellions. The main task was to preserve the union against burgeoning national interests (Lovén 1996:42). To clarify the antagonisms it is necessary to distinguish between the terms by means of dichotomies.

Conflicts whether the Roman Catholic Church should be Universal of National

In the 14th century the Holy See of the Roman Catholic Church was moved to Avignon, France. In 1377 there was schism within the church, which led to the existence of competing Holy Sees in Rome and Avignon. This led to the demand for reconstruction of the church. The Englishman John Wycliffe was one of those critics who claimed that the secular power of the Catholic Church went against Christian ideals. Wycliffe's teachings were very successful and resulted in the idea of establishing national churches. Especially in Bohemia this idea won support because of the animosity

between Czechs and immigrant Germans. The leader, Jan Hus, professor in theology and a Czech nationalist, was banned by the Catholic Church in Konstanz because of his heretic view and was burnt at a stake in 1415. To solve the tensions within the church the so-called Conciliarism was created, recurring Councils. In many countries the secular authorities gained influence over the ecclesiastical sphere. The result was that the Holy See was weakened and was forced to compromise with the Roman-German emperor and kings. The autonomy of the church was endangered (Losman 1970).

The Relationship between the Pope and the Monarchies

There were tendencies towards the establishment of national churches in Scandinavia too. During the late Middle Ages there was a twofold evolution, on the one hand the Pope tried to increase his influence in the church in each country. This was achieved by the Pope reserving the right to him self to appoint bishops and other ecclesiastical posts. On the other hand the kings aimed at gaining the support of the Pope. Thereby they succeeded in being let off from certain to the church at the same time as they could appoint their own followers on ecclesiastical posts (Hugason 1997:190).

A Vague Borderline between the Ecclesiastical and Secular Spheres

When the monarchy encroached on the rights of the church, the latter responded by increasing its activities within the political sphere.

The archbishop was an ex-officio member of the Council of the realm. During the late Middle Ages its most important issue was the Union, the basic idea of which was Nordic cooperation. Much of the tensions concerned dynastic struggles and a devastating rivalry between the nobility and the monarchy.

The Church was deeply involved in this struggle. In the conflicts to do with the Union most bishops supported the Unionists and went against the Swedish regents. The Swedish bishops saw the Union as one of many political tools to preserve the autonomy of the church. Thus to achieve their goal the Union was a useful means. Conversely, the Swedish nationalist groupings and eventually the adherents of the Reformation instead experienced the Union as an obstruction. Swedish regents and kings represented this line of thought (Martling 1997:47f).

It was common that the bishops isolated themselves in their castles and in different ways obstructed the secular authority. The bishops, for instance, acted as commanders (Lovén 1996:236) and 1457 archbishop Jöns Bengtsson Oxenstierna instigated a rebellion against the Swedish king Karl Knutsson.

The same goes for his successor Jakob Ulfsson (Larsson 1997:285f).

The Relationship between the Monarchy and the Catholic Church

The antagonism between the monarchy and the archbishop dates back to the interpretation of the Canon Law that regulates ecclesiastical matters. The part of the Canon Law that was based on declarations by the Pope, decisions by the synod and the Bible had universal application. Therefore it was difficult for the king to gain control of the ecclesiastical posts without getting into conflict with the Holy See (Beskow 1995:133f). Even if the three Nordic countries were united via a union king, the three archbishoprics continued to function independently.

The Swedish church was fitted into a European Catholic network led by the Curia in Rome and was in reality independent of the monarchy. The basis for the power of the church was economic and social. The church levied tithes and other kinds of rates apart from the fact that it collected taxes from a large part of the taxed land. The church carried on trade, owned minds, employed bailiffs, soldiers, scribes, and tradesmen. The church was a state within the state. The bishops resided in powerful castles, belonged ex officio to the Council of the realm, took part in the wars with their own troops, summoned foreign princes but could overthrow them if the interests of the church were threatened (Johannesson 1987:124f).

The church and the state, represented by the king headed for a collision. Also the king approached the Pope in order to control the officials of the church. Another example of the conflict was the acquisition of property by the church, which went against the interest of the state, the nobility, the townsmen and peasantry

Regimen Regale and Regimen Politicum

By applying the concepts of the Swedish historian Erik Lönnroth, regimen regale, a strong royal power and regimen politicum, where constitutional provisions reduce the power, two rivaling forms of government can be contrasted. Simply put this means that regimen regale is a strong but not an absolute monarchical government while regimen politicum guarantees the right of consultation to the nobility and the Council of the realm.

In Sweden the monarchy was antagonistic to the nobility, to whom also the bishops usually belonged. Seen from an idealistic point of view the nobility, the priesthood could be said to safeguard the constitutional and individual rights (Lönnroth 1969:22ff). Since the monarchy in Sweden was split, it was possible for the church to act very independently and argue for the right of the church to cooperate with the Holy See. Since the monarchy exposed the church to threats when it tried to preserve its autonomy the ecclesiastical hierarchy joined forces to fight the King. A shift of the interests of the church from the theological to the political level is clearly discernible. The church demanded the right to consultation and worked to uphold regimen politicum. The aspiration of the King was to achieve autocratic control within

his territory. His goal was regimen regale. Eventually the monarchy used The Lutheran Reformation as its ideological tool to fight the church.

THE BISHOPRICS /STRONGHOLDS - A PART OF THE POWER POLITICAL DEVELOPMENT

In Sweden the struggle for power resulted in hard fights to control territories. The mandate of the Swedish monarch was to keep the large territories together. This is why the bishoprics played an important part as pawns in the power political struggle between the church and the king. The purpose of the ecclesiastical strongholds was to consolidate the position and autonomy of the church. The power of the strongholds equaled the power over Sweden.

From the line of argument above it is obvious, in other words, that it is necessary to situate the individual bishopric in its historical and power political context. An investigation of the military importance of the ecclesiastical strongholds would not be complete, unless these bishoprics were examined as a part of a larger unit, that of the permanent defense of the whole of Scandinavia.

The bishoprics can be divided into two main categories depending on their geographical location. The first category is situated inland, inside or in the vicinity of cathedral cities. The second category is situated in more exposed positions; along the coasts, waterways or borders. The latter group is as a rule more powerful from a military point of view (Lovén 1996:191). The first category will here be called interior bishoprics, while the second category will be called exterior bishoprics. Naturally, the military capacity between individual bishoprics differs considerably, but by means of my analysis of the network of bishoprics, I want to uncover the strategic scheme of the bishoprics in Scandinavia.

The clear-cut military aspects of our bishoprics and their adjacent strongholds become obvious by looking at their location and spread both to cities and to strategically important sites such as waterways. For the monarchy whose goal it was to establish a subordinated national church the task must be either to destroy these bishoprics or alternatively capture/take over them.

The fifteenth century is characterized by military political changes. To be able to control a territory politically was a matter of being in command of the castles. The permanent strongholds of the king were castles situated close to important cities such as Stockholm, Kalmar, Lödöse, Nyköping and Åbo. Other castles were situated in militarily exposed areas such as Borgholm, Åland, Stegeborg by the coast of Östergötland, Tavastehus and Viborg, Finland to uphold the defense to the east. The chain of castles was complemented by time. The Castles became centers of the royal administration and were fed by the surrounding countryside (Lönnroth 1940:137).

The control of the administration of the castle counties was the key to controlling the state. To the central state here was the possibility to control the country and do away will illoyal members of the nobility.

During the late Middle Ages the split up between the monarchy and the Council of the realm remained, to which the bishops usually belonged. During the period of 1434-1470 there is a marked decentralization of the chain of castles, resulting in the impairment of the monarchy. The Bishops controlled the counties that surrounded their fortified bishoprics, where also military troops were placed. Thereby the bishops controlled some of the most powerful castles (Lönnroth 1940:191ff; Olsson 1947:43f).

The bishops of Skara had built several fortified structures during the late Middle Ages: Husaby, Brunnsbo, Säckestad, at the same time as Läckö had been considerably enforced. In the episcopate of Växjö there were fortified constructions in Vembo, Vissefjärda apart from the stronghold of Kronoberg. The bishop of Linköping had at his disposal, apart from his fortified residence in Linköping, also Skänninge, Bro, Munkeboda, Skällvik and Rönö. In the episcopate at Strängnäs there were strongholds in Tynnelsö and Sigtuna plus a fortified estate next to the cathedral in Strängnäs. The bishop also owned the strong Kustö and Korois. The military stronghold of the archbishop of Uppsala was Almarestäket, which like the main residence by the cathedral had been equipped with a ring-wall. In addition, the fortified estates at Biskops-Tuna and Biskops-Arnö were at the disposal of the archbishop (Lovén 1996:268).

In Sweden it is possible to see a clear pattern of interior and exterior castles of the Catholic Church. The main residence in Uppsala was an interior castle, which was protected by the militarily stronger exterior castle, Stäket. The bishop of Skara had at his disposal the strategically situated exterior castle Läckö by Lake Vänern. The bishop of Strängnäs fortified the exterior castle Tynnelsö, situated on an islet in Lake Mälaren. The bishop of Växjö had Kronoberg by Lake Helgasjön at his disposal. The bishop of Linköping controlled the exterior castles at Rönö and Skällvik. The bishop of Åbo had the coastal castle Kustö at his disposal. As a rule the priesthood supported the Union thereby going against the nationalistic aspirations of the king for autonomy. For a long period of time the adherents of the Union controlled the majority of the castle counties, but once they had lost that power, their adversaries got the upper hand.

THE AUTHORIZED TERMINOLOGY OF TODAY

The basic terminology of a castle can be includes many aspects: according to position (topographic location), geographical position, from a political perspective a functional description, typological classifications and by a chronological label (Eriksson 1995:11f). Usually a broad frame of interpretation is used such as castle, stronghold, tower house, fortified estate, etc. These terms are accepted as terminology for a specific kind of castles, but they do not reveal anything about the purpose of the castles.

When morphological interpretations are applied, i.e. the way in which a castle can be defined, three aspects are in focus; purpose, concept and requirements. In order to classify a castle as a stronghold, three basic elements must be fulfilled; a grounds capable of defense, a housing capacity and the possibility of an overview of the surrounding territory (Eriksson 1995:15).

There can however be variants from these three elements. A fortified edifice can be defined as a castle where the housing capacity has not been cut out but where the defense capacity is too weak to avert organized attacks (Lovén 1996:27). Classic quadrangular castles were first erected for military reasons. The wall only refers to stone or brick-wall in mortars (Lovén 1996:197). During the 14th and 15th centuries a new kind of fortification castle was introduced in Scandinavia known as *det fasta huset* in Swedish. It is the term for a castle whose only fortified building in stone was a multistory building (Lovén 1996:35). All the functions of the fortified house, that in older castle were distributed onto several houses. The housing, the hall, and the defense was now concentrated in the same building (Hansen 1992:46f). The defense of the fortified house was passive.

The definitions discussed above refer to the degree of militarized buildings. They leave a lot to be desired. These terms describe the characteristic of these kinds of castles, but they all lack descriptions of their purpose, symbolism and function as parts in a larger context.

The evolution of ecclesiastical buildings during the 15th and 16th centuries as stated above, during the 15th century the castles were distributed between the king, the church and the nobility. The power over a territory presupposed control of the societal administration. The essential thing for those in power in Scandinavia was the control of the castles and their surrounding counties. Consequently the tug-of-war about the counties runs like a red thread through the last period of the Middle Ages. The principal agents were the king and the priesthood. Around these two poles the nobility gathered split up in fractions. These castles were at the very core of the power politics.

During the late Middle Ages the fortification architecture adds another important element to the Swedish bishoprics. At that time they enclosed their residence after a classic quadrangular ground plan that sometimes included square flank towers. This kind of castle consisted of a wall and within it there were wings in stone or wood. The yard was quadratic or rectangular. This type of castle was called a "kastell" (citadel), a term that dates back to the Roman word 'castellum' meaning army camp. The area of the castle was reduced when a wall was constructed around a rather small area so that the buildings were concentrated to a smaller area. The offices and workshops were either moved inside the wall and became part of it or placed outside of the enclosed area. The majority of the Nordic bishoprics had good locations situated at crossroads or next to churches.

It is of vital interest to see if the reconstruction of the ecclesiastical buildings occurred during the same period, that is the period when the monarchy started encroaching upon the rights and the autonomy of the Catholic Church. These circumstances must be taken into consideration when examining the ecclesiastical castles from the late Middle Ages. A circumstance that indicates the residence of the church is that it went against the ban of the monarchy to build defense establishments. During the reign of Queen Margareta a ban was enforced geared at persons which not belonged to the kings manor, and which lasted from 1396-1483 (Lovén 1996:27ff). However, it seems as if the church did not heed this ban, since a long row a strongholds were built.

A DIALECTICAL APPROACH BETWEEN ARCHAEOLOGY AND HISTORY

With this dialectical approach in mind, one should start documenting the wall belonging to an ecclesiastical building. However, every time a change of the building is demonstrated one should on the one hand see if these changes are due to the reconstruction of the immediate surroundings. But on the other hand investigate whether these changes have anything to do with a larger reconstruction on a higher political level. Could the changes be caused by an altered need in a new political climate? Are there parallels to changes in other castles and how can we distinguish a demand for a function in a larger geographical context? By applying a dialectical approach the interaction between archaeological and historical sources, a concordant picture of what caused these changes can be offered.

Concerning the fortification of the bishoprics in the 15th century (see above) it is possible to see that the reconstruction of the ecclesiastical buildings indicate that the church did everything in its power to maintain its autonomous position. This was in order to make them militarily stronger castles in addition to increasingly frequent interference of the bishops. Different epochs have different characteristics which makes it important to understand the all-embracing framework. As concerns the ecclesiastical castles in Scandinavia at the end of the Middle Ages it is important to see them as central in the last struggle of the Catholic Church in Scandinavia and as a periphery in the Catholic Church, situated in western Europe with its center in Rome. Since the purpose of the ecclesiastical castles was the very opposite of that of the royal castles it is a mistake to study these two types of castles as one category of construction with reference to the fact that they were built in accordance with the same building principles.

It is very important not to see the investigations in building archaeology isolated from the context. A difficulty to interpret a wall is that there are no artifacts to help establishing the main purpose of the castle's function. In addition, several castles are built at the same period in the same material and with the same design. The difference for instance between a royal castle and an ecclesiastical one can be minimal as the

exterior goes. It is therefore easy to cross-reference the two castles to each other. Naturally, the similarities and differences should be studied and the results from these studies are used. But it is very important to remember that two similar buildings can have been built for very different purposes. By applying a dialectical approach between archaeology and history it becomes much easier to discern the different purposes.

THE PROBLEMS CONCERNING THE ARCHBISHOPRIC IN UPPSALA

To be able to demonstrate my claim I have chosen to discuss a castle that till this day has confused scholars in Sweden, much due to the fact that they have worked too one-sidedly. The building in question is the Swedish Archbishopric in Uppsala. The first time the archbishopric in Uppsala is mentioned in written documents is in age 1298. In two later documents two other estates belonging to the archbishop, "lilla"and "stora", are mentioned (DMS 1984). The research around the archbishopric in Uppsala has focused on the question which buildings that can be tied to two castles during the late Middle Ages. Since it has been difficult to separate which functions that belong to which residence the picture has become very split.

The help of maps and old written documents has established two castles as the main residence of the archbishop during the final years of the Middle Ages. One of the buildings that still exists today is called Gustavianum, and is a so called double complex, where two buildings, one facing north and one facing south, have been joined. Gustavianum has been examined several times by building archaeologists. The second residence, which is destroyed, was a quadratic castle from the Middle Ages. When the University building was constructed in 1886 in Uppsala there were extensive removal of soil, which uncovered the castle, but it was very summarily documented by means of a photo and a plan. At that time substantial parts of the wall remained but it is unknown how many of these walls that were destroyed. However, a major part of it is situated outside of the walls of the present university building. In 1996 a small part of the wall of the archbishop's palace was examined, revealing that walls as tall as 1.7 meters had been preserved and that two different building stages could be identified. The ceramics dated from the late Middle Ages alternatively from the 16th century (Elwendahl 1996).

During the inter-war period when the Swedish national self-esteem was being confirmed, the castles often were regarded as national monuments. It is characteristic of this period that August Hahr (1929) was interested in the research of castles. Hahr treats Uppsala archbishopric as belonging to one category of castles. He studied plans, types of plans fortification details in the architecture. Hahr claims that the quadratic castle was the main residence of the archbishop.

During the 1960s there was a lively discussion between historians basing their evidence on written material and building archaeologists. At this time there were building archaeological excavations of Gustavianum by Nils Sundqvist (1969). He shared the ideal of his time to describe what he has found. The material is therefore treated very narrowly. He claimed that Gustavianum was the main residence of the archbishop.

It is not until the end of the 1980s and the beginning of the 1990s that there was a more scientific approach. Gunilla Malm (1993), who carried out building archaeological excavations of Gustavianum has initiated a discussion on whose initiative, the king's or the archbishop's that Gustavianum was built. Malm does not treat the question which of the buildings that was the main residence of the archbishop during the final years of the Middle Ages.

The Art historian Christian Lovén (1996) has studied the Swedish castles among others the archbishopric at Uppsala and the evolution during the Middle Ages from an architectural point of view. It is interesting that he separates the ecclesiastical castles from other castles. From an architectural perspective he claims that it was the quadratic castle that was the main residence of the archbishop.

By way of conclusion it can be said that the picture that the historical and architectural sources jointly give of the archbishopric in Uppsala is contradictory. The absence of archeological material has given the scholars free rein to create their own interpretations based on written material. This is due to the fact that the archbishopric had not been problematized before the excavations started but only afterwards. If in the future new excavations of the destroyed walls of the quadratic castle will be carried out, given that parts of the walls are preserved, it is imperative, that a dialectical approach is applied. Which reconstruction has occurred? When? Is it possible to link the reconstruction to the written material? What can have caused these changes?

It is important that when such an investigation is carried out the findings should be linked to the reconstruction of the wall. Do they suggest an ecclesiastical or a royal owner; does the castle have a military or a symbolic importance? If it is an ecclesiastical castle, in what way does it differ from the findings of a royal castle? If there are no archaeological artifacts as reference material, stratified dating of the wall could indicate the adherence of the owner, issuing from written sources around the castle. But if there are no sources a geopolitical study like the one above could indicate during what period for instance ecclesiastical representatives reconstructed their castles. If these questions are uppermost in the mind, it is much easier to go in depth trying to find those changes that can convey further knowledge. For instance, the period after 1450 when several of the Swedish bishoprics were rebuilt serve as an important part of a building archaeological study in order to find out whether the destroyed quadratic castle also went through this reconstruction at this time. In 1521 the archbishop's palace was burnt down according to written sources (DMS 1984:289). If this will be documented, it would supply the excavation with a much better certainty of the chronology. By means of a dialectical approach already at the time of an excavation archaeologists would be able to answer questions that would be impossible later when writing reports. It is, however, important to remember that much of the information that can be extracted during an excavation cannot be supported by historical sources. The archaeological results must have priority, but be supplied by a dialectical approach by using historical sources.

CONCLUSION REMARKS

By separating the established terms for castles, residences and fortified edifices in subdivisions in the future, it will be easier to distinguish what is typical for ecclesiastical castles in contrast to other types of castles. Because of the, ever improved methodology within building archaeology new possibilities open up for a dialectical approach. By means of a more exact division of the changes and reconstruction of stone walls together with historical sources and findings from one castle, the function, purpose and symbolism of the castle during various periods will be identified with much more certainty.

Without a dialectical approach, regardless of good stratigraphic investigations of a castle, the interpretation will be hypothetical and not as well supported. If for instance there are many findings of weapons it might suggest that the castle had a military importance. The absence of it suggests that the castle had more symbolic importance in spite of other military artifact. In the same way findings from different periods of time reveal the main purpose during that time. Often written information has been used as a proof of the establishment of a building as well as when reconstruction of the building occurred. These data are then used as a basis for the dating of different phases of construction. Other kinds of information are often left out, even if they too can reveal something about life in the estate.

Finally I want to underline that I also in the future will be focused on building archaeological excavations. In no way should written sources or historical research be the only key for what is to be found in building archaeological excavations. The important thing is that the questions are not posed from the written or historical sources, but from archaeological perspectives. Scholars, however, must realize the great benefits of a dialectical approach at the same time as innovation is achieved if the terminology of preceding studies is questioned and redefined.

Antikvarie Ingvar Mårald
Slussgatan 14:11
S-211 30 Malmö
Sweden
Telephone: +46 (0)40-978501
E-mail: kariningvar@swipnet.se

References

BESKOW, P. HELLSTRÖM, J-A. and NILSSON, N-H., 1995. *Den kristna kyrkan. Från apostlarna till renässansen.* Stockholm.

DMS., 1984. *Det medeltida Sverige 1:2.* Ed. Dahlbäck, G. Ferm, O. and Rahmqvist, S. Stockholm.

ELFWENDAHL, M., 1996. Universitetsparken. Riksantikvarieämbetets arkeologiska undersökningar. *UV Uppsala rapport 1996:33.* Uppsala.

ERIKSSON, A-L., 1995. *Maktens boningar. Norska riksborgar under medeltiden.* Lunds Studies in Medieval archaeology 14. Stockholm.

HAHR, A., 1929. Uppsala forna ärkebiskopsborg. *Upplands fornminnesförenings tidskrift 43. Bilaga.* Uppsala.

HANSEN, S.I., 1992. *Senmiddelalderlige herregårdsbygninger.* Århus.

HUGASON, H., 1997. Religionen. *Ur Nordens Historia 1397-1997. 10 Teman.* Köpenhamn.

JOHANNESSON, K., 1987. Reformationen och renässansen – en periodöversikt. *Den svenska Litteraturen. Från forntid till frihetstid 800-1718.* Band 1. Ed. Lönnroth, L; Deblanc, S. Uddevalla.

LOSMAN, B., 1970. *Norden och reformationskonsilierna 1408-1449.* Göteborg.

LOVÉN, C., 1996. *Borgar och befästningar i det medeltida Sverige.* Kungl. Vitterhetshistorie- och antikvitetsakademins handlingar. Antikvariska serien, fyrtionde delen. Uppsala.

LÖNNROTH, E., 1940. *Statsmakt och statsfinans i det medeltida Sverige, Studier over skatteväsen och länsförvaltning.* Göteborgs Högskolas årsskrift XLVI. Akta Universitatis Gothenburgensis. Göteborg.

LÖNNROTH, E., 1969. *Sverige och Kalmarunionen 1397-1457.* Studia Historica Gothoburgensia X. Andra upplagan. Göteborg.

MALM, G., 1993. Qustions concerning the Medieval Archbishop's and King's Manors in Uppsala. *Castella Maris Baltici 1.* Stockholm.

MARTLING, C.H., 1997. *De nordiska nationalkyrkorna-från Kalmarunionen till Borgådeklarationen.* Stockholm.

NORDEIDE, W.S., 1997. Aktivitet i erkebispens anlegg i norge, belyst ved gjenstandsmateriale. *Meta.* Nr. 4. Lund.

OLSSON, G., 1947. *Stat och kyrka i Sverige vid medeltidens slut.* Göteborg.

PERNLER, S-E., 1999. *Sveriges kyrkohistoria. 2. Hög- och senmedeltid.* Stockholm.

SUNDQVIST, N., 1969. Biskopsgården och "Styrbiskops"-gården i Uppsala. Ett "kapitel i sten" i Sveriges politiska historia och kyrkohistoria under unionstiden och äldre vasatiden. *Kyrkohistorisk årsskrift.* Sextionionde årgången. Stockholm.

COUNTRYMAN, TOWNSMAN, CITIZEN. DEVELOPING URBAN IDENTITY IN NORWEGIAN TOWNS AD 1000-1700

Axel CHRISTOPHERSEN

Abstract: During the 11th century,a number of small urban nuclea developed in Norway. Based on a spatial analysis of a large number of archaeological investigated urban dwellings, this paper discusses how, and to what extent, people with different social and geographical backgrounds established an "urban" community different from the rural surroundings. The discussion leads to a hypothesis on how *countrymen* became *townsmen* who during the 16th and 17th century finally became *citizens*, in the sense of an uprising social group within towns held together by common social, economic and political interests. One conclusion is that up to the late medieval period, the townsmen were landowners from the surroundings, bringing their rural way of life (i.a. reflected in the dwellings) into the towns. This situation conflicted socially and ideologically with the emergence of a *proper* group of townsmen - mainly tradesmen and workers - living quite differently from this small aristocratic elite with their cultural identity rooted in rural tradititions. When these townsmen gradually became *citizen*, the dichotomy between the rural elite and them became spatially expressed in new types of visually dominating, urban dwellings and a restructuring of urban space that gradually changed the norwegian towns from a medieval to a modern townscape.

1. THE CONSTRUCTION OF SPACE

A general feature of post-processual archaeology's use of modern theory of space is that it perceives space as being *constructed* with its basis in a particular social and cultural practice. This idea can be traced back to Hillier and Hanson's book, among others, where the structure of space is depicted as "architecture's syntactical grammar" which codifies a social and cultural practice (Hillier og Hanson 1984). It is not as simple as this, for at the same time as space is constituted through social practice it also appears as a *medium* which opens up possibilities and places limitations upon interaction and action. We influence, but at the same time are influenced by the space around us, which in this sense appears as a produced and relational category which is formed and re-formed through people's practical, sensory and interpretative interaction with the world. The relationships between space and the individual assume the form and content of a dialogue, a dialogue which in principle can adopt unpredictable directions and consequences. In the meeting between the individual and the organization of space there arises a social translation which is experience-related. Space represents therefore something *more* than an imprint of social and cultural forms of practice, or that which Hillier and Hanson can, in the empirical sense, read and interpret. If space is viewed as an action-related and relational structure there are therefore grounds for adopting a strongly critical attitude to the idea of spatial structure as a "syntactical grammar", this being nothing more than a simplification and barbarisation of the concept "social use of space".

The geographer *Ed Soja* uses the notion of *"the re-presentation of space"*, or *"social spatialisation"* to describe that which arises in the encounter between human perception and experience and spatial order. It is in this dynamic and uncontrollable phase of re-presentation that the social significance of space is given a real experiential content, and which ultimately makes the study of spatial structures into something which points *beyond* an analysis of area, volume, form and physical boundaries verk (Aspen og Pløger 1997).

The intensionality and functionality of space can alternatively be described in terms of *social meaningfulness* which is mediated through spatial signals and expressions, in, for example, architecture and spatial organization.

2. SPACE AS AN ARENA FOR CULTURAL PRACTICE

The relationships between norms, action, and spatial structure can be made apparent and be reinforced as social categories within the concepts of *mode of living, lifestyle and identity*. The Norwegian social anthropologist *Marianne Gullestad* has in a number of studies focused on everyday life as a modern cultural expression (Gullestad 1989:103). A fundamental axiom in her work is that everyday life in all its variety expresses people's efforts to create integration and meaning in life. It is through the actions of everyday life that norms, attitudes and opinions are developed which give structure and meaning to our lives. But *what* is understood

Map

as meaningful, and *how* the meaningful is expressed in the norms and attitudes which govern everyday life are in the broadest sense contextually determined and represent equivocal possibilities for interpretation in an ananalytical context. *Identity and identity-creating action* is an important aspect in seeking integration and meaning in life, but also these are actions the expression and consequences of which are subject to relational and contextual contexts. Maintaining and strengthening the identity of self or the group will probably emerge as more significant and meaning-related actions in periods of class conflict, intervention, multilateral conflict etc. During such periods of social and cultural stress one might expect that the patterns of identity-creating action and symbolic functions challenged and placed established normative systems under strain. Gullestad has pointed to the importance of social identity in *our* time, and has shown how this has created a time- and resource-squandering "lifestyle competition" where "the prize is an affirmed and accepted social identity" (Gullestad 1989:105). In other contextual situations the need for, and the means of expressing identity will, as a matter of course, take different forms, by, among other things, taking other social arenas and communication forms into use. Nonetheless, we must maintain the condition that the need of individuals and groups to find a meaningful place in society is, in a decisive way, formed and expressed in and through the norm-related patterns of action of everyday life. Another expression for this is *"mode of living"*, which embraces both the economic, organizational and cultural aspects of the way life is lived, and which, with the help of symbolic systems and symbolic values, is communicated to the surrounding world. Important arenas for such communicative actions can be the dwelling house and its domestic fittings, clothing, food preparation, recreational activities, social gatherings etc (Gullestad 1989:104f). In situations where identity-promoting actions are reinforced in order to maintain integration and meaning, it is within such areas that identity-forming statements are expressed and given a social form and understanding.

The development of identity-preserving/-promoting lifestyles creates a clearer sense of belonging to social environments and places, which has a clear functional intention through the creation of stronger social environments and a clearer attachment to place. At the same time as the social and cultural boundary between "us" and "them", or between "here" and "there" is made clearer, the "sense of differences are also made evident. This will in its turn lead to the increase of barriers built against the outside world. By creating safety, integration and meaning through the strengthening of identity and a sense of solidarity within society, at the same time a potential for contradiction, conflict and destabilisation vis-à-vis external relationships is produced. Material culture is one of many communicative media created by society through which belonging to and opposition can be expressed and be made visible. But the opposite can also occur; namely, that social antagonisms and conflicts are concealed. As an "agent" in this social game material culture constitutes in the broadest sense a potential for description and interpretation of the processes which contribute to the formation of the urban environment generally, and the culture of urban habitation in particular, especially during the Middle Ages. I shall make such an attempt in the course of the following.

3. SOCIO-CULTURAL CHANGES IN THE URBAN MODE OF LIVING - A CASE STUDY

To build a dwelling house involves, among other things, the organization of private space in accordance with norms and conventions relating to the ways in which individuals relate to each other - and to the outside world - within the private sphere. It also involves the way in which the dwelling communicates patterns of activity which are identity-creating. The urban dwelling house therefore becomes not just a physical framework around the organization of private life, and which passively expresses an historical custom, but on the contrary, an *active participant which expresses and represents the private sphere's qualities and characteristics.* In the dynamic and transformative meeting between the individual and space, the private dwelling therefore not only represents a meaningful, identity-forming and organizing element in our worldly existence, but also something which at the same time can generate *opposition, conflict and disintegration.* In given circumstances this can find expression in individual and/or collective actions and restructuring of space. I will now exemplify the way in which this theoretical standpoint can be used in an analysis of the structured inhabited environment in Norwegian medieval towns.

4. DWELLINGS, NORMS AND SOCIAL CUSTOM IN THE TRANSITION TO HISTORICAL TIME

In Oslo, Tønsberg, Bergen and Trondheim archaeological excavations have documented hundreds of examples of the most common type of dwelling house on the urban tenements; namely, the single-storeyed, two-roomed, notched-log building of *laft* construction (ie. a technique employing cogged or cross-jointed interlocking logs). This was usually equipped internally with a corner hearth, wall benches and planked flooring. This type of building was described already during the 1860's by the sociologist *Eilert Sundt*, who called it the *"stue med forstue"* (a living room with anteroom), and who considered it to be the oldest and most widely distributed type of building in the Norwegian countryside. According to Sundt it represents an archaic form of dwelling, developed in, and adapted to, rural norms and conventions of social and cultural behaviour. On urban sites this building appears from the very start, in Trondheim already from the 970's, and somewhat later in Oslo and Tønsberg. In Trondheim something over half of all the buildings consist of such two-roomed *laft* buildings, and the major proportion of these are equipped with a hearth, placed either in a corner or positioned centrally (Christophersen og Nordeide 1994). In Oslo the two-roomed *laft* buildings with hearths appear around 1100 and predominate as dwelling houses throughout the rest of the medieval period (Fett 1989). A decisive, and frequently discussed problem, is whether the two-roomed *laft* building with a hearth is a building category which was *transferred* from its rural context *into* the urban centres at a very early point in time, or whether this represents an entirely *new* type of dwelling house within the towns. Discussion has concentrated almost exclusively on the question of whether or not the *laft* technique was known and used at the end of the Viking Age. Opinions on this have changed over time, and arguments for and against have been advanced (Grieg 1938, Hauglid 1980, Berg 1989, Hinz 1989, Fett 1989, Comber 1989). The norwegian archaeologists *B.Myhre* (1982), *D.Skre* (1995) and most recently H. Sørheim (1999) have discussed the problem in a broader context than that relating purely to building techniques. On the basis of a broadly based data analysis covering all of eastern and western Norway Myhre has concluded that the functionally divided house known from written sources builds upon traditions which can be traced right back to the later Roman Iron Age. He therefore dismisses the earlier claim that the introduction of the *laft* technique led to the subdivision of the long house into smaller functional units. An important result of Myhre's research is that *the use of a particular construction technique is not exclusively associated with a particular building type, nor is it confined to a particular region.* For example, he shows the manner in which the long house, or parts of a long house, can be constructed using the *laft* technique. Myhre does not state explicitly *where* and *when* the *laft* technique first appears in the country. For him the construction technique as such is not the decisive factor in understanding and explaining the development of the dwelling house from the Viking Age through to the Middle Ages. Instead, Myhre takes as his starting point the way in which the house was *functionally divided*, and arrives at the surprising conclusion that "...one should perhaps use the same terms for the most important rooms (in houses from) the early Iron Age as those which were used in the medieval period: *eldhus, stove og bur* (cook house, living room and store)" (Myhre 1982:215). Myhre bases this on a detailed study of the spatial division of functions within the Iron Age long house compared with archaeologically derived building evidence from Iceland and stipulations in the Gulating Law. According to Myhre the construction technique itself is therefore an element which is subordinated to the building's adaptation to the functional needs and social organization of rural society (Myhre 1982). Also Skre, who has recently undertaken a nation-wide collocation and evaluation of the building-related archaeological material from the Iron Age to the medieval period, is of the opinion that the purely technical aspects of buildings are of subordinate status: Skre has found that an important change in building practices occurred already during the Merovingian period when the part of the long house which contained functions connected with animal husbandry was distinguished as a separate unit. At the same time the long house was was divided up into two or three rooms of which two were living rooms with hearths and a storeroom. In the 7th or 8th centuries AD there is a tendency in western Norway towards the separation out into separate building units of functions which were previously localised within the long house, and during the course of the Viking Age there occurs increasing differentiation within the building mass in rural areas. With regard to the special two-roomed buildings equipped with a hearth (the "*stova*"), which is the preferred building in urban environments, Skre emphasizes that, functionally-speaking,

there is little difference between the 9th or 10th-century long house without animal stalls and the two-roomed buildings from 12th-century Oslo. This ground plan is also known from south-western Norway and the Gudbrandsdal area (south-central Norway), though not combined with the *laft* technique, however. That the use of the *laft* technique came to be particularly widespread in the towns, is, in Skre's opinion, possibly connected with the forcing of the urban building mass into a structure composed of small-scale surface areas, causing a sharp, functional subdivision of the building mass. The circumstances were therefore well-suited to the use of the *laft* technique, which is essentially best-suited to the construction of smaller houses with a restricted span between the walls. Against the background of the evaluated material Skre concludes that *"....changes in building techniques have played a minor role in the development..."*. Neither does he find that the changes are strictly functionally motivated, but instead seeks a wider discussion where the development of building types and construction techniques are placed within *"....a broad social and cultural context..."* (Skre 1995:69). I subcribe to Myhre's and Skre's opinion that construction technique is an element within building practice which is subordinated to other and more important aspects of the ways in which buildings are formed and organised spatially. In this sense the questions as to whether the *laft* technique emerged in the town or in the countryside, and whether it was introduced from outside or developed locally, are of secondary importance to the question as to whether the rural forms of building which accommodated the private dwelling function at the end of the Viking Age, when towns such as Oslo and Trondheim emerged, portray *a spatial-functional structure which also occurs in an urban context.* In his article *"Acts of identity, ethnicity and architecture in the Viking Age"* (Price 1994) the archaeologist *Neil Price* presents a study of the spatial structure of buildings in areas colonised by the Vikings using the access analysis method. He has noted a clear similarity in the way in which the Scandinavian settlements organised private space in contrast to, for example, Anglo-Saxon buildings: *"It does seem reasonable to propose the existence of a specifically Scandinavian way of thinking about and structuring space which is encoded with social meaning.... Whatever the pattern means, it appears to be consistent in buildings of very different types and appearances in many parts of the Viking world: Perhaps it cuts across many levels of status, power etc..."* (Price 1994:67). Implicit in Price's research is that, among the Vikings who colonised Iceland, Greenland, northern England and the islands of the north Atlantic during the 9th and 10th centuries, there existed a common conception of how the living area should be arranged and structured in accordance with social norms and conventions in the area of private and public interaction. Price has distinguished three types of building, each with its own characteristic spatial structure, and which can also be arranged in chronological sequences. We shall here concentrate on the earliest type 1, since this represents a principle of spatial organization which the colonists must have brought with them to Iceland, principally from western Norway and the Trøndelag region in mid Norway. The type is characterised by the presence of a single entrance placed in one of the house's long side walls. The entrance leads into a neutral reception area. From this point one had access to two distinct, separated areas, one being a large room with a central hearth and wall benches, the other a more private area which, among other things, may have included the women's workplace. Price has found that this type was common used during the 9th and 10th centuries. This conclusion is strengthened indirectly by a study undertaken by Bjørn Myhre (1982) into the functional divisions in known Viking Age houses from western Norway. On the basis of the location of the hearths and the distribution of artefacts relating to household economy, Myhre arrives at a functional division of the living area which in principle conforms with the functional divisions into *stove, eldhus og bur* (living room, cook house and store) which are known from the Gulating Law. This functional division is expressed in three different types of ground plan which Myhre claims can be identified among the earliest house sites in Iceland (Myhre 1982:209).

The conclusion to this excursus is that both Price's and Myhre's research have, from different starting points, revealed a fundamental conformity with regard to functional division and spatial structure in building traditions in Iceland and in western Norway during the 9th and 10th centuries. On the basis of this it would appear that at the end of the Iron Age there existed *a fundamental core of socially and culturally determined conceptions about the organization and use of private space, existing independently of the buildings' technical construction and size.* The central question is, however, to what extent corresponding norms and ideas might also have lain behind the spatial organization of the dwelling houses which appear at about the same time, or shortly afterwards, in urban contexts.

We have formerly identified these buildings as mainly comprising a type of two-roomed *laft* building containing a large living room with a corner hearth, or occasionally a centrally placed hearth, and benches placed along the walls. This room is entered via an anteroom, essentially a neutral dispersal area (Berg 1989). In a number of instances the anteroom can be internally partitioned in such a way as to form a small room immediately in front of the entrance to the living room. From here one also had access to the back room which functioned as a store room. This functional division is practically identical with Price's type 1 and with Myhre's western Norwegian house with a two-roomed ground plan. An access analysis of the ground plan and functional divisions based on the examples at Rapstad, Klaufenes and the two-roomed laft buildings with fireplaces from urban contexts *shows a fundamental agreement in the spatial organization which is independent of the buildings' other technical and architectonic characteristics.* From an entrance in the building's long side one is led first into a neutral dispersal area from which one can either continue into a store room (*buret*) or into a large communal living room which accommodates the service and recreational functions required of a place of abode and food consumption. A characteristic qualitative feature which is found in both the western Norwegian Viking Age house, in the early settlement buildings in Iceland and in the urban two-roomed *laft* buildings is that the communal area's recreational zone is situated furthest in within the room's interior and is therefore surrounded by optimal social control, while the food preparation zone has a more exposed and inviting location in the communal area's foremost area. Lying behind the spatial structuring principle we have described above we must look for the contemporary norms and attitudes associated with social gathering within the private sphere. A possible "social translation" of the spatial structure we believe we have uncovered as a shared feature of houses from the western Norwegian Viking Age, Iceland and the earliest urban centres in Trondheim and Oslo can on the one hand express an intention for social control over the private space's activities, while on the other hand, this room, *in itself* an open and outward-looking structure, favouritises an integration of the recreational and social activities which took place in the room. In other words, the private sphere was not *so* private that it could not also include the like of friends, guests and other visitors in the room's social activities; in fact, on the contrary, such an effect may have been intentional and set the norm for the physical form taken by the room. The exposed nature of the hearth and food preparation can in such a context be interpreted as an expression that ritual surrounding food preparation and meals might have played a central role in the social life which unfolded within the room's four walls.

A natural conclusion to that which has been advanced above is that, in its spatial structure, the *laft*-built two-roomed dwelling house ("*stua*") displays clear parallels with Viking Age dwelling houses in western Norway and in the areas which the Vikings colonised. As the physical framework around the inhabitants' private lives this building type expresses, in my opinion, *the presence of a rural (and archaic) culture of habitation.* That the urban "*stua*" was constructed using the *laft* technique, which was a known but not widespread construction technique in Viking Age Norway, does not alter this conclusion.

5. DID AN URBAN CULTURE OF HABITATION EXIST IN NORWEGIAN MEDIEVAL TOWNS?

That the two-roomed lafted dwelling house equipped with a corner hearth became the standard form of abode in urban society throughout most of the Middle Ages can be interpreted as an expression that the people who occupied these buildings *sought to maintain and reinforce a rural culture of habitation in an urban context.* This is an interesting possible interpretion when seen against the background that from the end of the 12th century a *new social practice* was in the process of development in the Norwegian towns. The *skjøtstuer* (public rooms used for social gatherings), which we hear of in Bergen from around the beginning of the 13th century, taverns and public bathhouses comprised public spaces which can be connected with the emergence of new norms and conventions for urban social behaviour. The establishment of these types of public spaces, which quickly constituted important arenas for social intercourse and communication, indicates that, not only was a new social custom in the process of development, but in some areas this was incompatible with the private life encapsulated in the conventional culture of habitation.

This situation confronts us with a labile and contradictory social reality: While an attempt was made within the private sphere to maintain the norms and conventions of social and cultural behaviour with roots in traditional agrarian society, *a new social custom which is expressed and internalised in the high medieval urban building mass* forced itself into the public sphere. To the extent that the urban tenement's central dwelling house maintained and reproduced earlier social customs, this contributed to *emphasize the inhabitants' social and cultural relationships with the towns' rural hinterland* - one lived in the town but marked and reinforced one's "mental" roots and identity in the town's agrarian surroundings. This raises the questions: *who* used the "*stua*" and *how* did they use it? I can only suggest some possible answers. To begin with, the dwelling house was the only building of permanent character which was built on the marked-out urban plots in Trondheim. The building was placed centrally within the plot, somewhat set back from the earliest street. The place between the house and the street was reserved for various forms of productive activity connected with the household or sporadic craft production. Gradually, as the number of buildings on each plot grew, a development which intensified from the second half of the 11th century, the dwelling houses moved further back within the row of buildings which formed the urban tenement. This can be immediately explained by the economic significance eventually adopted by the combined storage, workshop and trading buildings which stood beside the street. However, productive and economic activities were no less important in the 17th-century town, although at that time the dwelling house fronted directly onto the public area, with access direct from the street. With regard to function, a customary withdrawn siting of dwelling houses is therefore neither obvious nor a prerequisite. The marked withdrawn siting of the dwelling house can alternatively be interpreted as an *intentional screening off of the private sphere from public space.* The social psychologist Irwin Altman has discussed the mechanisms for social behaviour in relation to what he calls "privacy" (Altman 1975). Individuals or groups always react to situations affected by crowding, or dense population, by employing one or another form of screening-off of the private sphere, although the strategies can vary from situation to situation: One could expand the personal space, one could increase the use of non-verbal means of communication or in other ways reinforce the demarcation of territory. The withdrawn dwelling houses can, in my judgement, be an expression of such a strategy for *screening and the establishment of a private sphere*, where one could live life according to norms and conventions to some extent free of consideration for, or interference from, the outside world. It might be tempting to see this as a result of the urban space's increasing subdivision into more demarcated and denser physical environments, something which must have led to a growing degree of crowding.

In the course of the above we have not taken into account the fact that the urban dwelling is not an unambiguous phenomenon. It was not the case that everyone in the towns lived in their *own* dwelling house - that was first and foremost reserved for the tenement owner and his family. We will return to who these people were later. Who, then,

were all the *others*, those who represented the real core of permanent town inhabitants, and who eventually came to form the nucleus of the urban citizenry? How did they reside and live their lives? In the case of the former, it is clear that the dwelling house was not the only building in the tenement which was occupied. Written sources speak of, among other things, *lofts* which were obviously used as living rooms. The *loft* was probably not an independent building, but rather the second storey in a building in which the ground floor appears, on the basis of archaeological observations, to have been reserved for storage, workshops etc. In the case of Trondheim, it has been suggested that the buildings which stood beside the street had a second storey which was reserved for accommodation purposes. It is natural to think that those who lived in these *lofts* were the craftsmen and tradesmen who had bought their own accommodation in the form of a portion of a tenement, or the many who *rented* accommodation in the town for shorter or longer periods of time. The single-storeyed heated and withdrawn dwelling houses could on the other hand have been reserved for the tenement owner and his family. Generally speaking we know little about who they were, but in Bergen the conditions are better known than in the other urban centres thanks to a better written source material. Even though we do not know how representative the situation in Bergen was generally, I believe that in the first volume of the Bergen town history the historian Knut Helle provides a description which in principle could also apply to the other Norwegian towns: *"The majority of tenement owners of whom we know in Bergen during the latter part of the high Middle Ages were prominent town men or women..... They often had one foot in the town and one foot in the countryside. From this state of affairs light is thrown back onto the earliest circumstances of tenement ownership in the town."* (Helle 1982). That the tenement owners, or at least many of them, had their social and economic roots in agarian society is nothing new. But the tenements' withdrawn dwelling houses indicate moreover that the relationship with the agrarian community was not just of socio-economic character, but also socio-*cultural*, in the sense that they internalised a rural pattern of norms and behaviour. In this manner those who lived in the large urban tenements represent not only a social and economic upper class, but also a *cultural elite* which on the one hand held fast mentally to its identity in agarian society, and which on the other hand displayed *in its social customs* patterns of interaction developed in a completely different social and cultural context. In my opinion the urban tenement, with its many buildings and large volume, becomes the element in the urban landscape which most clearly makes visible the interweaving of economic, social and cultural dominance in the towns which the landed aristocracy represented, and which in addition expresses a depth and complexity in contemporary town-countryside relationships which points beyond simple social and economic relationships. As such the urban tenement becomes an ambiguous symbol which on the one hand expresses relationships of social, political and economic dominance in urban society, but which on the abstract and mental plane expresses town-countryside relationships as a *cultural* relationship with a contrasting social and cultural content.

For all the others who made up the urban community's *active* social core, tenants, craftsmen, vendors, and so on, living conditions were completely different. They were abandoned to the uncertainties of the rent market. They were forced to live their lives in spatial surroundings which they themselves could have no influence upon to any notable degree. The division between private and public space was for them less clear-cut and consistent than it was for those who who lived in the withdrawn dwelling houses. They all lived closer to their workplaces, with close association with other tenants, guests, servants, and in many instances also the street life. In such a context the possibility of maintaining privacy through physical screening against the outside world was barely attainable. Public space, its life, people and activities, was an element which impinged more closely on the everyday life of the town dwellers, a reality which one could both influence and be influenced by, and which therefore became the basis for new and alternative experiences and reflections. Established norms and conventions must have to an increasing degree have pushed against social custom which established itself within the frameworks of the high-medieval town's physical and social reality. The chaos which the urban landscape of the High Middle Ages expressed is therefore not fortuitous. *This complex, labile and confused social situation contains within itself a potential for generating conflict, the embryo of a social dynamic the consequences of which we do not see expressed in the structural environment before a completely new culture of habitation develops as the frame of reference for the leading citizens' self-perception of what it was "to be in the world".* But this probably did not occur in the Norwegian provincial towns before the chronological end of the Middle Ages. In Trondheim, for example, this appears to have occurred during a period when a capital-accumulating patrician class of merchants assumed the leading positions in the towns during the first half of the 17th century, erecting ostentatious, panelled residences on street frontages and on corner properties in order to dominate the cramped street area from a number of angles (Berg 1951). One is immediately tempted to interpret this as the new power elite's display of newly acquired power and dominance (Thommason 1997). At the same time these "bourgeois houses" are a physical manifestation of the new urban elite's historical roots within the public space, in the street and on the square . The street area is in this way not just a medium of communication and transport, a specific sosio-spacial structure that generates an urban way of living (Simmel 1981), but also a cultural space which represents a meeting between bygone power structures and those who carried the future in their hands, heads and hearts.

Axel Christophersen
Institutt for arkeologi og kulturhistorie,
Vitenskapsmuseet,
Norges teknisk-naturvitenskapelige Universitet
Erling Skakkes gt. 47 b
N-7491 Trondheim

Bibiliography

Altman, I. 1975. *The Environment and Social Behavior*. Monterey.

Aspen, J. og Pløger, J. (red.) 1997. *På sporet av byen*. Oslo.

Bauman, Z. 1993. *Postmodern Ethics*. Oxford.

Bender, D.R. 1967. A Refinement of the Concept of Household: Families, Co-residence, and Domestic Function. *American Anthropologist 69.*

Berg, A. 1989. *Norske tømmerhus frå mellomalderen. Bnd.1. Allment* oversyn. *Norske Minnesmerker*. Oslo.

Berg, A. 1995. *Norske tømmerhus frå mellomalderen. Bnd. 5. Hus for hus. Norske Minnesmerker.* Oslo.

Berg, H. 1951. *Trondheim før Cicignon. Gater og gårder før reguleringen 1681.* Trondheim.

Bourdieu, P.1977. *Outline of a Theory of Practice.* Cambridge.

Carsten, J, Hugh-Jones, S. 1995. *About the house. Levi-Strauss and beyond.* Cambridge.

Chapman, J. 1988. From "Space" to "Place": A model of dispersed settlement and Neolithic society. *I Burgess, C., Topping, P., Mordant, C, og Maddison, M. (eds.): Enclousure and Defence in ther Neolithic of Western Europe.* Oxford.

Christophersen, A. og Nordeide, S.W. 1994. *Kaupangen ved Nidelva. Riksantikvarens Skrifter nr. 7.* Trondheim.

Christophersen, A.1990. Dwelling Houses, Workshops and Storehouses. Functional Aspects of the Developement of Wooden urban Buildings in Trondheim from A.D. 1000 to A.D.1400. *Acta Archaeologica vol. 60.* København.

Elias, N. 1991(1989). *The symbol theory*. London, New Dehli.

Elias, N. 1994(1939). *The Civilizing Process*. Guildford.

Fairclough, G. 1992. Meaningful constructions - spatial and functional analysis of medieval buildings. *Antiquity 66 (1992).*

Fett, T. 1989. Bygninger og bygningsdetaljer. *Schia, E. (red): De arkeologiske utgravninger i gamlebyen, Oslo. Hus og gjerder.* Oslo.

Gansum, T.1996. Strukturasjonsteori - om arkeologers behov for handlingsteori. *META 1996:3.* Lund.

Giddens, A.1993(1989). *Sociologi 2.* Lund.

Grenville, J.1997: Medieval Housing. London.

Gregory, D og Urry, J. (eds.) 1985. *Social Relations and Spatial Structures*. London.

Grieg, S. 1938. Vikingtidshus i Gudbrandsdalen. *Årbok for Dølaringen 1938.*

Grøn, O., Engelstad, E. og Lindblom, I. (eds). 1991. *Social Space. Human Spatial Behaviour in Dwellings and Settlements. Odense University Studies in Hstory and Social Sciences vol. 147.* Odense

Gullestad, M. 1989. *Kultur og hverdagsliv*. Otta.

Hannertz, U 1980. *Exploring the City. Inquieries Towards an Urban Anthropology*. New York.

Hauglid, R. 1980. *Laftekunst. Laftehusets opprinnelse og eldste historie.* Oslo

Helle, K. 1982. *Bergen bys historie. Bnd. 1: Kongssete og kjøpstad fra opphavet til 1536.* Bergen, Oslo, Tromsø.

Hillier, B, Hanson, J. 1984. *The social logic of space.* Cambridge.

Hougen, B. 1944. Gamle fjellstuetufter. *Viking 1944.* Oslo.

Hinz, H. 1989. *Ländlicher Hausbau in Skandinavien vom 6. Bis 14. Jahrhundert.* Köln

Kent, S. 1990. *Domestic Architecture and the Use of Space.* Cambridge.

Komber, J. 1989. Jernalderens gårdshus. En bygningsteknisak analyse. *Arkeologisk Museum i Stavanger Varia, nr. 18.* Stavanger.

Landmark, T. 1998. *Makt, ideologi og materiell kultur. En studie av arkitektur i Oslos middelalder og renessanse.* Upubl. hovedfagsoppgave i nordisk arkeologi, IAKN, Universitetet i Oslo.

Lefebvre, H. 1991(1974). *The production of Space.* Oxford.

Lindh, J. 1992. Arkeologi i Tønsberg I - Søndre bydel. *Riksantikvarens Rapporter 20.* Oslo.

Myhre, B. 1982. Bolighusets utvikling fra jernalder til middelalder i Søvest-Norge. *Myhre, B., Stoklund, B. og Gjærder, P. (red): Vestnordisk byggeskikk gjennom to tusen år. AmS-Skrifter 7.* Stavanger.

Orderud, G. I. 1995. Tid og rom i vitenskapen. *NIBR Rapport 1995:6.* Oslo

Parker Pearson, M., Richards, C. 1994. *Architecture and order. Approaches to social space.* London, New York.

Pløger, J. 1996. *Gaden som social arena. Rummet, det sociale-og den sociale romliggjøring.* Norsk Forms høstkonferanse «Hvite flekker-sorte hull», okt.1996.

Price, N. 1994. Acts of Identity? Ethnicity and Architecture in the Viking Age. *META 1994: 3-4.* Lund.

Price, N. 1995. House and Home in Viking Age Iceland. Cultural Expression in Scandinavian Colonial Architecture. Benjamin, D. (ed): *The Home: Words, Interpretations, Meanings and Environments.* Ipswich.

Rapoport, A. 1969. *House Form and Culture.*

Samson, R. 1990. *The Social Archaeology of Houses.* Glasgow..

Saunders, T. 1990. The feudal construction of space. Power and domination in the nucleated village. In Samson, R. (1990): *The Social Archaeology of Houses.* Glasgow.

Simmel, G. 1981. *Hur är samhället möjligt? Och andre essäer.* Lund.

Simonsen, K.1993. *Byteori og hverdagspraksis.*

Simonsen, K. 1994. Rummet i samfundsteorien -en gang til. I *Nordisk Samhällsgeografiska Tidsskrift Nr. 18.*

Soja, E.1996. *Postmodern geographies. The reassertion of Space in Social theory.* Oxford.

Skre, D. 1996. Rural Settlements in medieval Norway, AD 400-1400. *Ruralia I. Conference Ruralia, Prague 1995. Pamotky Archeologické - Supplementum* Praha.

Sundt, E. 1976. *Om bygnings-skikken på landet i Norge.* Oslo.

Sørheim, H. 1999. De første laftehus? Lotte selsing og Grete Lillehammer (red): *Museumslandskap. Artikkelsamling til kerstin Griffin på 60-årsdagen. AmS-Rapport 12B. Bind B.* Stavanger

Tollnes, R. 1973. Hustuft på Søndre Rauland i Numedal. *Nicolay nr. 13.* 1973.

Thomasson, J. 1997. Private Life Made Public. *Andersson, H, Carelli, P., Ersgård, L. (eds): Visions of the Past. Trends and Traditions in Swedish Medieval Archaeology.* Stockholm.

Tringham, R. 1995. Archaeological Houses, Households, Housework and the Home. Benjamin, D. (ed): *The Home: Words, Interpretations, Meanings and Environments.* Ipswich.

Fig 1: Two-roomed, lafted buildings from urban excavations in Norway
(after Hinz 1989, Fett 1989, Lindh 1992 and Christophersen & Nordeide 1994.)

Fig 2: The Uv stove from Rennebu, Norway, dated to the 13th century.
Drawing from before 1846 (after Sundt 1857, 1976).

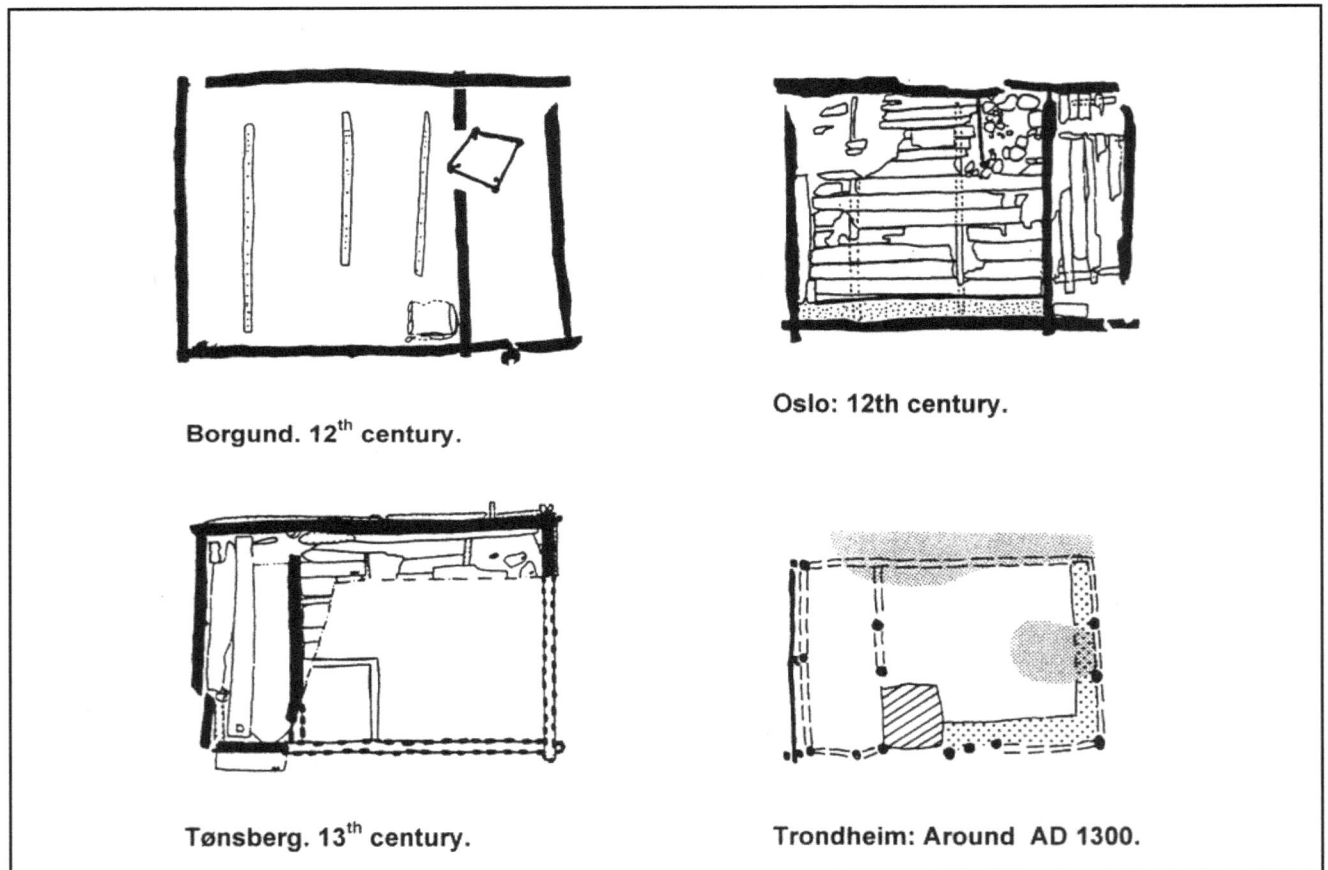

Borgund. 12th century.

Oslo: 12th century.

Tønsberg. 13th century.

Trondheim: Around AD 1300.

Fig 3: Reconstruction of building K 60, Library Site, Trondheim. The building is dendro dated to ca. AD 1010
(photo: Per E. Fredriksen, Vitenskapsmuseet, NTNU). after Christophersen & Nordeide 1994).

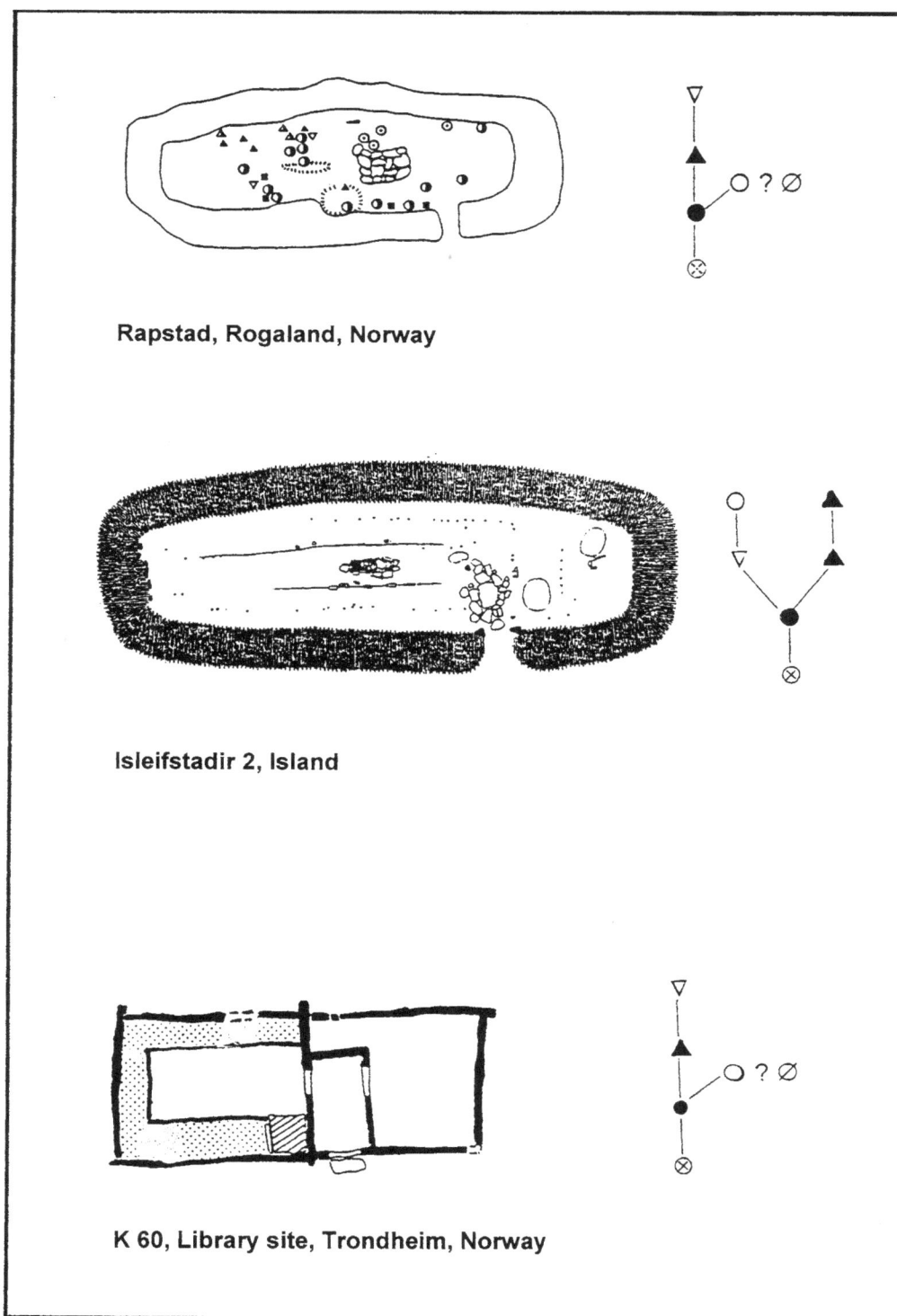

Rapstad, Rogaland, Norway

Isleifstadir 2, Island

K 60, Library site, Trondheim, Norway

⊗ **Neutral entrance** ● **Transit area** ▲ **Cooking area with fireplace ("stofa")**
▽ **Living area ("skåle)** ⊘ **Storing area** O **Unspecified area of use**

Fig 4: Room plans and access analysis of rural and urban buildings from Island (Isleifstadir) and Norway (Rapstad, Trondheim) in late Viking Age (after Myhre 1982, Price 1994 and Christophersen & Nordeide 1994).

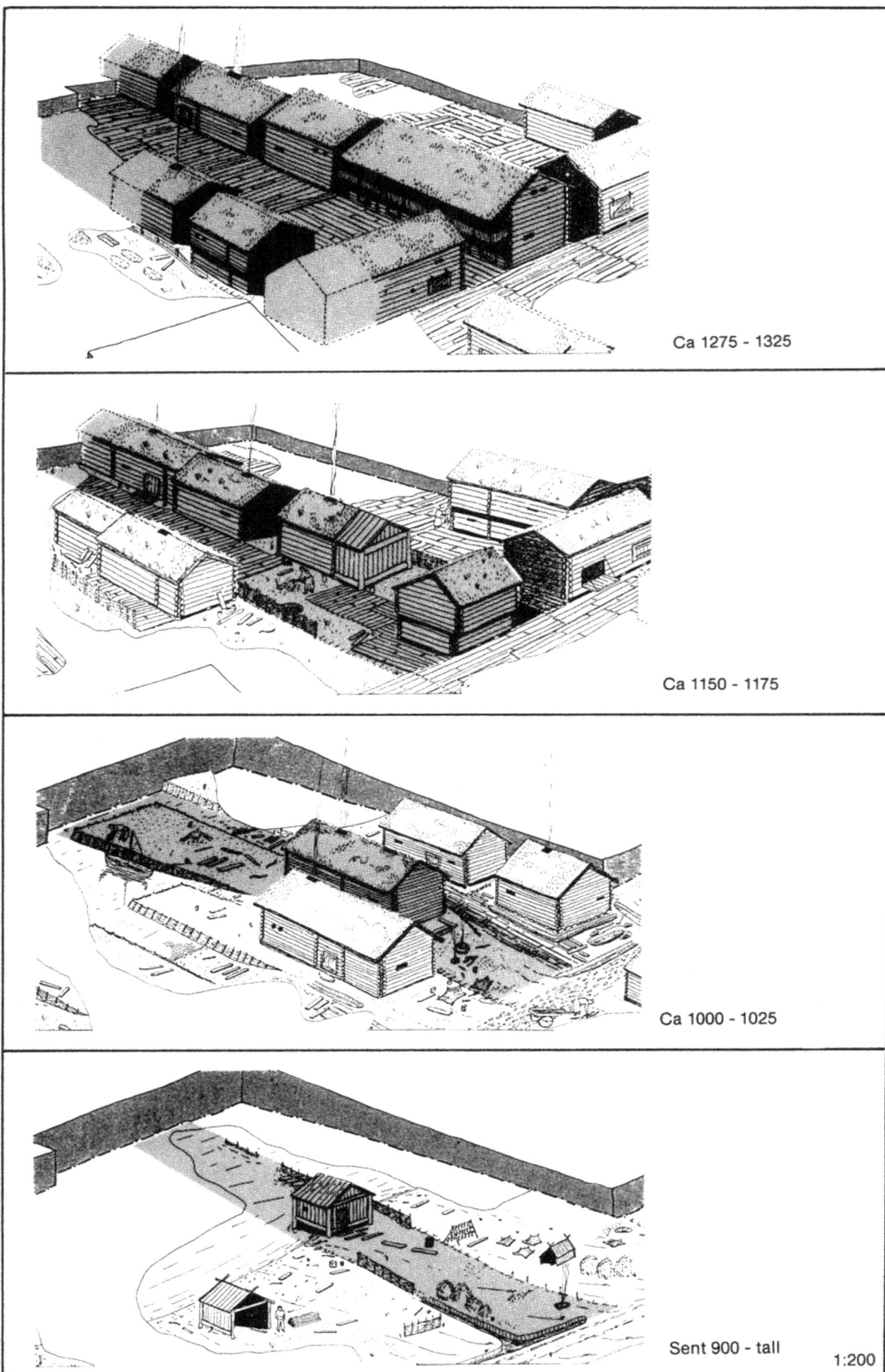

Fig 5: Development of the settlement pattern on a large plot in central medieval Tondheim AD ca. 970 - 1325 (after Christophersen & Nordeide 1994).

Fig 6: Booth buildings along the Kaupmanna strete, AD 1250
(after Christophersen & Nordeide 1994).

Fig 7: Print of Maschius, ca 1670, showing large wooden buildings
(behind the wharfs in fron) along the Krambugata
(photo: Per E. Fredriksen, Vitenskapsmuseet, NTNU).

THE NEVEH SHALOM SYNAGOGUE SITE IN SPANISH TOWN, JAMAICA

P. ALLSWORTH-JONES, D. GRAY, S. WALTERS

Abstract: It has long been known that there were once two synagogues in Spanish Town, Jamaica, an Ashkenazim synagogue on Young street and a Sephardim synagogue at the corner of Monk and Adelaide streets. The Spanish and Portuguese Jewish congregation was founded in 1692 and the land for the land for the Sephardim synagogue was purchased in 1704. An adjacent lot was used as a cemetery until about 1940. The synagogue received the name "Kahal Kadosh Neveh Shalom" or "Holy Congregation - Dwelling Place of Peace". A small building may first have been erected on the site, but the synagogue as it existed in its heyday was a late 18th century structure. It was struck by lightning in 1844 and although it was repaired it was again severely damaged by the earthquake of 14 January 1907. When Andrade wrote in 1941, he recorded that the building was in a deplorable condition, and it evidently was not used for worship. At about that time, the tombstones in the cemetery were removed and re-erected along its northern wall, and the whole area fell into a state of decay which has characterised it ever since. No harm came to the site, however, which is surrounded by land belonging to the Infirmary, otherwise known as Mulberry Gardens, west of the Rio Cobre. Given its antiquity, clearly this location is of great significance for the Jewish community in the New World as a whole. In 1997, Mr Ainsley Henriques, then Chairman of the Jamaica National Heritage Trust, proposed that the site of the synagogue should be excavated and the cemetery rehabilitated in order to make it once again a centre of Jewish cultural life, under the auspices of the newly founded Neveh Shalom Institute. A preliminary survey from the historical and architectural angle was carried out by Caribbean Volunteer Expeditions in October 1997. Two initial excavations have also been conducted at the synagogue in January 1998 and 1999. They were carried out by the University of the West Indies and the Archaeological Society of Jamaica under licence granted by the Jamaica National Heritage Trust, and with the participation of personnel from the Trust. The aim has been to clear the site and make a plan of it, to collect surface material, to begin to remove the heaps of rubble which cover the former structure in a controlled way, and to expose the foundations of the building which fell into ruin from 1907 onwards. A good beginning has been made in the achievement of these objectives. The areas excavated so far are on the south side of the main building, the outlines of which have been established. It seems likely that the mounds of rubble covering the site are themselves disturbed, and they could in future probably be fairly rapidly removed in order to expose the foundations of the principal structure. Quite a large quantity of 18th century artefacts have been recovered, including smoking pipes, glass vessels, and ceramics, in addition to material which has found its way onto the site in the present century. The latter is by no means irrelevant in terms of modern material culture studies, but from the overall historical perspective probably the material associated with the Jewish synagogue in its heyday will be of principal international interest. It is hoped that this report will stimulate interest in the site, so that the entire project can be completed within a relatively short span of time.

INTRODUCTION

Jewish people have played a significant role in Jamaican history, at least from the beginning of the British colonial period. Records show that a synagogue, known as "Neveh Zedek" - "Dwelling Place of Righteousness", was built in Port Royal between 1677 and 1686 (Andrade, 1941; Newman, 1989; Brown, 1996). After the earthquake in Port Royal, the majority of Jews moved to Kingston or to Spanish Town, where they are said to have numbered about 300 in 1774. There were once two synagogues in Spanish Town, an Ashkenazim synagogue on Young street and a Sephardim synagogue at the corner of Monk and Adelaide streets (Andrade, 1941). The Spanish and Portuguese Jewish congregation was founded in 1692 and the land for the

Sephardim synagogue was purchased in 1704. An adjacent lot was used as a cemetery until about 1940. The synagogue received the name "Kahal Kadosh Neveh Shalom" or "Holy Congregation - Dwelling Place of Peace". A small building may first have been erected on the site, but the synagogue as it existed in its heyday was a late 18th century structure. Andrade states that it was "built in red brick with a stone foundation rectangular in form" and that it was "a replica of Bevis Marks synagogue in London". The Bevis Marks synagogue itself was constructed in 1701. Pevsner (1962) described it as "unique in Britain in its preservation and wealthy appointment" but in form it was only a "plain parallelogram". As Barnett and Levy (1970) explain, it "somewhat resembled a Dissenters' chapel in its severely simple architecture", which is perhaps not too surprising, considering that it was built by a Quaker. The Neveh Shalom synagogue was struck by lightning in 1844 and although it was repaired it was again severely damaged by the earthquake of 14 January 1907. When Andrade wrote in 1941, he recorded that it was in a deplorable condition, and it was evidently not used for worship. At about that time, the tombstones in the cemetery were removed and re-erected along its northern wall, and the whole area fell into a state of decay which has characterised it ever since. No harm came to the site, however, which is surrounded by land belonging to the Infirmary, otherwise known as Mulberry Gardens, west of the Rio Cobre (Black, 1960). Given its antiquity, clearly

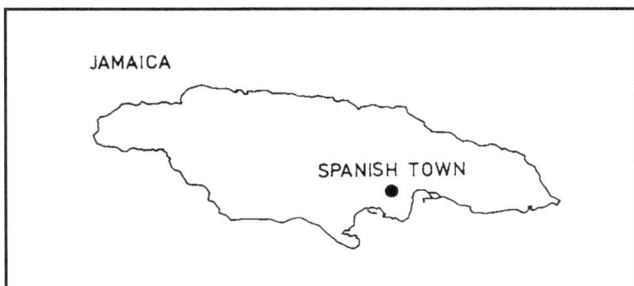

Map

this location is of great significance for the Jewish community in the New World as a whole.

In 1997, Mr Ainsley Henriques, then Chairman of the Jamaica National Heritage Trust, proposed that the site of the synagogue should be excavated and the cemetery rehabilitated in order to make it once again a centre of Jewish cultural life, under the auspices of the newly founded Neveh Shalom Institute (Henriques, 1997-98). A preliminary survey from the historical and architectural angle was carried out by Caribbean Volunteer Expeditions in October 1997 (CVE, 1998). They recorded information about 48 tombstones in the cemetery, and gave a detailed description of the standing wall around the synagogue compound. Excavations were subsequently conducted at the synagogue in January 1998 and January 1999 (Allsworth-Jones et al., 1998, 2000). Both were carried out by the Department of History of the University of the West Indies and, in principle, the Archaeological Society of Jamaica, under licence granted by the Jamaica National Heritage Trust, with the participation of personnel from the Trust. The aim of this paper is to present the main results from the excavations and the subsequent study of the material from the site. The first part of the paper (survey and excavation) is the responsibility of all three authors, who took part in the work at the site, while the second part (study of the material) is the responsibility of the first author, since it was carried out under his supervision, with the students who had participated in the excavations, at the University of the West Indies. The material recovered from the excavations has been or will be handed over for conservation and storage at the Neveh Shalom Institute, for whose support we are grateful.

SURVEY AND EXCAVATION 1998-1999
(P. Allsworth-Jones, D. Gray, S. Walters)

The work at the site took place on January 5-16 1998 and January 4-15 1999. The objectives were set out beforehand in a letter to the JNHT as follows. (1) A plan would be drawn, with baselines north-south and east-west, to serve as the fundamental reference grid for any further work at the site. (2) A contour map would be made of the present configuration of the site. (3) After clearing of the vegetation, a surface collection and record would be made of any loose material now on the ground at the site; it was expected that some of this might date back to the time of the structure's collapse, but that other items might be more recent. (4) Where walls were exposed, they would be recorded on the plan of the site. (5) In appropriate cases, such exposed areas would be extended by limited excavation; it was suggested that any building material excavated should be conserved with a view to its possible incorporation in any new structure that might arise on the site. (6) A location would be chosen for a possible stratigraphic control trench to establish the nature of the subsoil at the site. These objectives have been achieved, although no control trench has been dug as yet, and the excavations so far conducted have been concentrated on the south side of the synagogue only.

An east-west baseline 42 metres long was established, followed by a north-south baseline 26 metres long. A numbered grid of 4m² squares was established by reference to these baselines labelled 1-24 west-east and A-S south-north. In terms of this grid, the datum point for the two baselines is at the SW corner of square J21, in the eastern part of the site. All squares are numbered by reference to the coordinates of their SW corner. The resultant grid is at an angle to the axis of the property, which is tilted in a slightly NE-SW direction. In this, it follows the general angle of the layout of Spanish Town (Figure 1, after Black, 1960). The outside walls of the property, which forms a well-proportioned rectangle, measure some 26 by 41 metres, giving an internal area a little less than 1000m² (25x40m). Contouring was carried out by reference to the same datum point, taken as zero, and contour lines were drawn at 20 cm intervals.

Two areas were selected for excavation in 1998, having regard to the existing exposed walls. First, an area of 12m² was opened up in squares H16 and I and J17, at the south-east corner of what was evidently the main synagogue building. The rather massive stone foundations of the building were visible at this point. Second, an area of 40m² was exposed to the south and west of the main building in squares F-G 10-13 and E 13-14. This area was chosen because some red brick walls of what turned out to be auxiliary buildings to the main building were partially exposed. As the work proceeded, the main stone wall also came to light, and it was traced to its south-west corner. The length of the wall corresponds to the figure given by Andrade (1941: 41) where it is stated that it measured 52 feet from east to west. He also stated that the north-south wall measured 32 feet, and on that basis an extrapolated plan of the main structure has been drawn. It sits symmetrically in the middle of the property.

A map of the site as it appeared in 1998, combining the grid and the contour plans which were prepared in the field, is at Figure 2. The two field drawings were amalgamated in the laboratory by Mr Edward Coore, and were then replotted in a computer configuration at Leicester University by Ms Lucy Farr. The map shows the relationship between the number-letter grid and the layout of the compound. The walls of the compound are intact along Monk and Adelaide Streets (to west and north) but elsewhere they have mainly collapsed. The foundation of the main building (in part hypothetical) is indicated, as are the squares of the grid in which excavations took place in 1998. The contour lines reveal the main features in regard to the elevation of the site. At the south-west and the north-east corners, material was heaped up (it is suspected, some time ago) to a height of 1.40 metres. In general the ground slopes gradually up from east to west by about 40 cm, which is to be expected, since the Rio Cobre is away to the east and the site is still on the valley slope. Most noticeably, the gradual slope from east to west is interrupted by three mounds up to 1.80, 1.20, and 1.00 metres high above datum. Two of the mounds lie outside the bounds of the former main building, but the highest is inside the limit of the structure. Also inside the structure is a depression at the centre of the three mounds. The existence of these mounds obviously determines the nature of the work to be done at

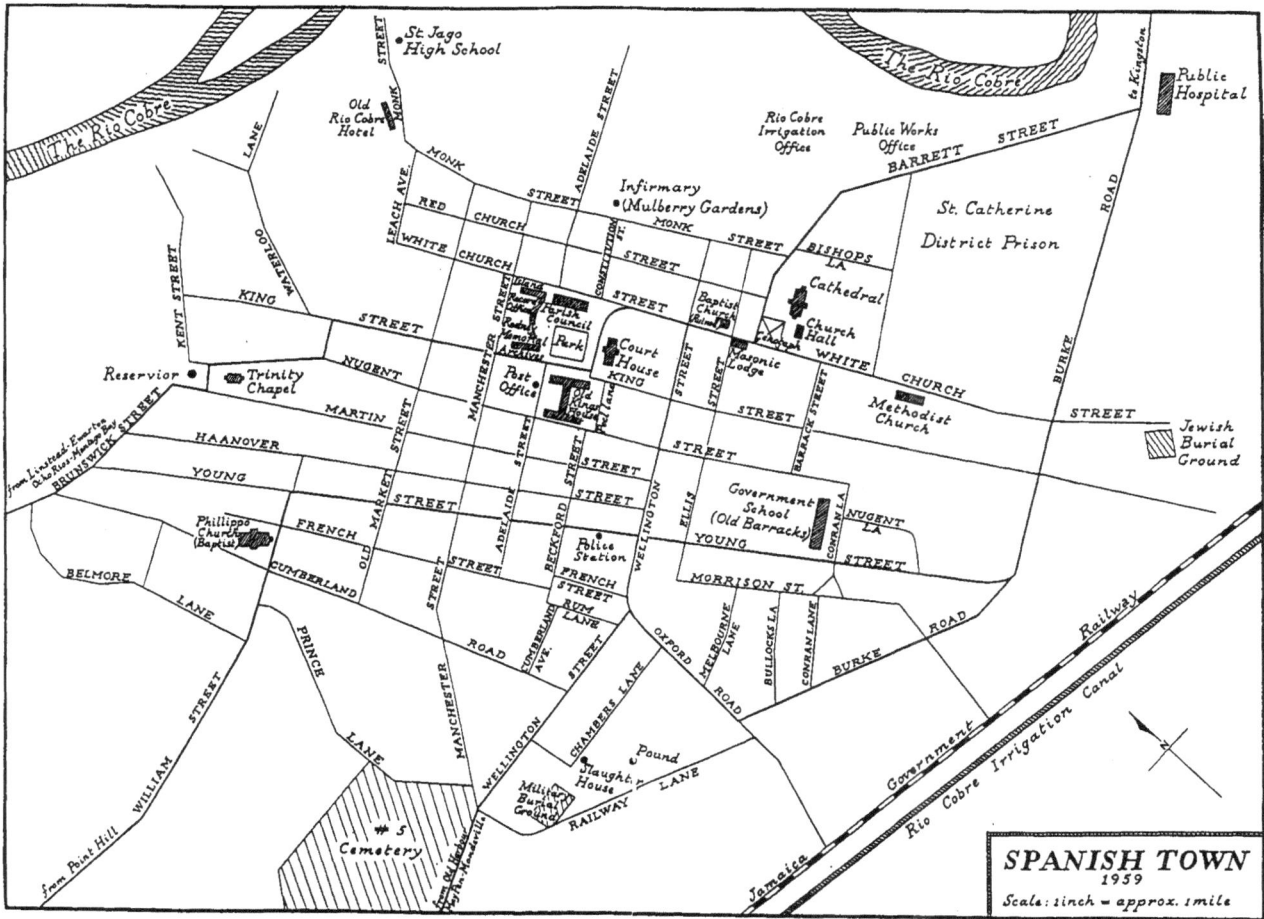

Figure 1

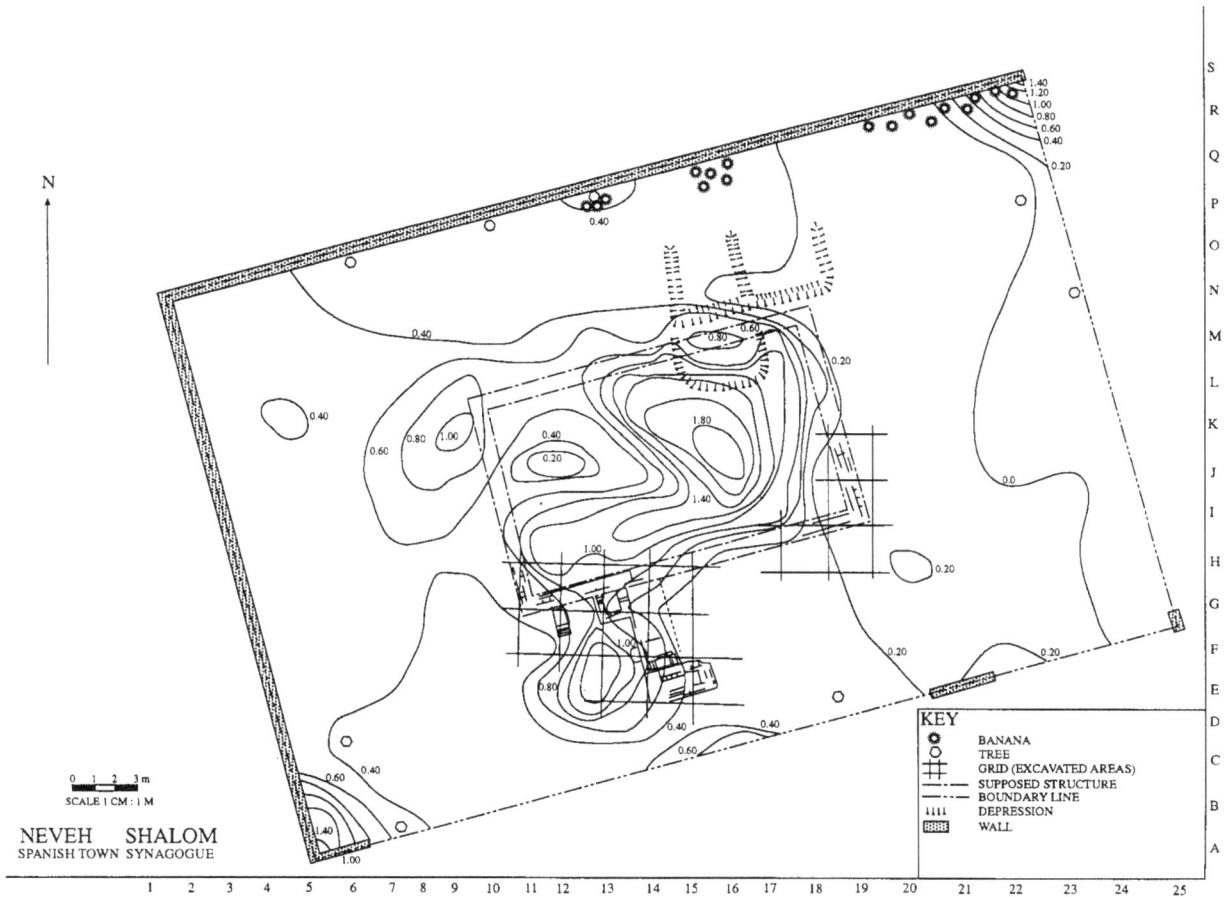

NEVEH SHALOM
SPANISH TOWN SYNAGOGUE

Figure 2

the site since they must be removed if any reconstruction is to be carried out. It is clear that (apart from the deposition of rubbish) the heaping up of the mounds is not the last thing to have happened at the site. Just beyond the line of the main building, to the north-east, there are some small trenches, and the large mound has also been cut into at that point. It is assumed that these features are due to agricultural activities carried out in the recent past. There are a number of economically useful trees in the compound, including bananas, ackee and guinep, and there were some traces of cassava in the vicinity of the trenches. Despite this, however, it is obvious from the material recovered that the site has really been very little disturbed over the years.

The map at Figure 2 shows the extent of the excavations and the structures uncovered in 1998. The south-east corner of the main building is uncomplicated, the only feature apart from the foundation itself being an aperture presumably for drainage purposes in the east wall. The situation on the south and west is a good deal more complex. A number of brick foundations were revealed immediately to the south of the main foundation and to the east of the mound at that point. It was obvious that the whole of the mound would have to be removed in order to make sense of these structures, and that was the main purpose of the excavations in 1999. In that year a further 32 m² was opened up in squares D-E 10-12, D13 and F14. These squares contained the main mass of mound material. The total area excavated over the two years in this part of the site therefore comes to 72 m². The excavation of squares F11-12 and E13 extended over the two years, since they were not completed in the first year. As a result of the work undertaken in 1999, the plan of the entire complex in this area was revealed. Figure 3 is an isometric drawing by Mr Coore showing the excavated structures viewed from the north-east. Figure 4 (A) shows the south-west part of the excavated structures in more detail, and Figure 4 (B) is a plan of the complex in relation to the foundation of the main building and in particular its south-west corner.

Already in 1998, the excavation of the mound itself when its sides were being scraped back at the edges of squares F12

and E13, taken in conjunction with evidence from E14, revealed fairly conclusive proof of the manner in which it had been heaped up. In E14 right on the foundations of the brick structure there was found a circular chrome fitting identical to two which were observed at the top of the sequence on the mound at the boundary of E13. We cannot be sure of the exact date of these fittings, but they must be fairly recent, and being so similar they indicate that there was no great gap in time between the top of the mound and the base. That in itself is something, but the value of these observations was much increased by further discoveries made in F12, when, at a stratigraphically intermediate level between the upper and lower chrome fittings two more artefacts were found: first, a "snap-off" metal can top of a distinctly modern kind, and second (a few cm above it) one of the best preserved 18th century smoking pipes so far discovered at the site. One could hardly ask for a more convincing stratigraphic "sandwich" than this, a conclusive demonstration not only that the mound is recent but that it consists of randomly heaped up material where old and new have been indiscriminately jumbled together. Subsequent excavations have confirmed these observations in that there is throughout the same admixture of old and new.

The mounds as you look at them today give no external indication that they may not have represented something else, the gradual stratigraphically steady collapse of a structure or structures, but it seems that the reality was otherwise. They were heaped together in the fairly recent past. While exercising all due caution, it seems that the lesson for further excavation at the site is plain. The mounds could be demolished relatively quickly in order to reveal the foundations of the synagogue, since their own stratigraphic value is very slight.

The nature of the excavated complex south of the main synagogue building can be discerned in Figures 3 and 4. Broadly it is a T shaped structure which abuts that building and is later than it, since the brickwork bonds into the foundation in such a way that it must post-date it. At the base and the top of the T are two "box-like" brick squares which

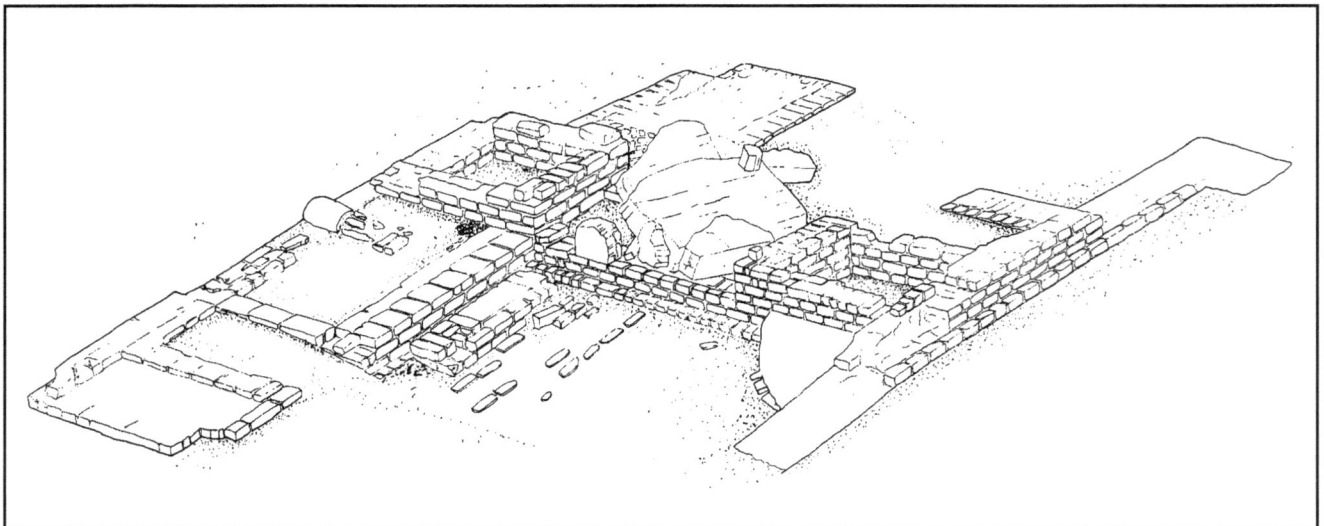

Figure 3

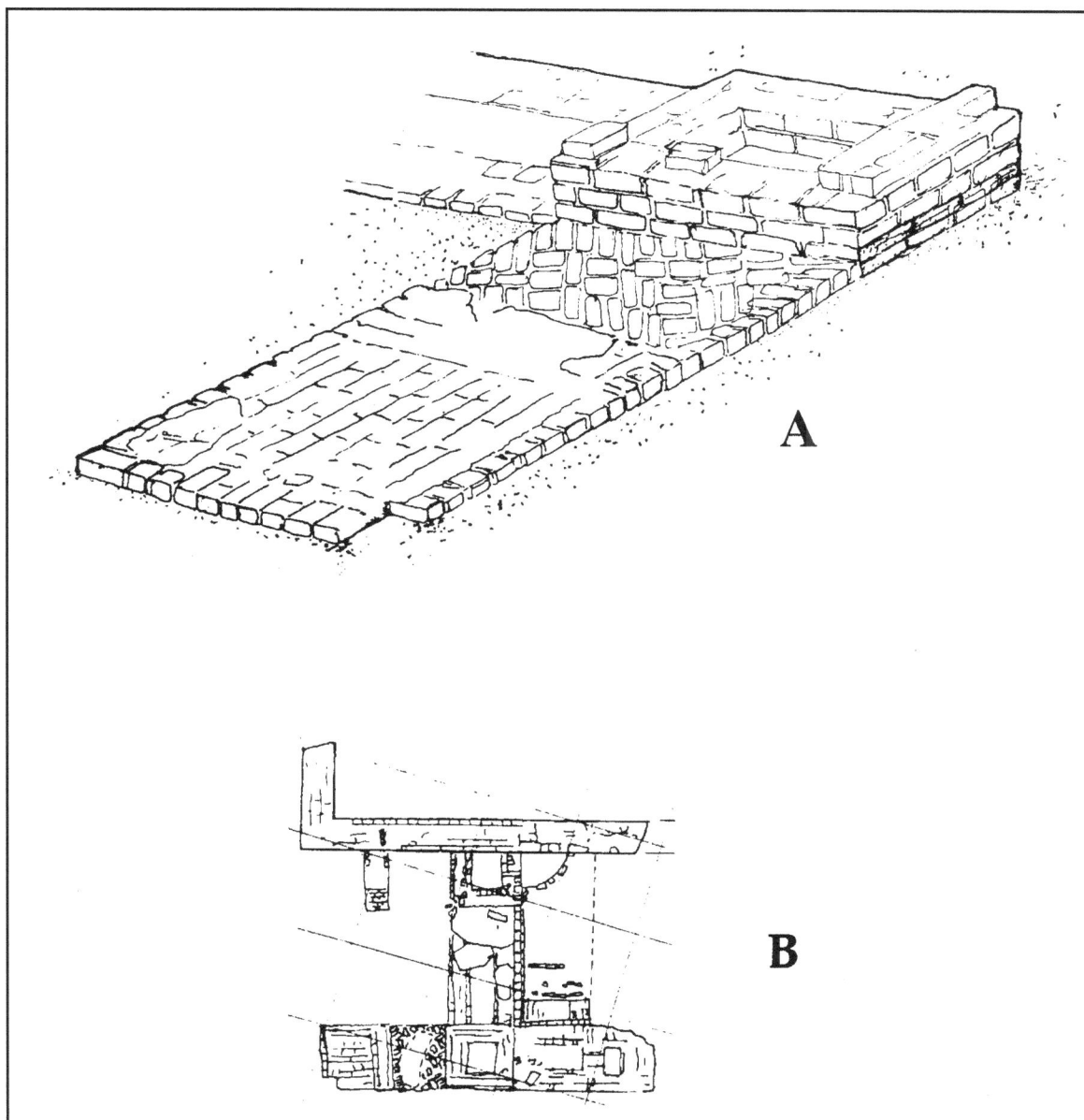

Figure 4

have remained quite solid. They are joined by a further brick foundation, and, as shown in the isometric drawing, there is now a portion of a fallen brick wall in this space. If there are any deposits in situ in this area, they should be beneath that wall, which has been left undisturbed for the time being. The eastern branch of the T structure is also a solid and apparently simple brick foundation, but the situation is more complex in respect of the western branch shown in Figure 4 (A). There are three components here. Outermost is again an apparently simple brick foundation, but then there is an area of mortar followed by a pavement of bricks at an irregular angle to the "box-like" square at the top of the T. On the east side of the T by the main synagogue foundation there is a triangle of plaster and bricks in situ and it possible that this may have formed part of a walkway. On the west side of the T and separated from it is an isolated possibly fallen brick wall. While we cannot be certain as to the function of the excavated features, it seems likely that an answer can be found in the account given by Andrade, who recorded that the Ladies

Gallery was reached "from the yard by a brick staircase with steps of tiles" (Andrade, 1941:41). Probably this was the staircase.

In the course of the excavation of the mound, a rather puzzling feature came to light in the area of the T structure's western branch. Here a stack of bricks was revealed, oriented north-south in an orderly fashion, measuring 1.5 by 0.3 metres and 0.7 metres high, but apparently not a wall, since the bricks were not laid uniformly nor were they held in place by mortar. Clearly this was not a permanent feature. The stack was removed and the foundation shown in Figure 4 (A) was uncovered beneath. Again one is left to speculate, but presumably at some point during the synagogue's collapse these bricks were heaped together perhaps for greater safety. How they were then incorporated into the mound in general is not certain. While therefore the future dismantling of the mounds may not pose great problems stratigraphically, the possibility of surprises in store cannot be entirely excluded.

A STUDY OF THE ARTEFACTS
(P. Allsworth-Jones)

The material recovered and analysed comes both from the excavated squares, totalling 84 m², and from the surface area included within the synagogue compound, totalling approximately 948 m². A little surface material was collected from the squares subsequently excavated prior to their excavation. The material, apart from the fauna, has been divided into two broad categories, that presumed to belong to the 18th or 19th centuries, and that presumed to belong to the 20th century. All the finds have been plotted by square. Generally speaking, the modern material found on the surface tends to be concentrated at the western end of the site, and represents for the most part rubbish which has been thrown over the wall from Monk Street. The older finds are concentrated in the central and eastern parts of the synagogue compound, but there is considerable spatial overlap between the two categories, and the distinction betweeen them is far from clear cut. The total number of finds is listed in Table 1. All together there are 14850 pieces, of which 11483 come from the excavated squares and 3367 from the surface. All classes of material are present both in the excavated squares and on the surface, but not in equal numbers.

Presumed 18th-19th century material

Smoking pipes

The majority of the smoking pipes are of white clay and are assumed to be of European manufacture, but a minority are of brown terracotta and are assumed to be of local manufacture (Hume, 1991; Barber, 1994; Deetz, 1996). The white smoking pipes consist of 966 stem fragments, 114 bowls, and 24 pieces with parts of both. One of the most complete examples comes from excavated square F12 and constitutes an important part of the argument suggesting that the mounds now characteristic of the site consist of mixed material, since it occurred in association with objects which are far from being 18th century in character. A few of the pieces are distinguished by heels, spurs, cartouches, and other inscriptions, for example SCOTLAND and GERMANY, the letters D and T also being popular.

Wine bottles

Globular-bodied dark-green glass wine bottles are some of the most frequent artefacts found at the site. They are of a type well known from British colonial contexts where an evolution can be detected in their form from the mid 17th to

Table 1: Neveh Shalom 1998-99: Inventory of Finds

presumed 18th-19th century material	1999	1998	surface
smoking pipes:			
white	494	204	406
brown	18	6	9
wine bottles	2380	522	587
other glassware	153	5	23
European ceramics	1668	458	777
Afro-Jamaican earthenware	789	309	219
nails and other metal objects	435	202	8
miscellaneous	2		
total	5939	1706	2029

presumed 20th century material

	1999	1998	surface
glassware	1370	348	711
ceramics	101	1	38
iron objects	436	35	86
metal containers	626	3	100
other metal objects	86	37	32
plastic containers	3	1	36
other plastic objects	169	5	92
footware	149	7	48
other clothing items	70	5	28
miscellaneous	261	22	64
total	3271	464	1235

fauna 1998 only

		1998	surface
bones		70	57
teeth		7	4
shells		26	42
total	**9210**	**2273**	**3367**

the early 19th century (Hume, 1991: Figs. 8-13). The finds consist of 327 bottle tops, 2413 fragments of bodies, and 749 bases. The bases are all round except for 9 which are square.

Other glassware

A smaller number of fragments belong to 18th or 19th century vessels of a different type, either drinking glasses or pharmaceutical bottles (Hume, 1969, 1991: 72-76, 184-202). The latter usually take the form of small pale green phials (Hume, 1969: Fig. 36) whereas the former are mainly represented by rather heavy pieces of stems (Hume, 1969: Figs. 4-5).

European ceramics

Evidently this is a very important class of finds, which, if located in proper stratigraphic conditions, would have fairly precise chronological as well as cultural implications (Hume, 1991; Deetz, 1996; Barber, 1994; South, 1977). The total of excavated and surface material comes to 2903 pieces which can be divided into a number of categories as indicated in Table 2. As would be expected from the history of the site, the majority of the ceramic types clearly indicate an 18th or possibly a late 17th century date, the style of decoration found being generally not dissimilar to what obtained in Port Royal (Mayes, 1972: Figs. 17, 20, 21, 23). The commonest types present are creamware, delftware, pearlware, and stoneware. White salt glazed stoneware, a typical English product of the mid 18th century, is well represented, and there are a few examples of other stoneware types: Westerwald, Frechen, Nottingham, Staffordshire, Fulham, Jasperware, and American. Porcelain and slipware are also

well represented in the collection, the latter including many characteristic decorative types. A particularly fine porcelain dish fragmented into three parts was found beneath fallen masonry in excavated square F12 in 1999. Other minor categories include black-glazed redware and Wieldon and Agate refined earthenware. It is interesting and possibly significant that diagnostic early 19th century material, including Yellow ware, Mocha, and especially White ware, is not abundant. In their very careful study of the excavated material, Ava Tomlinson and Michele Bogle-Douglas distinguished a number of vessel forms among the finds, mainly bowls, cups, plates, and dishes, but also jars, saucers, handles, lids, covers, tureens, bottles, candle holders, and chamber pots.

Afro-Jamaican earthenware

Apart from indisputably European ceramics, quite large quantities of earthenware were also found at the site. As is common in Jamaica, some of this earthenware was glazed, as indicated in Table 3. Since Mathewson's excavations at Old King's House in Spanish Town, it has been common to refer to this type of pottery as Afro-Jamaican (Mathewson, 1972 a and b). At that site he discovered not only European ceramics (of the same kind which have now been found at Neveh Shalom) but also what he termed "a most interesting folk pottery". It formed a "tradition", which had not hitherto been duly recognised in Jamaica, with "a long history of development in West Africa prior to its introduction into this country". The excavations at Old King's House in his view demonstrated "the evolvement of an indigenous ceramic tradition consisting of the blending of both African and European influences", such that it could "only be adequately described as Afro-Jamaican". The blending

Table 2: European ceramics

Ceramic type	1999	1998	surface	total
pearlware	248	66	150	464
creamware	492	145	239	876
slipware	168	47	65	280
porcelain	141	28	74	243
stoneware	276	57	86	419
delftware	271	99	155	525
other	67	7	5	79
undetermined	5	9	3	17
total	1668	458	777	2903

Table 3: Afro-Jamaican earthenware

Earthenware type	1999	1998	surface	total
unglazed	573	256	203	1032
glazed	216	53	16	285
body sherds	673	265	192	1130
rim sherds	116	43	24	183
lids & handles	-	1	3	4
total	789	309	219	1317

affected both the forms of the vessels and the fact that they were at times glazed, a practice which is not characteristic of traditional pottery in West Africa. Afro-Jamaican pottery forms part of a larger continuum which it is customary to refer to as "Colono" ware (Deetz, 1996: 236-244), and it has continued to be made up to this day by Ma Lou and her family in Spanish Town (Ebanks, 1984). The pieces found at Neveh Shalom are characteristic of the ware in general. Measurements carried out on 271 of the excavated rims and body sherds showed that they had a modal thickness of 0.8 cm, with a moderately skewed distribution, and a range from 0.4 to 2.0 cm.

Nails and other metal objects

Most metal objects at the site cannot confidently be assigned an 18th or 19th century date, but some if not all of the nails probably do belong here. It is no accident that they are concentrated in the mounds of rubble, since, to a considerable extent at least, these must incorporate constructional material from the collapsed synagogue. Of the 197 nails excavated in 1998, 135 could be positively identified. According to Norman Rose, who studied them in detail, approximately 82 were wrought, 17 were cut, and 36 were wire nails. Of the wrought nails, about 42 were rose headed, 19 and 21 were L and T headed respectively. According to Hume (1991: 252 and Fig. 81) wrought nails were used throughout the 18th and well into the 19th century. Cut nails were first produced in about 1790, and wire nails came into use from the middle of the 19th century onwards. Of the 409 nails detected in 1999, 249 appear to be wrought and 160 are wire.

31 other excavated objects have tentatively been classified as belonging to this period, including household items (a three legged cooking pot, three forks, a thimble, a lock, and three flat irons) and six possible synagogue fittings. There are a number of objects definitely associated with horses, including stirrups, horse shoes, and parts of bridles. The recognition of the latter is due to brilliant detective work by Nicole Patrick, who observed a similarity between three or four of the pieces found and 18th century bits illustrated by Hume (1991: Fig. 75, 2 a solid-mouthed bridoon and 5 cheekpieces for a jointed-mouthed curb).

Miscellaneous

Two items are definitely resonant of the Colonial period in Jamaica: one half of a blue glass bead found in F14, and a gun flint of presumed English manufacture found in D12.

Presumed 20th century material

The pace of things, and the nature of the finds, changes when we come to consider those objects which can more or less confidently be regarded as modern, i.e. post-dating the collapse of the synagogue in 1907. A posssible course of action would have been to bundle these finds together and immediately seek to consign them to the municipal rubbish dump. After all, Neveh Shalom itself did clearly serve as a rubbish dump in recent years. However, this would perhaps not have been in accord with the spirit of present day archaeology, when, as William Rathje has taught us, "contemporary garbage" may make a significant contribution to "modern material culture studies" (Rathje, 1979, 1989; Rathje and McCarthy, 1977; Rathje and Murphy, 1992). To the exasperation of the students considerable time was expended upon the collection of this material and later its study in the laboratory. Exasperation lessened when it became clear that this material did in some sense reflect the daily existence and the life style of the present day inhabitants of this part of Spanish Town as well as certain changing patterns of production and consumption in Jamaica in general. This experiment in testing the possible correlates between material culture remains and socio-cultural realities will hopefully have some resonance in time to come. The categories of objects found are listed in Table 1.

Glassware

This is one of the largest categories present, both in the excavated and the surface material. The totals in the two cases come to 1718 and 711 pieces. The majority of the finds consist of broken fragments and otherwise unidentified bottles. In other cases it is clear that these bottles were for beer, spirits, wine, soft drinks, sauces, medicines, perfumes, and cosmetics. Well known Jamaican and imported brands feature prominently, e.g. Red Stripe, Guinness, Dragon Stout, Wray and Nephew, Kelly's, Coca Cola, Pepsi, Liquid Foods, Heinz, Vicks, Morses Indian Root Pills, Afro Sheen, Ponds, and Nadinola (for "bleaching"). There were also some louvre and window glass fragments. One of the excavated cosmetic jars was of a distinctive blue colour, which enabled the broken pieces to be traced over three squares (F13, E10 and 11) and the broken container to be reconstructed. This product, probably a jar of cold cream, is still available, but now comes in blue plastic holders of the same shape. The glass container seems likely therefore to date to a period between the 1960s and the 1980s, and the way in which the remains were scattered is also indicative of the manner in which the material now forming the dumps was heaped up. An ash tray excavated in G10 provides a stratigraphic marker, since it bears an inscription indicating that it was made by R. Hanna & Co for Independence Day on August 6 1962.

Ceramics

The items which can be definitely classified as modern are not so numerous. They include various imported cups, plates, and dishes (one specifically said to be for the microwave oven) mainly from China but also from the United States, as well as presumably local earthenware in the form of roof and floor tiles, pipes, and flower pots.

Iron objects

It is not altogether easy to classify these materials, amounting to 557 pieces all told, in part because of their fragmentary and corroded state, in part because of the multifarious uses to which they were put. Utensils include knives or machetes, and there are other domestic items, including bottle tops, as well as toys. There are some car or bicycle parts. There are many pieces of wire, possibly curtain wire, possibly wire for fencing or electrical purposes. A distinct category is formed by those artefacts which can be regarded as constructional material, such as roof sheeting, pipes, hinges, straps, washers, screws, nuts and bolts. The remainder of the finds have to be classified as miscellaneous. Apart from large numbers of unrecognisable fragments, these include components which once formed part of larger appliances, the purpose of which is now hard to determine.

Metal containers

There are 729 items which popularly would be known as "tin cans". Most of the excavated examples are very fragmentary and there is not much that can be said about them, although one evidently contained paint, dried portions of which were found elsewhere. One important stratified find in F12 consisted of a "snap-off" metal can top found in close proximity to the 18th century smoking pipe already mentioned, thus providing proof of the heterogeneity of the deposits making up the mounds at the site. So far as the surface material is concerned, we were more fortunate than Rathje (Rathje and McCarthy, 1977: 278) in that for most of them the former content could be specified. 66 contained food or drink, mostly well known brands. Tinned foods included sardines, mackerel, corned beef, and Vienna sausage, the first three imported from Canada, Thailand, and Brazil, the last canned locally by Grace Kennedy. Drinks included Coca Cola, condensed milk and various juices, as well as the still popular "Nutrament" and "Supligen", made by Mead Johnson (USA) and Nestle (Jamaica) respectively. Both are marketed as "fitness" drinks "for strength and energy". The 34 remaining surface finds were mainly aerosol containers for various domestic and cosmetic purposes.

Other metal objects

These objects, of which there are 155, include parts of vehicles, domestic appliances, various articles of enamel, electrical fittings, pieces of mesh, and items connected with clothing such as buckles and shoe eyelets, as well as unrecognisable scraps. It must be emphasised again that the stratified finds include three chrome circular fittings, two in excavated square E12 (at the top of the mound) and one in E14 (at the base), which form a significant part of the sequence that also includes the 18th century smoking pipe and the modern "snap-off" metal can top found in F12.

Plastic containers

Plastic products are a characteristic 20th century phenomenon, and Neveh Shalom has its fair share of them. They can be divided into two broad groups. Only four out of 40 containers were excavated, all the rest were found on the surface. Once again well known brands are represented, including containers for drinks, medicines, cosmetics, and various domestic needs. Some of the brands are Jamaican, for example a ginger beer made by a firm known as VAP once based at White Marl, but the majority appear to be from either Trinidad or the USA. Then there is a whole miscellany of other objects.

Other plastic objects

174 of these objects were excavated, the remaining 92 items were found on the surface. They constitute a veritable cornucopia of products, among which certain items are a recurring feature: pens, combs, hair curlers, buttons, clothes pegs, cups, forks, spoons, plates, 45" records, toys, and electrical items. In the excavated material there were a considerable number of melted or burnt scraps. Among the complete objects which defy categorisation is an Oxford mini dictionary cover and another for a pack of playing cards.

Footware

156 items of footware were excavated, mainly rubber soles but also some of leather. The 48 pieces found on the surface were better preserved and more heterogeneous, including "sneakers" with well known brand names, and other more or less complete childrens' shoes. 10 ladies' shoes, gold, black, yellow, with spiked high heels, made in Taiwan and elsewhere, were unmistakeable.

Other clothing items

75 other items of clothing were excavated, mainly scraps of material of various colours. Some of the 28 pieces found on the surface were also no more than scraps of cloth, but there were some more complete items, mostly clothing belonging to women and children, including undergarments and school uniforms.

Miscellaneous

Of the 347 objects classified as miscellaneous, 245 or 70% belong to five categories only: pieces of formica which were found in large numbers in 1999, scrap pieces of rubber, batteries, fragments of building material, and slates. The 29 pieces of building material excavated in 1999 are no more than a selection of what could have been obtained, and were collected merely as examples of what clearly were decorative items in the synagogue architecture. They consist of pieces of decorated plaster, in one case adhering to a brick foundation. The slates are quite different. They are grey, brown, and black, of different thicknesses, frequently with lines on one or both sides, sometimes carefully cut at the edges. Clearly they were the "schoolbooks" of yesteryear. These five categories of objects, and most of the others, were found both in excavated contexts and on the surface of the site. Five coins were found in the excavated area and two outside. Those coins found in excavated contexts were as follows: D11 a penny of 1953, F11 a 50 cent coin of 1987, F13 a half penny of 1958, F14 a 5 cent coin of 1989 and a 25 cent coin of 1996. The more recent coins were found near the surface and do not contradict the notion that the mounds were heaped up well before the 1980s or 90s. The coins found on the surface were as follows: L7 a 10 cent coin of 1991, N11 a 10 cent coin of 1994. It would be interesting to know more exactly the date and the circumstances in which one of the "miscellaneous" finds made in excavated square F11 came to be on the site: a spent cartridge from a gun, confidently pronounced by one of the students to be a .45

automatic. The 39 artefacts of a type found only on the surface include a very varied collection of items, among which those associated with women are prominent (lipstick containers, purses, and wigs of synthetic materials) as well as pure ephemera. Attention should however be drawn to certain of these finds which are unusual or significant in other ways.

(1) a Jamaican flag, "100% cotton, made in China". Since Jamaican flags were not that much in common currency before 1998, it can be assumed that the appearance of this flag is very recent, linked to the rise of the Reggae Boyz in that year. (2) two shaped stones, one of them in Q17 smooth and pointed and greenish in colour, broken at the base, looking rather like a fragment of a "celt" such as was characteristic for the Taino occupation of the island. (3) one or two pieces of leather, sewn into a rectangular form, acting as a container for an unknown object inside, found in F6; the appearance of this object suggests that it is an amulet, reminiscent of the practice of "obeah". (4) a lozenge shaped metal object inscribed with a "logo" as follows: "genuine - AJS - Kampala, Montreal, Cannes, Bangkok"; this seems to be a trade token of some kind. (5) a lead seal, found after the conclusion of the excavation, bearing a cross and a crown and the letters "SS&EC"; the appearance of the ampersand tells against the first appreciation of this piece as Spanish, and it appears that it may again be some kind of trade token or jetton (Hume, 1991: Fig. 62).

What are we to make of all this? Is it just random bric-a-brac, which it would have been wise to have jettisoned at the start? Not quite. There is a pattern here, of sorts. A predominance of womens' and childrens' items is fairly pronounced, although other items presumably relate to the whole family, a family marked by pronounced tastes and probable constraints. The Oxford mini dictionary and the amulet possibly indicative of "obeah" may if you like illustrate contrasting ideological tendencies, the Jews being long gone. The students' opinion was that many of the things recovered "indicate the activities of the low socio-economic strata of society", as one of them put it. There may be a measure of subjectivity in that, and the opinion would need to be substantiated by a more wide-ranging comparative study. What the site does demonstrate, indirectly at least, is certain broad trends in the products characteristic of the Jamaican economy as a whole in recent years, with technological replacement of one set of raw materials by another, and also the role of imported items, which clearly were objects of choice for these consumers. In the specific context of the archaeology of the site, the 20th century artefacts in the excavated area contributed in a vital way to an understanding of its chronology and the mechanism whereby the mounds were accumulated. For that reason alone, they could on no account be neglected. In all probability the mounds go back to the 1960s, when objects of many different kinds were heaped together to form the landscape we encountered.

Fauna

As indicated in Table 1, 103 bones teeth and shells were excavated at the site, and the same number were found on the surface, in 1998 (Chaplin, 1971; Humfrey, 1975; Mehring, n.d.). The faunal remains from 1999 have yet to be studied in detail. 54 bones, 4 teeth, and 19 shells from the excavated material found in 1998 were studied in detail by Esther Rodriques under the supervision of Professor S. Donovan and Mr M. Gardner (Geology and Anatomy Departments of UWI, respectively). There were 48 cow bones, 3 goat, 1 dog, 1 bird, and 1 rat, together with 2 cow and 2 goat teeth. Three of the cow bones showed signs of butchering. The majority of the bones on the surface seem also to have been cow bones, and at least half of them show clear signs of butchering. These signs are not what one normally encounters on archaeological sites: they are clean cuts, made by mechanical saws, indicative of the fact that the bones have been dumped here relatively recently. A complete dog skull is no doubt also a recent arrival. The shells found on the surface broadly coincide with those studied in detail, 19 of which could be identified as shown in Table 4.

The first three of these shells are marine, the last two terrestrial. The latter could well occur naturally at the site, but the marine shells must have been brought in. It is not likely that they were eaten by the Jews, because of the injunction contained in Leviticus 11: 9-12. Melongena melongena is often found at Taino sites, and it is tempting to link it to the possible "celt" fragment also found in the compound. It would be premature to suppose that there was a Taino settlement here, although as Mathewson remarked, "the occurrence of Arawak pottery and a considerable amount of sea shells in the lowest levels at King's House clearly attests to the nearby presence of Arawak communities during the early Spanish settlement of the town" (Mathewson, 1972a: 4).

CONCLUSION

In conclusion, for the moment, the following may be stated. The main foundation of the Neveh Shalom synagogue has been identified, and probably also the external staircase mentioned by Andrade. Large quantities of 18th and to a lesser extent 19th century material have been recovered both from the excavated squares and from the surface area within

Table 4: Shells 1998 only

Livona pica	West Indian top shell	4
Isognomon alatus	Flat tree oyster	5
Melongena melongena	Brown crown conch	1
Pleurodont sp.		8
Orthalicue Beck		1

the compound. The fact that these materials were discovered in such quantities suggests that the site has been left fundamentally undisturbed since those times. For the most part, the site has served as a dumping ground during the present century. An analysis of this material reveals that it is not random, and it can be used to reconstruct the discard patterns of the inhabitants of the area, which themselves reflect broader socio-economic realities. It is likely that the mounds of rubble covering the site were heaped up some time during the 1960s. They are themselves disturbed, and could probably be fairly rapidly removed in order to expose the foundation of the principal structure, although pockets of in situ deposits and stratigraphic surprises cannot be ruled out.

Neveh Shalom should not be seen in isolation. In the historical perspective, its investigation forms part of a larger endeavour to investigate the circumstances of the Jewish diaspora in the Caribbean (Newman, 1989). Michelle Terrell's archaeological research into the synagogue on Nevis, which was in existence from the late 1670s to the mid 1760s, and her attempt to place it within a wider context, is part of this general endeavour (Terrell, 1998, 1999). So far as the more recent material at the site is concerned, and the attempt to interpret it, this too has Caribbean parallels which are by no means irrelevant. Thus Richard Price, investigating "the dark complete world of a Caribbean store" in the fishing hamlet of Petite Anse in Martinique in the summer of 1983, concluded that "the products on its dusty shelves form a startling microcosm of the world-system, an astonishing testimony to the history of colonialism and the more recent organization of international commerce" (Price, 1985). At that time, the store stocked 213 different items or brands of which 84% were imported from outside Martinique, indicative of a process whereby local crops and products were systematically suppressed or undervalued in favour of metropolitan imports which had been half way round the world and back again. The stock of information on material culture which is available in the seemingly humble or unpropitious surroundings of the abandoned synagogue in Spanish Town is from the anthropological point of view no less rich than that which was at hand in Petite Anse.

In the end, the "mise en valeur" of the site ultimately depends on the Neveh Shalom Institute. There is no point in these excavations being undertaken, or in clearing the cemetery of the refuse which encumbers it, unless there is to be a continuing programme of investment, which will ensure that these locations are properly maintained and exhibited to the public in a worthy manner. It is to be hoped that the Institute and its Director will succeed in the achievement of these aims, and that this publication will bring the site and its potential to the attention of a wider audience.

Acknowledgements

Thanks are due to all who made the excavations a success, particularly the UWI students and the staff of the JNHT, as well as the members of the local community who supported our work. The JNHT team included Miss A. Brooks, Mrs A.M. Howard-Brown, Mr C. McKen, Mr R. Murphy, Ms C. McGeachy (photographer), and Mr E. Coore (artist-illustrator). The UWI students involved were Philippa DaCosta, Marlon Manborde, Esther Rodriques, Norman Rose, Ava Tomlinson, Lounette Williams, Nicole Patrick, Erica Simon, Pheonie Leveridge, Yolanda Silvera, and Michele Bogle-Douglas. Mrs Karen Spence, technician in the Archaeology Laboratory, not only helped with the surveying but saved us from getting completely tangled up in the numbers during the analysis of the artefacts. Mr George Barton (driver) made our travel carefree. Miss Yvonne Brooks, of 2 Adelaide Street, Spanish Town, provided an indispensable link with the local community, including those workers hired by Mr Henriques to clear the cemetery. We also thank the Matron of the Infirmary for tolerating our intrusion, and Mr Doug Wright (architect and planner) for his interest and for the provision of a plan of the entire area. Representatives of the Spanish Town Historic Preservation Commission (particularly Mr Leroy Dallas) and the District Steering Committee (particularly Mr Derryck Roberts), together with some interested persons from Kingston, including the late Mr E.H. de Souza and Mr M.J. Stoppi, visited the site on more than one occasion and made valuable observations on the history and construction of the building. Nor can we forget the great hospitality extended to us in Mr Roberts's (alas now defunct) wine bar, where the excavations wound up. May it rise again.

P. Allsworth-Jones (Department of History, University of the West Indies)

D. Gray, S. Walters (Jamaica National Heritage Trust)

References

Allsworth-Jones, P., Gray, D., Walters, S. (1998) Excavations at the Neveh Shalom Synagogue Site in Spanish Town, January 1998. *Jamaican Historical Society Bulletin*, 11 (1): 17-18.

Allsworth-Jones, P., Gray, D., Walters, S. (2000) Neveh Shalom, an ancient Jewish synagogue in Spanish Town, Jamaica. *Archaeology Jamaica*, 12 (NS): 4-7.

Andrade, J.A.T.M. (1941) *A Record of the Jews in Jamaica*. Jamaica Times Ltd., Kingston.

Barnett, R.D., Levy, A. (1970) *The Bevis Marks Synagogue*. Latimer Trend Ltd., Plymouth.

Barber, R.J. (1994) *Doing Historical Archaeology*. Prentice Hall, New Jersey.

Black, C.V. (1960) *Spanish Town. The Old Capital*. Parish Council of St Catherine, Spanish Town.

Brown, M.J. (1996) *An archaeological study of social class as reflected in a British colonial tavern site in Port Royal, Jamaica*. M.A. Thesis. University of Texas at San Antonio.

Caribbean Volunteer Expeditions (1998) *The Neveh Shalom Synagogue (c1700-c1940) Spanish Town, Jamaica*. unpublished report. Corning, New York.

Chaplin, R.E. (1971) *The Study of Animal Bones from Archaeological Sites*. Seminar Press, London and New York.

Deetz, J. (1996) *In Small Things Forgotten*. 2nd ed. Anchor Books, New York.

Ebanks, R. (1984) Ma Lou and the Afro-Jamaican Pottery Tradition. *Jamaica Journal*, 17 (3): 31-37.

Henriques, A.C. (1997-98). Jamaica Synagogue Ruins and Jewish Cemetery to be Protected, Rebuilt. *Jewish Heritage Report*, I (3-4): 20.

Hume, I.N. (1969) *Glass in Colonial Williamsburg's Archaeological Collections*. The Colonial Williamsburg Foundation, Virginia.

Hume, I.N. (1991) *A Guide to Artifacts of Colonial America*. Vintage Books, New York.

Humfrey, M. (1975) *Sea Shells of the West Indies*. Collins, Glasgow.

Mathewson, R.D. (1972a) Archaeological Excavations at Old King's House. *Jamaica Journal*, 6 (1): 3-11.

Mathewson, R.D. (1972b) Jamaican ceramics: An introduction to 18th century folk pottery in West African tradition. *Jamaica Journal*, 6 (2): 54-56.

Mayes, P. (1972) *Port Royal Jamaica Excavations 1969-70*. Jamaica National Trust Commission, Kingston.

Mehring, A.L. n.d. *Land Shells of Jamaica*. unpublished manuscript.

Newman, A. (1989) The Sephardim of the Caribbean. in ed. R. Barnett, W. Schwab. *The Sephardi Heritage: vol. 2: The Western Sephardim*: 445-473. Gibraltar Books Ltd., Northants.

Pevsner, N. (1962) *The Buildings of England: London, vol. 1: The Cities of London and Westminster*. 2nd ed. Penguin Books, Harmondsworth.

Price, R. (1985) The Dark Complete World of a Caribbean Store: A Note on the World-System. *Review*, IX(2): 215-219.

Rathje, W.L. (1979) Modern Material Culture Studies. *Advances in Archaeological Method and Theory*, vol. 2: 1-37.

Rathje, W.L. (1989) Rubbish! *The Atlantic Monthly*, 264 (6): 99-109.

Rathje, W.L., McCarthy, M. (1977) Regularity and Variability in Contemporary Garbage. in ed. S. South. *Research Strategies in Historical Archeology*: 261-286. Academic Press, New York.

Rathje, W.L., Murphy, C. (1992) *Rubbish! The Archaeology of Garbage*. HarperCollins, New York.

South, S. (1977) Revealing Culture Process through the Formula Concept. in S. South. *Method and Theory in Historical Archaeology*: 201-274. Academic Press, New York.

Terrell, M. (1998) *The Jewish Community of Nevis Archaeology Project*. mterrbu@bu.edu.

Terrell, M. (1999) *An historical archaeology of the Sephardic Jewish Diaspora*. summary. Symposium 068, WAC 4, Cape Town, South Africa.

INHERITED CITYSCAPES: SPANISH TOWN, JAMAICA

James ROBERTSON

Abstract: Spanish Town is a candidate for UNESCO's World Heritage status. The architectural and archaeological legacies of its long service as Jamaica's "capital city" are remarkable. How are these to be understood today? The town was the administrative and social hub for a rich sugar colony in Britain's eighteenth-century empire, and as such it supported a sizable number of building craftsmen, black and white, free and slave. Reporting the extensive opportunities for conservation and for further research offers a base for considering how these buildings, public, private and religious, should be presented to modern audiences.

In 1912, an American tourist returned to Kingston from a rural excursion by way of "Spanish Town (San Jago de la Vega) the one-time capital." He had enjoyed touring the Jamaican countryside, but his description of this section of his trip was brisk and dismissive: "The drive was delightful and we were all sorry to reach Spanish Town. This place may have justified the name at one time but it is very decidedly 'Black Town' now. Little of interest there, except the old government houses, now unoccupied, and some monuments." (Morton, 1912, p. 26).

It was a snap verdict offered by an outsider. During his Caribbean cruise the young heir to a Chicago salt fortune proved far more readily charmed by exotic scenery, lush vegetation, smartly turned out police constables or the modern buildings re-erected after Kingston's 1907 earthquake. Spanish Town might have a distinguished history, impressive buildings and a long-established African Jamaican population, but he remained under-whelmed. The items that this impatient tourist noted nearly ninety years ago remain key themes to be addressed today in any strategies for introducing modern audiences Spanish Town — Jamaican and non-Jamaican, groups who may well include visitors potentially just as unimpressed by the town's remarkable past. This essay examines the range of older buildings in the city and the questions that the preservation and interpretation of this complex historic townscape raise for archaeologists and historians.

The choices that the tour guides made in 1912 were straightforward enough: magnificent buildings were conspicuous in those "old government houses, now unoccupied." Indeed, in 1912 the complex of former government buildings standing in Spanish Town was far more substantial than those remaining in those other eighteenth-century capitals of trans-Atlantic British colonies, Virginia's Williamsburg or Maryland's Annapolis, never mind North Carolina's New Bern, all of which have now integrated historical tourism into their urban development plans (Lindgren, 1993, pp. 75-90; Potter, 1994, pp. 92-95; Barnett, 1993). In the eighteenth and early nineteenth centuries Jamaica was a far richer colony than all these. Floating new

architectural commissions on the island's Rum Duties allowed the Jamaican Assembly to erect a succession of substantial public buildings that embellished the site of the colony's legislature, law courts and administration. In 1872, when most government business was transferred to Kingston, the merchants' city, these public buildings proved a difficult legacy: a proposed Queen's College, reusing the buildings surrounding main square as a university quadrangle failed to attract students; some of the empty buildings were then leased to local schools or were later handed over to the St. Catherine Parish Council but, even during the shave-penny Crown Colony administration of the late nineteenth century, funds continued to be found for the upkeep of the former Governor's mansion (Brown, 1999). Despite a fire at the old King's House in 1925 (Brown, 2000) and another at the law courts in 1986 that reduced to brick shells two of the principal buildings open to those turn-of-the-century visitors, architectural historians continue to express well-merited superlatives about the square outside the old King's House (Crain, 1994, pp. 156-7; Binney, Harris and Martin, 1991, p. 98). Emancipation Square does remain an impressive testimony to the wealth produced during King Sugar's brutal reign in Jamaica. [Illustration 1: a-g]

Considerably more interesting architecture survives in Spanish Town than a single square, magnificent as it is, or even than an extensive array of public buildings, open and closed, large and small. For two hundred years the city was the site for meetings of both the island's Assembly and its Law Courts. A long parade of legislators, litigants, lawyers and, indeed, their households not only stayed there during law terms and Assembly sessions, but all knew that they were likely to return. Today a remarkable number of substantial eighteenth- and early nineteenth-century domestic buildings still remain, mostly built as town houses or as shops and taverns to supply all these visitors' appetites. The town also housed one of the largest concentrations of slaves on the island: with a total of 2,237 in 1829-32, during slavery's last years. This population was just over a sixth of the total number of slaves in Kingston, but otherwise only a hundred or so fewer than in the north shore port town of Montego Bay and a far higher concentration than in any other Jamaican town

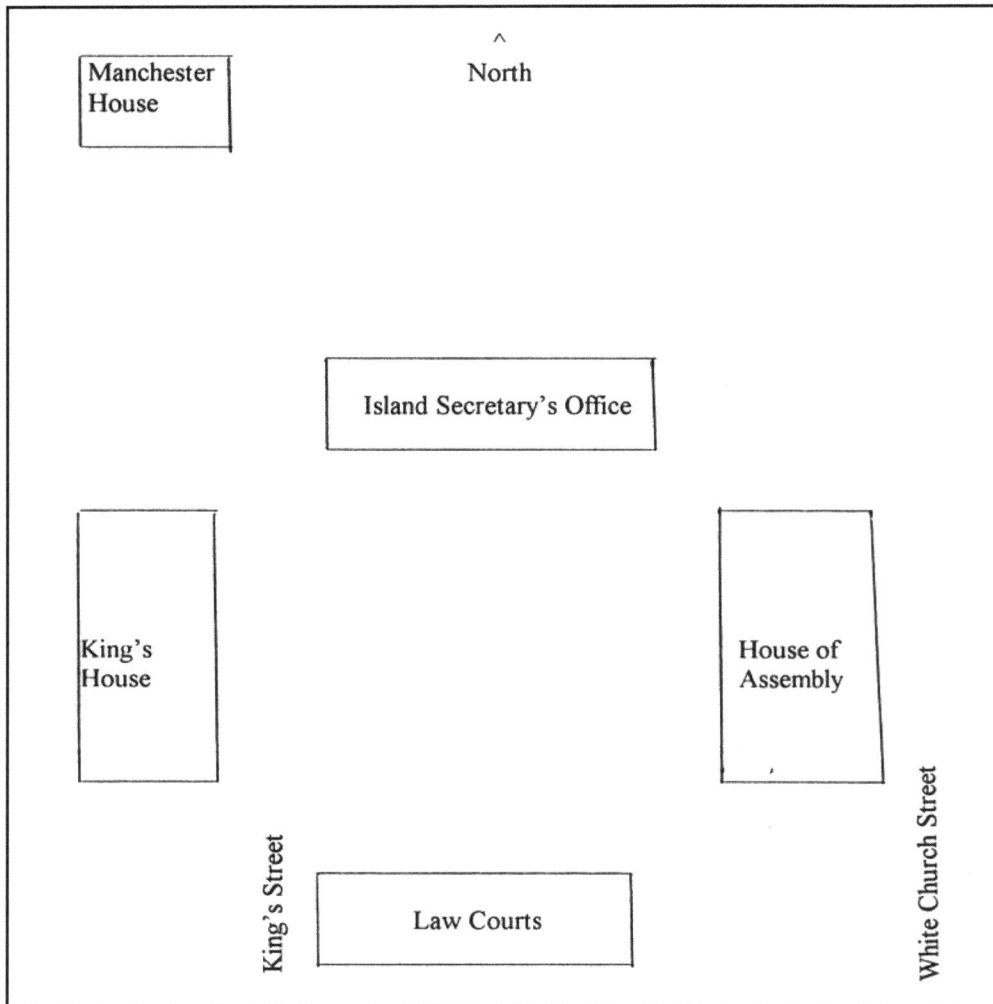

^
North

Manchester House

Island Secretary's Office

King's House

House of Assembly

King's Street

White Church Street

Law Courts

Illustration1) Spanish Town, Jamaica, Emancipation Square: formerly the *plaza maior* of the Spanish city and subsequently "The Parade" and "King's House Square" under the English.
a) Outline map (not to scale) of Emancipation Square

b) The south-eastern corner of Emancipation Square from White Church Street. The Assembly building is to the right, the ruins of the 1819 law courts are to the left. The former Archives building on the far side of the Square can be seen across the square. (author's photograph).

c) The west side of the square. The front of the old King's House. The wrought iron railings date from 1802. If the new pedestrianization scheme goes ahead, cars will be blocked off from this area. (author's photograph).

d) Looking east, the former House of Assembly, 1760, now the St. Catherine Parish offices. (author's photograph).

(Higman, 1976, pp. 58-59). In earlier years Spanish Town during its social seasons would have held an even larger proportion of the urban slaves on the island.

The town's permanent residents included a deeply rooted Jewish community and one of the most substantial free black populations on the island. Little work has yet been undertaken to identify the neighborhoods, houses and shops that framed either of these groups. High as the colony's social boundaries were, we should not expect the physical lines separating African Jamaican residents from the white townscape to be hard and fast. There were some areas that were settled by free African Jamaicans from an early date, but, at the same time, African Jamaican craftsmen, free and slave built many of the houses, ran shops and lodging houses and, of course, worked in individual households (Kerr, 1995; Boa, 1993).

Even if we do not yet have much idea about the development of particular neighborhoods in the city, there are still remarkable testimonies to the resilience of these communities

91

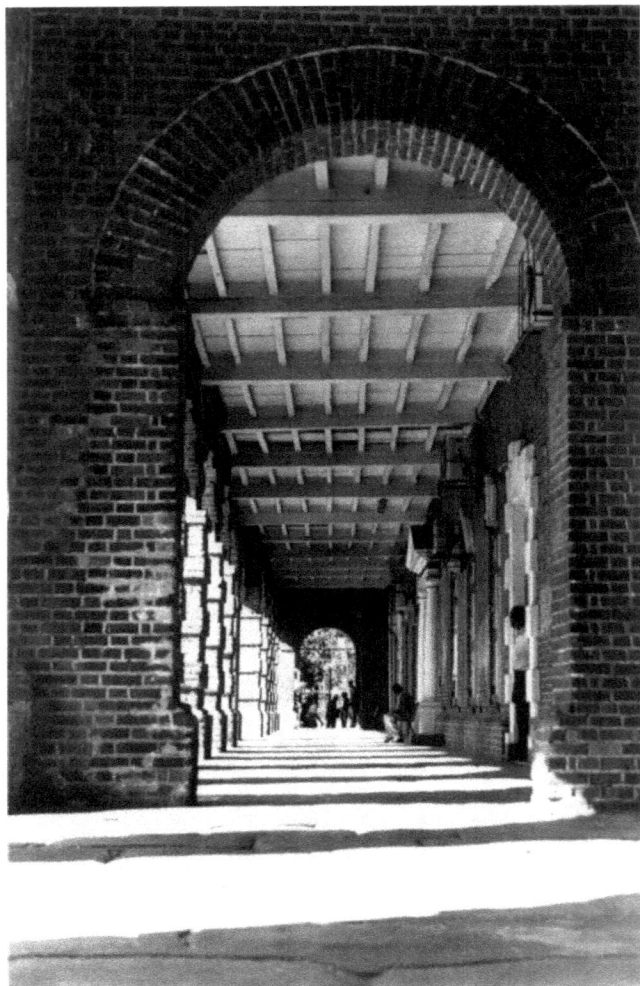

e) "Piazza" under the old Assembly building.
(author's photograph).

of residents in their places of worship. The Sephardic Jews' Neveh Shalom synagogue was the oldest of them. A further cluster of protestant chapels date from the early nineteenth century. The town's Wesleyan Church, which was expanded and re-opened in November 1828, was destroyed in the 1951 hurricane (Goldson, 1997, p. 8, Roberts, 1977, pp. 16-17). The ambitious Phillippo Baptist Church still stands. It was also expanded and rebuilt in 1827, after arson destroyed its predecessor, with the rebuilding drawing on the pennies and sixpences scraped together by its congregation, free and unfree. A second mid-nineteenth century Independent (Native) Baptist chapel on White Church Street, the product of a split in the Phillippo congregation in the mid-1840s, was another casualty of the 1951 hurricane (Stewart, 1984). Its site remains an empty lot. The continuing development of particular groups within the nineteenth-century city is reflected in the building of a new Anglican Trinity Chapel in the 1830s (consecrated in 1844) on the opposite side of the town from the old Anglican parish Church, the promotion of the main Anglican Church to become the Cathedral of St. Iago in 1842 and the elaborate rebuilding of its chancel in 1849-53, all along with the erection of St. Joseph's, a small brick-built Roman Catholic church in the 1872. The current worshipers at all of Spanish Town's chapels remain very proud of their inheritance but, as always, building funds are just one call on congregations' resources.
[Illustration 2: a-d]

Although Spanish Town did enter into a relative decline once it lost its administrative roles, the city was hardly dormant during the late nineteenth century. Even when the Governor and administration removed to Kingston, the colony's main prison stayed in Spanish Town. Today's St. Catherine District Prison incorporates massive late Victorian cell blocks. In 1907

f) South side of the square: the former Law Courts, constructed 1819, destroyed by fire in 1986 but still eminently restorable. The town's public clock used to be sited on the central tower (author's photograph). This was built over the site of the Spanish-era Abbot of Jamaica's Church.

g) The former Island Secretary's Office complex, looking northwest from the balcony of the House of Assembly. The "Rodney Temple" in the center, along with the linking colonnades was erected by an amazingly relieved Assembly after Admiral Rodney's unexpected victory at the Battle of the Saints in 1782 saved Jamaica from an invasion and almost inevitable conquest by combined French and Spanish forces. The cupola houses an expensive statue of Lord Rodney commissioned in 1784. The upper stories of the 1962 Jamaica Archives building can be seen behind the "Temple." The whole eighteenth-century complex was recently restored with the aid of a grant from the European Union. The sign in the center announces the source of the funding. (author's photograph).

tourists could add a visit to the prison into their itinerary, finding it "admirably managed and scrupulously clean" (Leader, 1907, p. 161). It is not seen as a tourist attraction now. The town retained further facilities from its period as the capital, particularly a pivotal place in the island's railway — begun in 1843, opened in 1846 and an early industrial phenomenon in its own right (Hall, 1959, pp. 35-36, 152-153). Although the Railway was closed for passengers in 1992 the station and some substantial marshalling yards remain on the southern edge of the old city. In the 1880s and '90s the line was extended out to the west and also across the Blue Mountains in the interior of the island, up to the new banana plantations and docks on Jamaica's north shore (Gunter, 1945, pp. 1-13; Rollinson, 2001, pp. 50-57). The lines joined at Spanish Town.

Economic development projects in the former capital's vicinity did not cease after the departure of the colonial administration to Kingston and the failure of the would-be colonial university, the Queen's College. During the 1870s the colony initiated an extensive irrigation canal system, centered on the Rio Cobre river. This helped to transform

Illustration 2: Places of Worship
a) The west tower on the Cathedral of St. Jago de la Vega (Anglican), formerly "The Red Church" rebuilt in 1712 after its Spanish predecessor was destroyed in a hurricane. Viewed from the south. The brickwork on the nave retains many more eighteenth century features than any other church on the island. The tower was erected just after the Napoleonic Wars. (author's photograph).

b) The Phillippo Baptist Chapel, William Street, opened 1827 (author's photograph).

c) Trinity Chapel (Anglican), Martin Street, consecrated 1844 (author's photograph).

the parish's agriculture from savanna grazing and fodder crops to sugar cane and later to bananas. From the late nineteenth century through to 1933 when "Panama blight" afflicted banana plantations across the St. Catherine's parish, the irrigated areas grew the premium bananas within the United Fruit Company's Jamaican banana plantations (Marquardt, 2001; Sealy and Hart, 1984). The Company finally sold its estate just to the east of the Rio Cobre to the colonial Government in 1946. From the 1890s too a tourist itinerary developed within the town for visitors breaking their train journey south or else taking excursions while their cruise ships anchored in Kingston (Taylor, 1993, pp. 55-95). As a result of these various activities the "black town" that Mr. Morton traversed continued to thrive and its domestic buildings include a further two or three generations of locally built bungalows which housed the administrators and skilled employees of all these enterprises (Green, 1985, also Green, 1984). Characteristic smaller late nineteenth- and early twentieth century houses, built of imported pine on a balloon frame and set up on posts, also survive (Crain, 1994, pp. 60-66). Deferring repainting under a tropical sun, together with a post-war shift towards using cement blocks in new building, now leave these vernacular buildings vulnerable to decay and demolition.

d) St. Joseph's Roman Catholic Church, King Street, 1872.
(author's photograph)

THE ARCHITECTURAL LEGACIES OF A LONG URBAN TRADITION

Today's city retains a palimpsest of earlier townscapes overlaid one onto another, with buildings from very different periods juxtaposed in the same street. The resulting "cultural landscape" is more complicated than many North American towns (cf. Alanen and Melnick, 2000). Even in the latest rapid expansion of the city during the 1980s and '90s, where new housing estates extend well out beyond the traditional core, aerial photographs demonstrate that these new neighborhoods continue to follow pre-existing field and farm boundaries (see Buisseret, 1996, p. 37).

As yet only scrappy evidence for any pre-Columbian Taino settlement has been found nearer than the White Marl site a mile to the east of the Rio Cobre (Mathewson, 1972). There was a Taino presence in the new Spanish city as laborers and later as herders and hunters, but by the time Spanish Town was founded in 1534, the island's Taino population had fallen drastically from the high levels Columbus encountered. The conscripted Taino labor force employed to build the royal fort and the magnificent cut-stone chapel in island's earlier capital at New Seville on the north shore were no longer available (Curtin, 1994). So while some Taino remained

among the townspeople, by the early seventeenth century they appear to have died out as a distinct urban group. Nor, in a peripheral colony that was losing its initial settlers to the golden prospects of mainland New Spain was it possible to populate the newly founded city with Spaniards. The royal grants authorizing the shift to the new site and granting the townspeople common fields were accompanied by further grants permitting the recruitment of thirty married settlers from Portugal and thirty African slaves (Wright, 1921, p. 77). The final population of New Seville had included African slaves. In Spanish Town, however, Africans were an integral presence in the new city from its establishment.

In 1655 this small Spanish colonial center was captured and held by an English army. The town's sixteenth-century founders had closely followed the general directions for locating a town laid down in the royal Laws of the Indies, being set well back from the coast and located in the fields. This might be healthy and defensible, but these Spanish criteria appeared downright incomprehensible to many English settlers, who were used to building their cities at their trading ports. Under both Spanish and English rule particular developments in Spanish Town often run counter to patterns that contemporaries expected for colonial cities.

Standing monuments are now sparse from either the Spanish or the earliest English periods. The principal church of the English settlement, today's Cathedral, retains the site and orientation of the Spanish-era Dominican priory and — despite not only extensive rebuilding after the 1712 hurricane but also a further heavy-handed Victorian rebuilding work in 1849 that inserted a properly neo-Gothic choir — its foundations are Spanish (Nelson, forthcoming). Similarly the standing ruins of the King's House date from the mid- and late eighteenth century (Mathewson, 1972, 1970); while even the gateposts decorated with heraldic eagles from Lord Inchquin's tenure as Governor in 1690, which earned his residence the local nickname of "the John Crow House," have now disappeared. Yet in the late seventeenth century Spanish Town or St. Iago de la Vega — both names were used — was one of the most distinctive cities under British rule. With its piratical wealth Port Royal, twelve miles away across the harbor, might upstage it, but the island's administrative capital was an impressive urban center in its own right. Traversing these streets led pedestrians past a series of re-used Spanish public buildings: first the old Red Church, whose chancel now held several English governors' tombstones (Wright, 1966, 106-114, 118-120); then, on the southern edge of the town where "the White Chapel" survived and for a short spell during the 1680s became a Roman Catholic church again (Osborne, 1988, 125-130). Over on the south side of the former *plaza maior*, where the law courts were erected in 1819, were ruins from the old White Church of the Abbots of Jamaica, the stubs of whose stone gateposts remained standing well into the eighteenth century (Long, 1774, II. p. 3). On the *plaza*'s west side stood the complex of the old wooden *Audiencia* building and the Spanish Governor's house, which now housed the new colony's Assembly and law courts along with the royal Governor. There was no public architectural component to the new English settlement. Instead, the major new buildings in the capital city for one of the richest colonies in the Stuarts' empire were private residences and these were interspersed among older Spanish houses. Here the importance that the new English settlers assigned to their property grants means that glimpses of the late seventeenth-century city can still be found in the runs of patents, plats and deeds preserved at the Jamaica Archives and the Island Records Office (Robertson, 2001(a), pp. 109-140). Manuscripts alone can not provide a substitute for the close-textured findings from archaeological fieldwork, but these documents already offer suggestive hints both for the scale of private building in the town and, indeed, for the town's role as a cultural meeting point.

The distinctiveness of this early synthesis would be highlighted for contemporaries by the contrasts that late seventeenth-century Spanish Town presented to Port Royal, the other major urban settlement in English Jamaica. At Port Royal, successive archaeologists along with Michael Pawson and David Buisseret, have shown how far this late seventeenth-century haven attempted to reproduce an English town set down on the sandy peninsula at the entrance to Kingston Harbour: Port Royal's streets fanned out from the main landing place at the "Chocolata Hole" and were lined with closely-spaced properties. Alleys then cut through the main blocks of buildings allowing pedestrians access to the wharves or to cross from one street to another (Pawson and Buisseret, 1975, n.e. 2000: also, Aarons, 1990; Hamilton, 1984, 1986, 1988; Hamilton and Woodward, 1984; Mayes, 1972; Mayes and Mayes, 1972). The former Spanish city was far less of an "English" town and always proved a far more alien place for its English residents. Despite being sacked by the English army in 1655 and then becoming a garrison center during six years of guerrilla warfare, the town retained its older Spanish grid of streets. Indeed, in his early eighteenth-century description of the island that he had visited in 1688, Sir Hans Sloane felt it necessary to explain to his English readers that the city "was very grand in the *Spaniards* time ... every Street running parallel to or else piercing the other at right Angles," besides being "broad and very long" (Sloane, 1707, p. lxv). Nor was this all. The properties lining these streets remained thoroughly unfamiliar, even though English houses were built on them and Sloane took lodgings in a four story brick house during his stay. Older Spanish properties endured interspersed among the new brick mansions. Furthermore, as the new settlers' land grants assigned title to Spanish houses or to blocks of land set within the inherited Spanish grid or, over time, assigned deeds to sub-divisions of these earlier properties, then the outlines of an older spatial lay-out were maintained. Lot sizes were generally bigger than in Port Royal, which might cover 35x35 feet, or even than the 60x60 feet blocks assigned over in Old Harbour, a haven twelve miles to the west. Instead a single grant in Spanish Town could allocate a rectangle of 158½x96½ feet, hardly customary English or English-colonial units, while streets and cross-streets were lined by walls or the backs of buildings that looked inwards. These remained compounds rather than house-plots.

This cityscape would look foreign to most English visitors, but the "foreignness" did not end with its buildings. Under the English the city housed a distinctive cultural and racial mix. From the first it had a Jewish presence. Its flourishing Sephardic community supported an ordained rabbi by 1683, well ahead of any of the mainland colonies in British North America (Faber, 1992, p. 23, also Arbell, 2000). From 1704 the synagogue, Neveh Shalom, was tucked away behind solid brick walls on Monk Street. The substantial brick-built building harked back to the plan of the Bevis Marks congregation in London (Allsworth-Jones, this volume, also Allsworth-Jones, Grey and Walters, 2000, and Newman, 1989, pp. 456-457). In 1790 Ashkenazi Jews established their own congregation, building a synagogue in 1796 (Faber, 1998, p. 105). There were Irish settlers too and here "teague" as a nickname among early grantees may well suggest Gaelic Irish backgrounds. Inter-mixing proved more pervasive. Under the Spaniards the city grid was surrounded by "straggling thatcht houses" for the unfree population, while under the English regime one edge of the common granted to the townspeople was soon lined with "Negro houses." However, an examination of the first English land patents suggests that urban spaces were never clearly polarized: grants in the early 1660s included "One House and yard" on the main square for "Anthony Rodrigues a Negro Soldier of the English Army," along with "the Negro Mr. De Camps House" — made at a time when "Mr." was not assigned to all English grantees. More grimly, from 1667 the Royal African Company, which held the official monopoly on importing slaves from Africa, had a compound a few hundred yards to the south-west of the Cathedral — apparently near the site of the current prison — just to the south of "The Old Spanish Market." The site lay across from some of the major settlers on the island, besides being within ear-shot of the town's principal market and church (Robertson, unpublished).

The eighteenth-century city, many of whose public and private buildings do survive, was re-established on foundations cleared of those ambitious brick-built mansions by natural disasters. The earthquake of 1692 not only destroyed Port Royal but across the island it levelled the magnificent houses that the first generation of English settlers erected (Robertson, 2001(b)). Meanwhile Spanish Town's wood-framed Spanish houses rode out the quake, to provide an increasingly archaic in-filling among the city's new eighteenth-century buildings. Then, when a hurricane struck in 1712 — the first to hit Jamaica since the English conquest — the Spanish buildings again survived better. The only Spanish houses that proved vulnerable were those that stood too near to English buildings, as they sustained damage from the debris as their neighbors shed their roofs. The architectural result of all this natural destruction was to encourage the increasing creolization of local building styles and techniques away from unsuitable English templates. In the process Spanish Town not only diverged from Port Royal's pre-1692 buildings but also from the new Kingston too. When Port Royal was rebuilt after the earthquake its residents chose to use wood, but their town then suffered a series of disastrous fires and hurricanes through the eighteenth-century (Priddy, 1975). These accidents all provided opportunities for Kingston and this new city, with its grid laid out on its quayside, then became a merchant city whose English-born residents preferred more resolutely English housing — albeit embellished with turrets and mahogany woodwork (Clarke,

1975, Williams, 1971, Ross, 1951, Young, 1946, and Buisseret, 1996, pp. 64-65). The merchants and traders based in this new commercial port persistently objected to the colonial government's continuing to use Spanish Town.

Nevertheless, in 1758 the residents of Spanish Town succeeded in defeating an attempt to have the administration, legislature and law courts of the colony transferred the thirteen miles over to Kingston. This political achievement encouraged further public building in Spanish Town. The major public buildings still standing today were mostly constructed in the second half of the eighteenth century. The mid-eighteenth century also saw the expansion of the city to the west and north, extending the older Spanish grid well beyond the street behind the King's House which, up until the early nineteenth century still remained known as "Western Street." The chronology for private building remains less clear, though it was underway by the late 1740s. However, the effort and enthusiasm of the late T.A.L. Concannon as architectural advisor to the Jamaica National Heritage Trust recognized a substantial number of domestic buildings erected in an impressive creole style, (Concannon, 1970), while an initial survey of surviving buildings across the city coordinated by Pat Green has highlighted the remarkable number of eighteenth- or early nineteenth-century shops and houses still standing (Green, 1995).
[Illustration 3: a, b]

Modern scholars are impressed by the domestic buildings from the eighteenth-century town. Local construction took advantage of local materials and adapted to the tropical climate. Perhaps even more than the Great Houses on the island's sugar estates, where building in stone presented a suitably confident public face for enterprises that always ran on merchants' credit, the wooden framed, veranda-ed and balconied houses and shops built in eighteenth-century Spanish Town adapted to the tropics. If the sugar planters' Great Houses were "the ultimate consumer object" then it is Jamaica's urban buildings that appear to "embody [their] attitudes towards material life and are shaped by new domestic activities and changing economic conditions" (adapting Chappell, 1994, p. 168). English visitors to the early nineteenth-century town still made scathing comments, reaffirming metropolitan standards. Hence in 1816 "Spanish Town has no recommendations whatsoever, the houses are mostly built of wood and the streets are very irregular and narrow; every alternate building in a ruinous state, and the whole place wears an air of gloom and melancholy" (Lewis, 1999, p. 100). But colonials would always find it difficult to please traveling diarists, whose brisk judgements remained unshakably dismissive about whatever was architecturally unfamiliar. Local builders could never win. Buildings "modelled on European forms, ... were deemed inferior and derivative by English critics, those that sought to incorporate indigenous forms, ... were disparaged as exotics" (Metcalf, 1999, pp. 589-590). Yet, despite the persistent derogatory comparisons with Kingston where, in between major fires, its English-born merchants continued to erect more familiar buildings, local artisans, free and unfree, working in Spanish Town did construct some impressive public and private buildings. The nineteenth-century plantocracy's profits collapsed after the Napoleonic Wars, but the local planters' confidence remained strong enough for the Assembly to undertake further major building commissions until Emancipation in 1834 and, indeed, until the Westminster Parliament's abolition of differential sugar duties in 1846. This last measure left West Indian sugar to compete for the English market against both slave-produced sugar from other

Illustration 3: Domestic and Commercial Properties
a) Late eighteenth or early nineteenth-century brick buildings on Old Market Street.
(author's photograph)

b) Manchester House, on the corner of Manchester and King Streets. The Duke of Manchester, Governor during the 1820s, lived here. The building was restored in the mid-1960s but it proved insufficiently resilient to house the school that was put in it. It is now unused and vulnerable, demonstrating the need to find effective uses for historic buildings once they are "saved." (author's photograph).

empires, beet-sugar's increasing domination of many European markets and, increasingly, with more efficient production elsewhere (Hall, 1959, pp. 37-42; Curtin, 1954). Besides the brick law courts erected in 1818, the nineteenth-century city also saw the building of various chapels; of a number of substantial brick houses and bungalows and, of course, the Jamaica Railway in 1843-6. These projects dating from the era of high sugar prices would still be followed by the extensive remodelling to transform the old Red Church into the cathedral of St. Iago de la Vega during the late 1840s, the Rio Cobre Irrigation Canal's works from the 1870s, the rebuilding of the municipal "Workhouse" in the 1880s, along with the massive expansion of the St. Catherine District Prison in the mid-1890s. These all provided substantial additions to the town's institutional building stock.

Public buildings dating from the twentieth-century are scarce, since major architectural commissions are generally located in Kingston, but the Jose Marti School erected in 1976 by the Cuban Government as a gift to the people of Jamaica is a distinctive complex. As a Euro-Cuban design erected in a Jamaican field on the edge of the town, the school remains very different from most other buildings on the island. Archeology provoked one more public commission in the shape of the Taino (formerly Arawak) Museum erected in 1963 on the Taino site at White Marl, alongside the road to Kingston.

Even though the nearly forty years since Jamaica's independence in 1962 have added few new monuments to the town's streets, they have seen the introduction of ambitious conservation legislation that recognizes the value of the streetscapes around the city's major buildings. Legal

protection for the older part of Spanish Town is incorporated in the Jamaican National Heritage Trust Act of 1985, which itself built on the 1964 Town and Country Planning (Spanish Town) Provisional Development Order. These both aimed to establish Heritage Zones extending out from the central square to include not only more of the "monuments" in a wider area including the eighteenth-century Barracks, along with the multi-period Cathedral, and the 1801 Iron Bridge. [Illustration 4] The 1985 Act extended the earlier area to incorporate a wider swathe of domestic buildings, chapels and shops. In 1987 Jamaica made a submission to UNESCO's World Heritage Committee for the inclusion of three sites on the new World Heritage List as a World Heritage Sites: Port Royal, the seaport mostly submerged in the 1692 earthquake; New Seville, the island's first Spanish capital; and Spanish Town. A further proposal is now in train for Falmouth, a remarkably well-preserved eighteenth-century port town laid out in the 1790s. The first two were rejected as being primarily of importance to Jamaican history, but the proposal for Spanish Town won conditional acceptance. The prospect of achieving full acceptance encourages continuing efforts at preservation. International grants have already funded the recent stabilization of the Iron Bridge, while a current project funded by a European Community grant has successfully refurbished the late eighteenth-century complex of government administrative buildings on the north side of the square, which had lain empty for three years after the civil servants who used them moved to a new complex on the road to Kingston. Plans now call for the extension of this renovation project with an elaborate pedestrianization scheme, which should take through traffic out of the narrow streets inherited from the city's sixteenth-century Spanish

Illustration 4: The Iron Bridge over the Rio Cobre, 1801, viewed looking up-stream from its 1930s successor. The cut-stone piers were recently restored. (author's photograph).

plan. Other proposals include undertaking further excavations on the site of the former Neveh Shalom synagogue and refurbishing the late eighteenth-century Barracks complex as storage and conservation facilities for the Jamaica National Heritage Trust's Archaeology Division. Individually, all these projects are feasible enough, although, in a period characterized by "scarce resources," they must compete with a host of other worthwhile projects.

When it comes to shaping public attitudes towards the historic area in Spanish Town, funding is not everything. The Government of Jamaica recently decided to rename Spanish Town's main square "Emancipation Square" — since it was from the steps of the old King's House that the royal proclamation ending slavery was read on August 1, 1834. Such initiatives can encourage fresh emphases. So too should a current island-wide project to survey Jamaican vernacular buildings organized by the Caribbean School of Architecture at the University of Technology in Kingston, (for comparable work on Guadeloupe's architectural patrimony, see Giordani, 1996). The survey has yet to tackle Spanish Town, but the findings from this work should help shape attitudes towards modern Jamaica's architectural heritage — and towards the island's elite and middling buildings as components in that inheritance — among a raising generation of Jamaican architects and planners.

OPPORTUNITIES AND CHALLENGES

A few foreign tourists continue to drive out to Spanish Town. However, once they reach the old capital their stay is very short. Their mini-buses circle the main Emancipation Square, but hardly stop. They may park at the Cathedral to photograph the tower and, if the traffic over the modern bridge across the Rio Cobre is moving very slowly, then an alert passenger can catch a passing view of the Iron Bridge as they leave town, but that will be all. This not only hardly does justice to the oldest iron bridge in the Western Hemisphere, nor, indeed, to the Cathedral, nor to the Square; such abbreviated itineraries also short-change Spanish Town and its current residents. The brevity of the tourists' visits mean that today no vendors' carts selling cold drinks, patties or post cards are stationed near any of the city's monuments. Their absence may well mean fewer distractions for would-be photographers (though there can still be heckling) but, when sight-seeing is not generating local incomes, townspeople can hardly be criticized if they find the regulations preserving a group of under-used buildings incomprehensible and, as with all pointless government regulations, they will ignore them. Then, when stories continue to circulate about the treasure concealed in the foundations of the Iron Bridge — just waiting for a crow bar to pry it free — and when socially conscious architects are eager to use recycled bricks to accent their new buildings so there is an excellent market for "salvaged" bricks in Kingston; under-appreciated buildings are not only fragile, but vulnerable. [Illustration 5: a-c]

There is a wider problem to recognize. Not enough has changed since Mr. Morton's visit in 1912, except that those earlier tourists did get out to wander around the major public buildings — and their evening drive back to Kingston was a lot faster. Current studies of "memory and geography" show that defining a monument can prove particularly contentious in post-colonial landscapes; involving what the cultural critic

Illustration 5: Illegal Demolition.
a & b) February 2000, at the corner of Red Church Street and Old Market Street, the illegal demolition of a substantial early nineteenth-century house in the historic preservation area in Spanish Town. Views from the front and the side. The interior was attacked first, with the removal of the floorboards and most interior beams. The unsupported walls were then pulled down from the window apertures. Both the wooden front porch and the wood-shingled roof have collapsed. The hand made bricks were carefully stacked on the pavement alongside for trucks to remove for resale. The demolition work was carried out by some local residents working in evenings and at weekends without any heavy machinery, so proved difficult to halt, despite the endeavors of the Jamaica National Heritage Trust's lawyers and surveying team and, indeed, despite the regrets uttered by other local residents while the destruction was going on. Further photography was actively discouraged. (author's photographs).

c) Early morning before the start of business: East Street, Kingston, "salvaged" bricks for sale. In January, 2002, the going rate was J$12.00 = US$ 26¢ each. (author's photograph).

Edward Said characterizes as "subtle and complex ... cultural struggle[s] over territory, which necessarily involves overlapping memories, narratives, and physical structures" (Said, 2000, pp. 175, 182, see also Mehrotra, 2001).

Despite the statutory protection for the townscape and its monuments there is as yet little public affection for the urban heritage surviving in Spanish Town. School parties do come into the city from the wider area: their choirs participate in the annual Emancipation services held at the Phillippo Chapel, while the history teachers in local schools bring their upper-level classes in for open days at the Jamaica Archives. So far, so good, but neither the city nor its range of vernacular and public buildings are incorporated into these educational visits. Here we can see that bad colonial-era history has a long half-life. A consequence of the emphasis by an earlier generation on the very high quality of so many of the town's surviving public buildings — which may indeed make them of comparable quality to the best work being commissioned in eighteenth-century England — is that attention was shifted away from the local contractors in Spanish Town, white, brown and black (Duncker, 1961, 94-100), or indeed from the African Jamaican artisans whose skill and sweat built these impressive buildings, never mind from the wider vernacular context of domestic buildings lining the surrounding streets. A narrow focus on official monuments built under slavery that commemorate a British imperial past made some sense in the 1890s, when tourism first became a cash-crop in the West Indies (Taylor, 1993), but such priorities no longer secure public interest in an independent Jamaica. Yet there is plenty more to emphasize. The town's main square itself retains most of a much older space, the former *plaza major* of the Spanish colonial capital. It has been a cultural cross-roads for four hundred years and provided the conclusion for the Emancipation Day procession that started at the Phillippo Chapel.

Public disinterest is something to address: "to survive, to flourish, historic sites must reach out to the public with a picture of the past that is more complete, more inclusive, and ultimately, more honest" (Schreiber, 2000, p. 50). Presenting fuller and better particulars should help to reshape both the tour guides' current motorized sprints and the local teachers' careful shepherding of their young charges through the town's historic center. When it comes to drafting such introductory material on Spanish Town the prospects are exciting. There is a well-developed West Indian historical literature dealing with late eighteenth- and nineteenth-century rural Jamaica, which is now the backbone for history teaching in the island's schools and universities (Higman, 1999; Brereton, 1998), while the rational offered for a recent study of towns and their influence on the historical geography of rural Ireland also applies in Jamaica. "Over much of its history, Ireland [and Jamaica] has been a relatively lightly urbanized society, and the bulk of its population has lived in the countryside. But towns and villages have been vital economic and cultural hubs, profoundly influencing, as well as being influenced by their rural hinterlands" (Whelan, 1997, p. 180). What's more, with modern Jamaica's rapidly growing urban population, it is now even more important to address the nation's urban past. This research is not only feasible, but timely.

The evidential base for Spanish Town is remarkably rich. Extensive late seventeenth-, eighteenth- and nineteenth-century record collections are held in Jamaican archives. Resources for work on the town's major buildings include the survival at the Jamaica Archives of two volumes of manuscript minutes from the Jamaica Assembly's Commissioners for Forts for 1769-1772, and 1773-1783, which provide estimates and contractors' names for several major public commissions in Spanish Town during a period of extensive official building, along with the parallel survival of the Vestry Minutes of St. Catherine's Parish from 1759, which offer further material on the maintenance and building of several smaller public buildings (Robertson, 2001, pp. 115, 121). For the nineteenth century, too, a group of more than three hundred plans and drawings deposited by the Rio Cobre Irrigation Company record the building and maintenance of this late Victorian canal system, its locks, viaducts and even individual culverts. When the cataloguing and conservation of the collection is completed it should offer a superb resource for future work on the industrial archaeology of these canals (Dacosta, in progress). Archaeologists and architectural historians who intend to work on any of these series will enjoy extensive opportunities of making further cross-linkages across to the even larger collections of personal inventories, wills and deeds at the Jamaica Archives and the Island Records Office.

Fruitful as the archival harvest certainly promises to be, there are further rich prospects for fresh insights from archaeological work in Spanish Town. If nothing else, because we do know so little about the town's growth, there is a great deal that can be found through opportunistic site-watching exercises, peering in whenever a utility company needs to dig a hole in the historic area. Still more exciting, through, are the opportunities for sustained excavation campaigns on sites currently lying open at the heart of the conservation area. The opportunities for exploring "the archaeology of transience and visitation" (Potter, 1994, p. 134) in the old capital are extensive: this was a seasonal town. However, the archaeological potential for investigating the communities and experiences of the permanent residents of the town is also remarkable, and could help to counter-balance the emphasis of much of the manuscript record on the island's planter elite.

The findings from the first two seasons' work at the Neveh Shalom synagogue site are among the few rigorously excavated sites in the city: they are also among the first to be published (Allsworth-Jones, Gray and Walters, 2000). Investigating urban sites of this quality offers not just archaeologists' answers to historians' queries — nice as it would be to have these — but also the foundations for posing a fresh set of questions about how this town's urban societies were constructed. Some work on these lines was proposed in the early 1970s, using the pottery found at the King's House excavations to address the patterns of cultural adaption and overlap between Spanish Town's social and racial groups (Mathewson, 1973). Current research on African Jamaican potters, on developments in local pottery and on its circulation up until the mid-nineteenth century looks to extend these opportunities (Ebanks, 2000, Hauser, 2001). Yet pottery will only be one strand within the broader cultural fabric that archaeology can disclose. Urban excavations and, indeed, their analysis, should allow the next generation to come to understand how a whole succession of cultural traditions overlapped, interacting and adapting, to produce a distinctively creolized urban culture.

This is an important story that deserves to be told. In Spanish Town we can hope to follow the particular ways that cultural interactions worked out in the successive societies that were compressed into the inherited grid of the Spanish city's plan.

A whole range of disciplines: archaeology, architectural history and, indeed, urban history and heritage studies can all be brought to bear on the research. If work of this sort can be undertaken, displayed, explained and integrated into Jamaica's own wider past then, unlike Mr. Morton and his bored travelling companions back in 1912, future visitors to Spanish Town should have plenty of interest to look at. Furthermore, these foreign visitors may yet find themselves standing in line with Jamaican tourists and, while they all wait together, there should be some local vendors' carts in the vicinity to peddle refreshments.

Acknowledgements

This essay was initially drafted while I held a University Research Fellowship from the University of the West Indies, Mona. Its final revision benefited from an opportunity to try these ideas out on Professor Patrick Bryan's graduate seminar in Heritage Studies at Mona. I am grateful to Janet Robertson and Linda Sturtz who both read and commented on earlier drafts.

Bibliography

Aarons, G.A. 1990. Port Royal Archaeological Adventures, the Past Fifteen Years: 1974-1989. *Jamaica Journal* **22**,(4), 33-40.

Alanen, Arnold R and Melnick, Robert. Z. (eds.), 2000. *Preserving Cultural Landscapes in America*, Baltimore: Johns Hopkins University Press.

Allsworth-Jones, Philip, Gray, Dorrick and Walters, S. 2000. Neveh Shalom: An Ancient Jewish Synagogue in Spanish Town, Jamaica. *Archaeology Jamaica* n.s. **12**, 4-7.

Arbell, Mordechai, 2000, *The Portuguese Jews of Jamaica*, Kingston: the Press, the U.W.I.

Barnett, Colin W. 1993. *The Impact of Historic Preservation on New Bern, North Carolina: From Tryon Palace to the Coor-Cook House*, Winston-Salem: Bandit Books.

Binney, Marcus, John Harris and Kit Martin, 1991. *Jamaica's Heritage: an untapped resource*, Kingston: Mill Press.

Boa, Sheena, 1993. Urban free black and coloured women: Jamaica 1760-1834. *Jamaican Historical Review* **18**, 1-6.

Brereton, Bridget, 1998. Teaching the Caribbean: An assessment of Texts for the CXE Caribbean History Syllabus. In *Before & After 1865: Education, Politics and Regionalism in the Caribbean* (eds.), Brian Moore and Swithin Wilmot, Kingston: Ian Randle, 88-98.

Brown, Annette Constance, 1999. The Old King's House, Spanish Town, 1872-1962. M.A. University of the West Indies, Mona.

Brown, Annette Constance, 2000. Old King's House destroyed by fire, *Jamaican Historical Society, Bulletin* **11**,(6), 153-157.

Buisseret, David, 1996. *Historic Jamaica from the Air*, Kingston: Ian Randle.

Chappell, Edward A. 1994. Housing a Nation: The Transformation of Living Standards in Early America. In *Of Consuming Interests: the Style of Life in the Eighteenth Century*, (eds)., Cary Carson, Ronald Hoffman and Peter J. Albert, Charlottesville: University Press of Virginia, 167-232.

Clarke, Colin G. 1975. *Kingston, Jamaica: Urban Development and Social Change, 1692-1962*, Berkeley: University of California Press.

Concannon, T.A.L. 1970, Our Architectural Heritage: Houses of the 18th and 19th Century with Special Reference to Spanish Town, *Jamaica Journal* **4**,(2), 23-28.

Crain, Edward E. 1994. *Historic Architecture in the Caribbean Islands*, Gainesville: University Press of Florida.

Curtin, Margaret, 1994. Carvings from the well at New Seville. *Jamaica Journal* **25**,(2), 19-23.

Curtin, Philip, 1954. The British Sugar Duties and West Indian Prosperity. *Journal of Economic History* **14**, 157-164.

Dacosta, Philippa, in progress, The Industrial Archaeology of the Rio Cobre Irrigation Canal System, University of the West Indies, Mona, M.Phil. thesis.

Duncker, Sheila, 1960, The Free Coloured and their Fight for Civil Rights in Jamaica, 1800-1830, London University, M.A. thesis.

Ebanks, Roderick, 2000. Jamaican Ceramics, 1655-1850. M.Phil. thesis, University of the West Indies, Mona.

Faber, Eli, 1992. *A Time for Planting: The First Migration 1654-1820*. Baltimore: Johns Hopkins

Faber, Eli, 1998, *Jews, Slaves and the Slave Trade: Setting the Record Straight*. New York: New York University Press.

Giordani, Jean-Pierre, 1996. *La Guadeloupe face à son patrimoine: Itinéraires et modalités d'une reconnaissance et d'une revalorisation*, Paris: Karthala.

Goldson, Terence O.B. 1997. *Warmed Hearts: Stories of Early Methodism and its Heroes and Heroines in Jamaica*, London: Avon Books.

Green, Patricia E. 1984. 'Small Settler' Houses in Chapleton: Microcosm of a Jamaican Vernacular, *Jamaica Journal* **17**,(3), 39-45.

Green, Patricia E. 1985. The Development of a Jamaican Architectural Style 1907-1951. *Jamaica Journal* **18**,(3), 2-12.

Green, Patricia E. 1995. *Proposal for the Preparation of a Preservation Scheme Master Plan for the Spanish Town Historic District*, UNDP/UNESCO/Government of Jamaica Project, JAM/91/008, typescript, copy at Jamaica National Heritage Trust, Kingston.

Gunter, Sir Geoffrey, 1945, *Centenary History of the Jamaica Government Railway*, (typescript draft, 30 May, 1945), Jamaica Archives, Ms. 4/97/1, Gunter Papers.

Hall, Douglas, 1959. *Free Jamaica 1838-1865: An Economic History*, New Haven, Yale University Press.

Hamilton, Donny L. 1984, Preliminary Report on the investigation of the submerged remains of Port Royal, Jamaica, 1981-1982, *International Journal of Nautical Archaeology and Underwater Exploration* **13**, 11-25.

Hamilton, Donny L. 1986, Port Royal Revisited, In *Underwater Archaeology: The Proceedings of the Fourteenth Conference on Underwater Archaeology* (ed)., Calvin R. Cummings, San Marino, Cal: Society for Historical Archaeology, 73-77.

Hamilton, Donny L. 1988, Underwater excavations of 17th-century buildings at the intersection of Lime and Queen Streets, In *Underwater Archaeology: Proceedings from the Society for Historical Archaeology Conference, Reno, Nevada, January, 1988*, San Marino, Cal: Society for Historical Archaeology, 9-12.

Hamilton, Donny L. and Robyn Woodward, 1984, A sunken seventeenth-century city: Port Royal, Jamaica, *Archaeology* **37**, 38-45.

Hauser, Mark W. 2001. Peddling Pots: determining the extent of market exchange in eighteenth century Jamaica through the analysis of local coarse earthenware. Ph.D. thesis, Syracuse University.

Higman, Barry, 1976. *Slave Population and Economy in Jamaica 1807-1834*, Cambridge: Cambridge University Press.

Higman, Barry, 1999. *Writing West Indian Histories*, Baisingstoke: Macmillan Caribbean.

Kerr, Paulette, 1995. Victims or Strategists? Female Lodging-House Keepers in Jamaica. In *Engendering History: Caribbean Women in Historical Perspective*, (eds)., Verene Shepherd, Bridget Brereton and Barbara Bailey, Kingston: Ian Randle, 197-212.

Leader, Alfred, 1907. *Through Jamaica with a Kodak*, Bristol: John Wright & Co.

Lewis, Matthew, 1999. *Journal of a West India Proprietor*, (ed)., Judith Terry, Oxford: Oxford University Press.

Lindgren, James M. 1993. *Preserving the Old Dominion: Historic Preservation and Virginia Traditionalism*, Charlottesville: University Press of Virginia.

Marquardt, Steve, 2001. 'Green Havoc': Panama Disease, Environmental Change, and Labor Process in the Central American Banana Industry, *American Historical Review* **106**, 49-80.

Long, Edward, 1774, *The History of Jamaica*, 3 vols. London: T. Lowndes.

Mathewson, R. Duncan, 1970. The Old King's House Archaeological Project, *Jamaican Historical Society, Bulletin* **5**,(11), 140-150.

Mathewson, R. Duncan, 1972. History from the Earth: Archaeological Excavation at Old King's House, *Jamaica Journal* **6**,(1), 3-11.

Mathewson, R. Duncan, 1973. Archaeological Analysis of Material Culture as a Reflection of Sub-Cultural Differentiation in 18th Century Jamaica. *Jamaica Journal* **7**, 25-29.

Mayes, Philip, 1972, *Port Royal, Jamaica: Excavations 1969-70*, Kingston: Jamaica National Trust Commission.

Mayes, Philip, and P.A. Mayes, 1972. Port Royal, Jamaica: The archaeological problems and potential. *International Journal of Nautical Archaeology and Underwater Exploration* **1**, 97-112.

Mehrotra, Rahul, 2001. Bazaars in Victorian Arcades: Conserving Bombay's Colonial Heritage, In *Historic Cities and Sacred Sites: Cultural Roots for Urban Futures* (eds.), Ismail Serageldin, Ephrim Shulger, Joan Martin-Brown, Washington, D.C.: The World Bank, 154-163.

Metcalf, Thomas R. 1999, Architecture in the British Empire, In *Historiography* (eds.), Robin W. Winks and Alaine Low, (Oxford History of the British Empire, **5**) Oxford: Oxford University Press, 584-595.

Morton, Sterling, 1912. *On the Spanish Main: Account of a Trip from New York City to the West Indies, Panama, Columbia and Venezuela, January 17 - February 20, 1912*, unpublished typescript, Chicago, Chicago Historical Society, Sterling Morton Papers, Box 1, folder '1908-1914'.

Nelson, Louis, forthcoming, Building 'Cross-wise': Reconstructing Jamaica's Eighteenth-Century Anglican Churches. *Jamaican Historical Review*. **22**.

Newman, Aubrey, 1989. The Sephardim of the Caribbean. In *The Sephardi Heritage: Essays on the history and cultural contribution of the Jews of Spain and Portugal: II, The Western Sephardim* (eds.), R.D. Barnett and W.M. Schwab, Grendon, Northamptonshire: Gibraltar Books, 445-473.

Osborne, F.J. 1988, *The History of the Catholic Church in Jamaica*, 2nd. ed. Chicago: Loyola University Press.

Pawson, Michael and David Buisseret, 1975, n.e. 2000, *Port Royal, Jamaica* Oxford: Oxford University Press, 2nd. edition, Kingston: the Press, University of the West Indies.

Potter, Parker B. 1994. *Public Archaeology in Annapolis: A Critical Approach to History in Maryland's Ancient History*, Washington, D.C.: Smithsonian Institution.

Priddy, Anthony, 1975. The Seventeenth- and Eighteenth-Century Settlement Pattern of Port Royal. *Jamaica Journal* **9**, 8-10, 17.

Roberts, Franklin A. 1977. *The Origin and Development of Methodism in Spanish Town and Its Environs, 1791-1841* Kingston: Methodist Book Center.

Robertson, James, 2001(a). Jamaican Archival Resources for Seventeenth and Eighteenth Century Atlantic History. *Slavery and Abolition* **14**, 109-140.

Robertson, James, 2001(b). Jamaican Architectures before Georgian. *Winterthur Portfolio* **36**, (2/3), 73-95.

Robertson, James, unpublished, Late Seventeenth-Century Spanish Town: Building an English City on Spanish Foundations.

Rollinson, David. 2001, *Railways of the Caribbean* Baisingstoke: Macmillan Caribbean.

Ross, Marion D. 1951. Caribbean Colonial Architecture in Jamaica. *Journal of the Society of Architectural Historians* **10**, 22-27.

Said, Edward W. 2000. Invention, Memory, and Place. *Critical Inquiry* **26**, 175-192.

Schreiber, Susan P. 2000. Interpreting Slavery at National Trust Sites: A Case Study in Addressing Difficult Topics, *Cultural Resource Management* **23**,(5), 49-52.

Sealy, Theodore and Hart, Herbert, 1984. *Jamaica's Banana Industry: A History of the Banana Industry with particular reference to the part played by The Jamaica Banana Producers Association Ltd.* (ed.). Clinton V. Black, Kingston: Jamaica Banana Producers Association.

Sloane, Hans, 1707. *A Voyage to the Islands of Madeira, Barbados, Nieves, S. Christopher and Jamaica ...* vol. I, London: B.M. for author.

Stewart, Robert, 1984. Conflict in the Jamaican Baptist Church: Thomas Dowson and J.M. Phillippo, 1842-1850. *Jamaican Historical Review* **14**, 28-41.

Taylor, Frank Fonda, 1993. *To Hell with Paradise: A History of the Jamaican Tourist Industry* Pittsburgh: University of Pittsburgh Press.

Whelan, Kevin, 1997. Towns and Villages. In *Atlas of the Irish Rural Landscape* (eds)., F.A.H. Aalen, Kevin Whelan and Matthew Stout, Cork: Cork University Press, 180-196.

Williams, Wilma, 1971. Old Kingston, *Jamaica Journal* **5**,(2-3), 3-8.

Wright, Irene A. 1921. The Early History of Jamaica, 1511-1536. *English Historical Review* **36**, 76-95.

Wright, Philip, (ed.), 1966. *Monumental Inscriptions of Jamaica* London: Society of Genealogists.

Young, J.G. 1946. Who Planned Kingston? *Jamaican Historical Review* **1**, 144-153.

CAPE DUTCH TONGAAT: A CASE-STUDY IN 'HERITAGE'

Peter MERRINGTON

Abstract: This paper explores the phenomenon of the model village and accompanying landscape architecture which was built, from 1937, on the Tongaat-Hulett sugar estate in the South African province of KwaZulu-Natal. Buildings were designed as replicas of particular instances of seventeenth- and eighteenth-century Cape Dutch baroque and Palladian architecture, transplanting this style from a 'Mediterranean' into a subtropical region. The paper interprets the Tongaat-Hulett project in terms of the inventing of heritage, and begins by a historicization of the concept of heritage, arguing that this concept enjoyed a particularly full range of meanings in the years of the 'new imperialism', roughly 1880 to 1930. This is followed by a brief survey of the Cape vernacular architectural revival at the beginning of the twentieth century, which was the mainspring for a 'typical' South African architectural idiom in the first half of the twentieth century. The links between this vernacular revival in the Cape and the Tongaat-Hulett project are pointed to, in the work of the impressionist painter and amateur architect Robert Gwelo Goodman. The paper then explores the application of Goodman's emphasis on aesthetics, in the reconstruction of Tongaat from the 1930s, subsequent to a severe malaria epidemic in 1930. The Tongaat project is then described in terms of the range of meanings which are entailed in the old 'heritage' discourse of the early twentieth century.

This paper is about the way in which a dominant tradition of South African national heritage evolved in the early twentieth century, and how it was applied in a particular instance, for the purposes of civil improvement and landscape beautification, within an agricultural and industrial context that was singularly remote from the origins of this heritage tradition. The proprietors of the sugar cane plantation of Tongaat, at the neighbouring towns of Tongaat and Maidstone in the Natal Province (now KwaZulu-Natal) of South Africa, began an experiment in social upliftment in the 1930s, initially to control a malaria epidemic. This project was expanded and over the next three decades became a pilot scheme for social improvement and town planning as well as race relations. It was described in extended narrative form in 1960 in a book, *Tongaati: An African Experiment,* written by the general manager of the estate, and has been the subject of specialist town-planning debate.[1]

There is a variety of possible ways of discussing the Tongaat experiment, from sociological analysis to questions of agricultural history, but this paper focusses on two aspects: the use of architecture as primary means of social improvement (and the choice of style for this architecture); and the way in which a sense of dynasty and heritage has been encouraged as a means of interpreting Tongaat. In South Africa as elsewhere, there has been a close connection between architectural innovation, renovation, conservation, and heritage. This paper explores the implications of such a connection, in the context of a South Africa, in the early twentieth century, where the nexus includes questions of race relations, multiculturalism and municipal planning, tradition and architectural styles which were deemed appropriate for the new nation, and the important role of family trusts, patrimony, and dynastic pride.

HISTORICIZING 'HERITAGE'

The context of this study is a broad research project which scans the range of initiatives that were undertaken by South Africans, in the first two decades of the twentieth century, for the 'inventing of heritage' for the new political entity of the Union of South Africa which came into being in 1910. Behind this broad project is a thesis which argues that the idea of heritage as we understand it, meaning roughly the public management of public cultural property, enjoyed its apogee in the late nineteenth and early twentieth centuries, within the European colonial and British imperial world. It is argued that the concept of heritage, in this period, served as a means of reinforcing traditional metropolitan and national identities and values in a rapidly modernising society, and a means of staking out and asserting particular cultural and political identities within the expanding colonies and dominions of the European (in particular British) overseas empires. The inventing of heritage for the Union of South Africa is seen in relation to similar initiatives in the new Australian Federation (1901) and in Canada, as well as the British attempt to shore up imperial rule in India at the turn of the century.

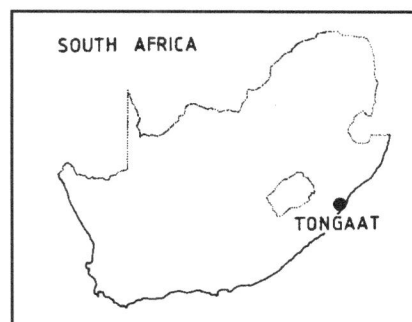

Map

---

[1] R.G.T. Watson, *Tongaati: An African Experiment,* London: Hutchinson, 1960.

The initiatives to establish a public cultural identity for the Union of South Africa in the early twentieth century were conducted, broadly, by two opposing political groups. On one hand were Afrikaner or Dutch-speaking South African nationalists, of various backgrounds but loosely united in their antipathy to British imperialism, in the aftermath of the South African War of 1899-1901. Foremost among these were the theologians and writers from the Cape rural town of Paarl, who for some decades already had been working for the recognition of Cape Dutch or Afrikaans as a language of the white Afrikaner establishment. Less liberal than these in their outlook were various nationalists from the erstwhile Dutch republics of the Orange Free State and the Transvaal. Their chief spokesman, perhaps, was the historian Gustav Preller, who did much to rally Afrikaner sentiment around a newly forged strong sense of Afrikaner national history and destiny. Immigrants from Holland such as the artist J.H. Pierneef, based in Pretoria, joined in with the Afrikaner vision of their own identity and sought to represent South Africa, culturally speaking, from this particular perspective.

In the Cape Province (formerly the Cape Colony, a British colony since 1806, but largely Dutch or Afrikaans-speaking in the country districts), sentiment was pro-British and pro-imperial in the capital city of Cape Town, and more or less 'loyalist' among the Dutch population. Those who joined forces against the British in the war and sided with the Dutch republics were known as 'Cape rebels' and were regarded by the authorities as traitors. Thus, the Cape was politically pro-imperialist (though not exclusively so), combined with a strongly Afrikaner or 'Cape Dutch' social and cultural character.

As would be expected in the colonial ethos of the day, these initiatives were driven exclusively by white South Africans, and were elitist in character. This political and social fact has bearing on what was then meant by the concept of heritage. At the root of the heritage concept is the idea of family, of legacy or bequest, genealogy, and lineage. It is argued that this set of metaphors, drawn from legal and social custom or practice, becomes bonded with nineteenth-century concepts of race, resulting in a powerful discourse about the nation as family, about sister states and brother races, motherlands and fatherlands, and ultimately, in the British sphere, the Commonwealth 'family' of nations, driven, at the time, by fantastic visions of an 'Anglo-Saxon' world order (even, as Cecil Rhodes fantasised in his first will and testament, an 'Anglo-Saxon' world government). These notions are reinforced by the popular culture of the day, and in particular literary practices, where every novel worth its salt concluded with a good marriage and a good inheritance. There are scores of popular novels in English from the late nineteenth and early twentieth centuries with the terms 'heritage' or 'inheritance' in their titles, while elite authors such as Joseph Conrad (*The Inheritors,* 1901, in collaboration with Ford Madox Ford) and Vita Sackville-West (*Heritage,* 1919) bear witness to the trend.

The inventing of heritage for the new nation state of the Union of South Africa is thus considered in this broad context of ideas of racial or national or imperial heritage. Under this broad umbrella, though, there are numerous particular usages of the concept of heritage, which range from the legal to the spiritual, social-Darwinian, family-dynastic, and cultural. At the most literal level of the meaning of 'heritage', we observe the phenomenon of wealthy South Africans, in the early years of the twentieth century, making large public endowments or bequests. The Rhodes Trust with its Oxford Rhodes Scholars scheme is the most well known, described in detail by the journalist W.T. Stead in *The Last Will and Testament of Cecil John Rhodes* (1902).[2] Other South African mining magnates, such as Sir Abe Bailey, and the Beit brothers, followed suit. The Alfred Beit Trust was publicized in book form by his nephew, Sir Alfred Beit, in 1957.[3] The unpopular Sir J.B. Robinson, another of the mining magnates from the turn of the century, died in Cape Town in 1929, and his will became the occasion for a severe philippic on the relationship between personal estates, civic duty, and public bequests. An entire page of the *Cape Times* was devoted to an analysis of his last will and testament. The editor of the *Cape Times,* Basil Kellet Long, wrote as follows:

> His immunity against any impulse of generosity, private or public, was so notorious that the name of J.B. Robinson became during his life-time proverbial for stinginess .... Any newspaper which has a claim to represent the public opinion of South Africa is under a stern duty not to mince words in condemnation of such a will as this. .... and those who in the future may acquire great wealth in this country will shudder lest their memory should come within possible risk of rivalling the loathsomeness of the thing that is the memory of Sir Joseph Robinson.[4]

Long — educated at Benjamin Jowett's neo-Hegelian Balliol College in the Oxford of the late nineteenth century — was, at the time of Union, legal advisor to the National Convention, compiler of a work published in 1908 by the Closer Union Society comparing the constitutions of the United States, Canada, Australia, Switzerland and other federal states, and editor of the pro-Union magazine *The State.* This magazine had been founded by more Oxford graduates of the same generation, members of Lord Milner's 'kindergarten', in order to propagandize the 'imaginary community' of Union. As an attorney and later the editor of the *Cape Times,* the Cape's foremost English-speaking newspaper, Long had a protracted commitment to what was meant by the Hegelian idea of 'civil society', an idea that demands of its citizens what Hegel called *sittlichkeit,* or an ethics based on mutual need and respect.

For Hegel, 'civil society' is one leg of a social triad composed also of his conceptions of the 'family', and of the 'state'. Civil society is a stage in the dialectical development from the family to the state. The concept of 'heritage' depends for its full force on its root associations with the family structure

---

2   W.T. Stead, *The Last Will and Testament of Cecil John Rhodes,* London, 1902, reprinted in Rhodesiana Reprint Library, Bulawayo: Books of Rhodesia, 1977.

3   Sir Alfred Beit and J.G. Lockhart, *1906-1956, The Will and the Way, being an Account of Alfred Beit and the Trust which he Founded,* London: Longmans, Green, 1957.

4   *Cape Times,* 7 November 1929.

and the idea of property as patrimony or family bequest. Where these root associations are so frequently metaphorized during the period in question, in such popular phrases as 'brother races', 'sister states', or 'family of nations', we may consider that the contemporaneous reformulation of Hegelian social ethics by the Oxford school of philosophy as practised by T.H. Green and F.H. Bradley at Jowett's Balliol provides us with an influential intellectual model for a reconstruction of the period meanings of 'family' and of 'heritage'. The recurring emphasis on the idea of 'the state' by Long and his fellow neo-Hegelians in the 'kindergarten' takes into account these ideas of the family and of civil society[5].

Thus, it is argued here, the common usage, at the turn of the century, of the idea of the family to describe society (not only the internal structures of a particular society but also relations between 'races' and 'nations' and 'dominions'), is underpinned by a major contemporary school of ethical and social philosophy which had direct links with significant parts of the British empire. The idea of 'heritage' appears to have enjoyed its most robust range of associations during the period in question, and these are given a particular social and ethical inflection by the contemporaneous neo-Hegelian philosophy which was imported to the Cape by men like Lord Milner and his team of administrators, and in particular by the appointment of the like-minded Alfred Hoernle to the first chair of philosophy at the South African College, in 1908[6].

Alongside this professional philosophical discourse we find, at the time, a host of more or less popular expressions of social responsibility couched in terms of 'heritage'. A considerable number of didactic books appear in this period with titles such as *A Goodly Heritage* (a popular title taken from Psalm 16.6), *The Heritage of the Spirit* (1896), *The Common Heritage* (1907), or *Our Heritage: Individual, Social and Religious* (1903). Three quotations from this last work (which specifically refers to all then-current interpretations of the theme, from orthodox Christian theology to Darwin, Herbert Spencer, Lamarck, and Galton) offer a sense of the urgency and cogency, and the ethical flavour, with which this new organic vision of society was proferred:

We are but links in a great continuous chain of ancestry. We are part of a society and a nation. We are members of a state. We belong to a people who have a national genius of their own which is partly the creation of their past history as well as part of their original endowment. .... Thus we are born into a nation, into a great heritage of national history, national temperament, national privilege, as well as into a family and a home.[7]

Every generation leaves to its successors a valuable legacy. That inheritance is stored up in some institution, in some

Art, in some accumulated wealth of Utility, in some Inheritance of History, or Poetry, or Science, or Literature, which make the world richer than they found it.[8]

As there is a natural and spiritual family, so there is a natural and religious heritage, ... a natural Brotherhood, constituted by bonds of blood, by ties of family, clan, nation, and race. And a spiritual Brotherhood, constituted by bonds of love .... The Church is no longer content to possess her inheritance. She wants to make the wide world share in her Heritage. To North, South, East and West the gates of the City of God by day and night stand open.[9]

The chapters in this book are titled 'Our Individual Heritage', 'Heredity and Responsibility', 'Our Social Heritage', 'Our Educational Heritage', 'Our Civil and Political Privileges' ('the patrimony of civil and political privilege'), and 'Our Trusteeship of the Great Heritage', which, while overtly an ethical-religious topic, also hints at the idea, prevalent during the nineteenth century, that Britain 'held in trust' the patrimonies of the peoples over whom she ruled as protectorates.

THE CAPE DUTCH VERNACULAR REVIVAL

The empire architect Herbert Baker wrote an essay published in 1910 entitled 'The Architectural Needs of South Africa'.[10] In it he discusses the architectural achievements of ancient Egypt, Greece, and Rome, and compares the South African climate with that of the countries of the Mediterranean seaboard. He recommends the old 'Cape Dutch' style of building as offering the appropriate sense of simple Palladian elegance and clean whitewashed expanses, best suited to the climate. He adapted the 'Cape Dutch' style for his own work in South Africa, and it became the standard style for the large personal residences of wealthy clients, propagated into the 1950s by several of his assistants and colleagues.

This eighteenth-century Cape baroque architecture was identified in the 1890s as of aesthetic and architectural value, the first published study of it being by Alys Fane Trotter, who wrote for the English *Country Life* magazine and, like Baker, was influenced by the new vernacular arts and crafts movement in England.[11] Trends in residential design by architects such as Baker's colleague Sir Edwin Lutyens, Ebenezer Howard's 'Garden City' concept, Gertrude Jekyll's promotion of the idea of the vernacular garden, and the emergence of *Country Life* magazine and the English National Trust in the 1890s all directly influenced events in South Africa. Alys Fane Trotter was followed by a coterie of writers,

---

5 See Bernard Semmel, *Imperialism and Social Reform*, New York: Anchor Books, 1968, for a concise account of the role of the Oxford neo-Hegelians at the time.

6 Andrew Nash, 'Colonialism and Philosophy: R.F. Alfred Hoernle in South Africa, 1908-11', unpublished MA thesis, University of Stellenbosch, 1985.

7 W.S. Bruce, *Our Heritage: Individual, Social and Religious*, London: Blackwood, 1903: 14.

8 Ibid: 93.

9 Ibid: 143.

10 Herbert Baker, 'The Architectural Needs of South Africa', *The State*, May 1909: 512-24.

11 Alys Fane Trotter, *Old Cape Colony: A Chronicle of her Houses and Men*, London: Country Life, 1903.

artists, and patrons of the arts, under the dominant patronage of Florence Phillips, wife of the Randlord Sir Lionel Phillips. Under their inspiration, and their patronage of Baker, the Cape baroque style became regarded as the national type for the new nation. With Phillips's active support the Cape author Dorothea Fairbridge produced, between 1910 and 1931, a series of documentary studies of old Cape homesteads, illustrated by the pioneer photographer Arthur Elliott, and by the impressionist painter Robert Gwelo Goodman.[12] The elegant Cape homesteads were identified by newly-rich Randlords and political figures as a means of their own gentrification. They bought old Cape wine estates and established themselves as gentleman farmers, or as lords of the manor, as landed gentry, with dynastic pretensions. Many of them managed, similarly, to gain titles in the English royal honours lists, especially the honours list of 1911 which recognised the efforts and success of the Closer Union Movement in uniting South Africa under Britain.

Sir Lionel Phillips bought the celebrated old Dutch estate Vergelegen, near Cape Town, as his Cape home, in 1917. His wife Florence Phillips was a patron of arts and culture in South Africa at the time, and both of them were leading figures in the Closer Union Movement. Florence Phillips understood her cultural activities as a means of reinforcing the fabric of civil society for the new nation, and a substantial aspect of these activities was the recording and preservation of old Cape architecture and 'antiquities', as well as the natural environment. She and a committee of interested individuals began, in 1905, a private association which was the forerunner of the South African National Monuments Council (now the SA Heritage Commission).

The homestead of Vergelegen, restored and modernized by C.P. Walgate, one of Herbert Baker's eminent colleagues, became a Mecca for artists, architects, writers, and antiquarians, as well as visiting dignitaries such as Field Marshall Jan Smuts and the Governors General of the day.[13] In 1927 Rex Martienssen, the foremost South African exponent of the modernist international style in architecture, stayed at Vergelegen on a student field trip, and developed from this experience a lifelong philosophical interest in the Cape vernacular building style. The Cape impressionist painter Gwelo Goodman was a frequent guest at Vergelegen, in a cottage on the estate set up for his convenience. He specialized in Cape landscapes and architecture, and saw himself as something of an amateur architect and restorer. As mentioned above his work was used to illustrate significant early documentary books on Cape architecture while Herbert Baker chose some of Goodman's paintings to decorate the interior of South Africa House, the South African High Commission building in Trafalgar Square, London.

TONGAAT, NATAL: AESTHETICS, CLASS, AND RACE RELATIONS

In turn of the century Natal several families had become wealthy sugar estate owners, their family heads described as 'sugar barons', the Natal equivalent of the Johannesburg 'Randlords'. Two prominent sugar dynasties were the Saunders of Tongaat and the Campbells of Natal Estates. The daughter of Senator Marshall Campbell bequeathed his property in her name to the University of Natal as the Killie Campbell Library, with one of South Africa's leading ethnographic collections, including Zulu artefacts and – later - the artist Barbara Tyrrell's celebrated paintings of tribal figures from around Southern Africa. This house, Muckleneuck, on the Berea, the elite residential suburb on a hillside overlooking Durban Harbour, was built in the Cape Dutch style in 1914 from a design by Herbert Baker[14]. Killie Campbell was introduced to Cape architecture and history by Dorothea Fairbridge when her father was in Cape Town for the parliamentary sessions, both women sharing interest in Africana, or South African antiques, books, and ephemera. Fairbridge's Victorian Cape Town father had compiled, in 1886, the first catalogue of Africana, and his own book collection, the Fairbridge Collection, was bought by the diamond magnate Sir Abe Bailey who presented it to the South African Library in 1925. Dorothea Fairbridge too lived in a house designed in the now traditional style by Francis Masey, a colleague of Baker. The artist Gwelo Goodman supervised the ornamentation of a Dutch-styled residence, Woodley, in Durban for the Mackeurtan family of bankers and accountants, intimate friends of the Saunders family, proprietors of Tongaat.[15] A pattern had emerged, by the late 1920s, for wealthy genteel white South Africans to pursue the concept of 'Africana' in its various forms, from book-collecting to art and antiques, and the establishment of homes (and gardens) in the approved new South African style.

Colonial society in the early twentieth century was governed by a strong sense of class, and it was virtually de rigueur for the 'ruling class' to act as patrons of the arts, arbiters of taste, and custodians of the nation's aesthetic heritage. National identity might be seen to have consisted in a kind of patriarchal aesthetics. In some liberal quarters, and notably at Tongaat, this was translated, through the various utopian social philosophies of the late nineteenth and early twentieth centuries, which ranged from the ideas of Ruskin and Morris to Fabianism, into schemes for social upliftment, and even for improvement in race relations. Thus, when Gwelo Goodman was invited in 1936 to redesign Amanzimnyama (isiZulu, meaning 'black water'), the home of the Saunders family of Tongaat, this became the wellspring of a long tradition at Tongaat whereby arguments drawn from aesthetics regulated all aspects of the sugar estate's society, including the lives of black male migrant workers, Moslem

---

[12] For information on Dorothea Fairbridge, see Peter Merrington, 'Pageantry and Primitivism: Dorothea Fairbridge and the 'Aesthetics of Union'', *Journal of Southern African Studies* 21,4: 643-56.

[13] A full account of the work of Florence Phillips in the cultural sphere in Unionist South Africa is given by Thelma Gutsche, *No Ordinary Woman: The Life and Times of Florence Phillips*, Cape Town: Howard Timmins, 1966.

[14] Fay Jaff, *Women South Africa Remembers*, Cape Town: Howard Timmins, 1975: 89.

[15] For background on Gwelo Goodman and his architectural experiments, see Joyce Newton Thompson, *The Story of a House*, Cape Town: Howard Timmins, 1968, and *Gwelo Goodman, South African Artist*, London: George Allen and Unwin, c.1960.

and Hindu families, and the managerial staff. Goodman, who had recently restored the eighteenth-century Newlands House in Cape Town, and transformed a derelict brewery building into a magnificent studio house for himself and his wife (Cannon Brewery or Cannon House, in Cape Town), made new facades for the Saunders' house, drawing effectively on the gabled, white-washed Cape Dutch style, and he redesigned some of the gardens.

Goodman had a strong following among the elite of Durban, partly due to his early painting career in India (Natal at the time having many Anglo-Indian connections, as well as a large Indian population, descended mainly from workers who were indentured to the sugar plantations in the late nineteenth century), partly because of the prestige attached to his impressionist botanical, landscape, and architectural studies. (These painterly subjects mirror the pre-occupations of the cultural elites of the period, who interpreted the cultural identity of the new nation precisely in terms of flora, land, and architecture).

He was invited, in 1937, to submit plans for the design of a 'model native township' at Tongaat, and developed a style which drew on traditional Cape architecture. This became known locally as 'Gwelo Colonial'. The primary reason for this project was a major outbreak of malignant malaria in Natal in 1930, which caused local authorities to focus for the first time on the conditions in the eighty-year-old shanty settlements inhabited by the Tongaat sugar workers. Goodman's own interest was, predictably, aesthetic[16]. While working on the home of the Saunders family, he proposed what he termed a 'Regent Street' plan to beautify the facades in the main street of Tongaat Village. His motto was, 'clean up the front street and the rest will look after itself'.[17] This 'shop window' idea of influence by benign example became the guiding philosophy of social and environmental improvement at Tongaat. R.G. T. Watson, the chief engineer of the estate, compares this with Aldous Huxley's term 'marginal activity', which Huxley used to describe the methods of doctrinal propagation that were used by agents of Cardinal Richelieu in seventeenth-century France:

Marginal activity is a method of inculcating a doctrine by imparting the idea to be propagated to a few selected disciples, or small groups, situated on the outer edge of a society, as Tongaat is situated in relation to the Central Government. When the persons or groups, because of their acceptance of the teaching, show signs of coalescing, they are sub-divided and dispersed, so that the marginal process may continue. The central citadel of authority is ignored. …. Successful marginal activity is the 'export' of religious, political, or sociological beliefs, export merely signifying transference from one community or locality to another, in an inward direction, so that if the movement survives, after

a time the centre is reached. The Tongaat plan was no longer to be looked upon merely as a scheme for cleaning up a village. It was a means of ameliorating the political and social disorders of a country.[18]

The success of this 'marginal activity' properly requires close monitoring, goodwill, and coherent strongly represented decentralized social groupings or communities. Watson regrets the lack of these qualities in modern society, and makes the following statement in this regard, which returns us to the topic of the dominant family or dynasty and the role of heritage:

In Natal … and doubtless in all young colonies, it is within living memory that the 'direct acquaintance' of the stalwart settler, himself a pioneer farmer, representing his own land and his own people in the legislature, and 'motivated by personal affection and a spontaneous and unreflecting compassion' for their needs, has been superseded by the self-interest and indirect knowledge of the careerist politician and the impersonal and pragmatic government of central authority and ministerial regulation. (Watson, 1960:19. The quotations are from Huxley, 1941:248)[19]

Watson's complaint here echoes a continuing dialectic in the internal discourses of the Tongaat tradition, whereby a staunchly independent Anglophone white liberal patriarchy abrogates to itself the right to conduct its own forms of racial and social experimentation over and against the legislation of the central Nationalist apartheid government. Tongaat paternalism became understood by its proponents as a liberal alternative to apartheid, and the Tongaat board coined the term 'aggregation' as their racial alternative to 'segregation'. Watson quotes the then proprietor and director, Douglas Saunders:

'Perhaps the wrong term has been chosen for race relations. Segregation implies breaking down, severing, or isolating parts from the whole; pain, degradation, humiliation, and injustice. "Aggregation" would be a better word. There is nothing repugnant in aggregation. It connotes building up, not destroying; strengthening and uniting, not weakening and humiliating. People *want* to be aggregated.' (Watson, 1960:25)[20]

The reconstruction of Tongaat estate and the building of model townships for the workers was undertaken some two decades before the onset of 'Grand Apartheid' in South Africa in the 1950s, yet early forms of legislated racial segregation already existed in the 1930s. Tongaat patriarchal discourse seeks to distance itself from the extremism of Nationalist Party apartheid while using such concepts as 'aggregation' and the cultural and religious differences of Zulu, Hindu, and Moslem communities to rationalize its own forms of racial separation in community management. Aesthetics is cited as an opportunity for local and liberal opposition to

---

[16] Dr P.N.H. Labuschagne, the highly respected medical officer at Tongaat who played a major role in combating malaria and establishing acceptable living conditions for the workers, also emphasises the aesthetics of the environment. A keen gardener, he writes articles for the company magazine on horticulture and the importance of beauty in the environment. (*The Condenser* III, 1, December 1953; III, 2, December 1955).

[17] Watson, *Tongaati*: 160-3.

[18] Watson, *Tongaat*: 17.

[19] Watson, *Tongaati*: 19. Quoting Aldous Huxley, *Grey Emminence*, London: Chatto and Windus, 1941: 248.

[20] Watson, *Tongaati*: 25.

harsh central government regulations, a noted instance being Gwelo Goodman's rejection of Pretoria bureaucratic requirements for the layout of black African townships. Law required that these townships should be laid out on a rectilinear grid pattern. Douglas Saunders writes to Gwelo Goodman, quoting from a letter of the Chief Native Commissioner of Natal, who was instructed by the central government concerning the proposed housing scheme at Tongaat:

> 'Kindly advise the Health Committee that in regard to the location lay-out, sites of not less than 60 feet by 50 feet, with streets of 40 feet width, at right angles to one another, enclosing rectangular blocks of sites ... must be incorporated in the location lay-out before the latter may receive approval.'[21]

Goodman replied as follows:

> If that rule from the Native Commissioner is applied rigidly, it reduces town or village planning to the work of an office boy with a foot rule and T square.

> The main roads may well be 40 feet though for what reason I cannot imagine. 30 foot seems to me to be more than ample. That every road should be at right angles to each other seems to be perfect madness. It simply cannot be done on our admirable sites. The main roads *must* follow the contour of the hill if only for the gradient & to provide for the gradient of drainage if at a remote period water borne drainage is provided.

> Frankly rectangular planning on that lovely hillside would be a disaster.

> If we can't get the officials to see reason I promise to make the lives of the responsible Ministers of Health a burden to them!!!

> It would be monstrous of any office to obstruct our scheme and leave the Natives in their present condition.

> What possible reason can they produce for such a fetish?

> Paris is designed on radiating lines from a centre! Pinelands (the only decent village planned in this country) is *not* rectangular. *Very much otherwise* & that is on flat ground. [Pinelands in Cape Town was the first 'Garden City' suburb to be laid out in South Africa, in the 1920s, in accordance with Ebenezer Howard's Garden City concept.][22]

Town planning in the new Tongaat was based on a conservative-liberal conception of racial and cultural difference, with a zone for black African workers' houses, one for Indian workers, one for 'Europeans' as white South Africans were termed in the mid-century, and an

'International Zone' where there would be no segregation at all. Much was made of the fact that two Indians were allotted to the five-man town management council in 1945, a move which was very much against the grain of the rigid official apartheid policies that emerged in post-war South Africa. The dominant personality of Douglas Saunders, the chairman of Tongaat, led to all policy being interpreted through his particular amalgam of utopian philosophy, social aesthetics, deism, and paternalism. His outspoken views rationalised Tongaat racial separation, while differentiating this from government policy, which was rightly seen as brutalizing and unjust. Despite the liberalism, Saunders's opinions are, to say the least, difficult to accept by present-day standards. They need nonetheless to be read as a genuine desire to improve the social situation of black workers, though wholly within the context of a colonial racist system:

> No single breed of man has been made the chosen favourite of the Gods because of the colour of a skin. But we are aware from history that the civilisation that was nurtured on the shores of the Mediterranean has built a people, known in general as Europeans, who since the days of Greece have proved to be ahead of those of other lands. Our object then is the gradual Europeanisation of Tongaat, and, as with Rome, the gradual improvement of our strength by bringing to full fruition the latent abilities of non-Europeans.

> ....

> We wish to rule as a Greek democracy; we wish to govern by discussion, and we welcome any race or class, but on grounds of excellence alone. We support any life-enhancing religion, for religion by its rules increases man's consciousness of his dignity as a human being and gives a motive for the good life. Further, as Nietzsche says, to ordinary men, those who have to serve and be useful, religion provides an inestimable contentment.

> ....

> The fundamental necessities, then, are food, family life, and freedom from fear. But this is not enough if 'the ultimate aim of life is right action'. We must add a fourth necessity – Beauty. If living is to be life-enhancing and man is to be humanised, beauty, whether visual, verbal, or musical, must be ever-present. The function of beauty, then, is didactic, furthering the purpose of evolution, giving man a deeper insight into the mystical. For beauty and the sublime are akin; both are aesthetic judgements.[23]

Gwelo Goodman died in 1938, before he was able to extend the Tongaat project. His direct involvement, apart from the homestead Amanzimnyama, is limited to the bachelors' quarters and the Community Centre in the new model village for black labourers, which was called Hambanati ('We walk together', the name in isiZulu of a nineteenth-century mission that had been located near Tongaat). However, over the next two to three decades successive architects kept to his blueprint. Labourers' cottages were designed to resemble

---

[21] Quoted by Douglas Saunders to Gwelo Goodman, correspondence, 21 May 1938, Tongaat-Hulett archives.

[22] Gwelo Goodman to Douglas Saunders, correspondence, 26 May 1938, Tongaat-Hulett archives.

[23] Douglas Saunders, 'A Philosophy for Tongaat', *The Condenser* III,4, December 1956: 3-4.

Cape artisans' cottages, particularly those which still stand in the quarter of Cape Town known as the 'Malay Quarter' or Schotschekloof. The façades of public buildings were all modelled on well known examples of Cape Dutch or Cape Georgian architecture. The Tongaat Health Centre (the public clinic) was designed in imitation of Cape Town's Parliament Street façade of the Old Supreme Court (once the Dutch East India Company's Slave Lodge and now the Cape Cultural History Museum). The Indian High School (1956) was a replica of the Adderley Street façade of the same building. The Municipal Market, Tongaat, with its popular Milk Bar, was modelled on Groot Constantia wine cellar, on the estate in the Cape Peninsula which was built in the late seventeenth century by the Dutch governor Simon van der Stel. The Tongaat Employees' Trading Company building in Maidstone Village had a front elevation which was derived from the eighteenth-century Customs House and Granary in Buitengracht Street, Cape Town, better known as 'Caledon Square'. The Engineers' Office was a simulacrum of the Cape Georgian townhouse, Grosvenor House, in Stellenbosch.

Tongaat Post Office was designed and built by the sugar company from drawings by Gwelo Goodman for a house he designed for his daughter in Johannesburg. This in turn is believed to have been derived from the Cape Palladian architect Louis-Michel Thibault's exquisite eighteenth-century De Wet House in the Cape Boland town of Tulbagh, which is considered to be an imitation of Gabriel's 'Petit Trianon' at Versailles. Goodman designed an elegant baroque gateway for the estate, based on Thibault's unused plan for a gateway to Cape Town's Government Avenue, as well as miscellaneous features such as baroque mortar garden seats. There is a summer house on Amanzimnyama Hill which is a perfect copy of the fine 'Kat' balcony in the inner courtyard of the Castle of Good Hope. The private owners of the Tongaat Hotel followed suit and remodelled the façade of their property on Cape Georgian lines, designed for them by Mary Alexander Cook who was, in the 1950s, South Africa's foremost expert on traditional Cape architecture. Other buildings in the Maidstone village were designed or remodelled to fit in with this scheme, including the Anglican Church in Maidstone, which was built in red brick in 1930 and entirely recast to match the trend, in 1949, complete with a copy of the Elsenburg farm slave bell. Most old Cape homesteads had, close to the main house, a 'slave bell' which would summon the workers to their meals, and measure the time of day. These were built in a customary style, with a whitewashed narrow elongated-H masonry frame, roughly four metres high, from which the bell was hung. There are sixteen imitations of these bells around the lands of Tongaat, all modelled on a particularly elegant example which is at the estate of Elsenburg, in the Cape. The architectural landscape affords an astonishing impression of baroque Cape buildings from a 'Mediterranean' region, famed for its old imported oak trees and stone pines, transplanted into a sub-tropical environment among cane fields, banana palms, bougainvillea and coral trees.[24] (See illustrations.)

Two other eminent South African artists became involved in the Tongaat project: Edward Roworth, friend (and rival) of Goodman, and Professor of Fine Art at the University of Cape Town, and the Cape sculptor Ivan Mitford Barberton. Roworth painted a masterly portrait of the proprietor Douglas Saunders, and a large-scale set of landscape murals by Roworth were removed from their original Cape homestead of Monterey when it was redecorated, and altered for installation in the Saunders house, Amanzimnyama. Mitford Barberton designed the stucco reliefs which were placed in the pediments of the neo-baroque public buildings of the new Tongaat and Maidstone, in a direct emulation of the eighteenth-century work in the Cape of the noted sculptor Anton Anreith and his colleague, the architect Louis Thibault. Where Anreith and Thibault modelled Palladian figures drawn from classical mythology, Mitford Barberton designed groupings of plantation workers, and allusions to the Saunders family. Mitford Barberton also undertook free-standing sculptures for public spaces and garden features on the Tongaat estate.

Thus, a concept which derived from the turn of the century Cape colonial vernacular architectural revival and its related concerns with local and national heritage, came to be understood as a means of transforming social conditions and attitudes in a region of the Natal Province. Further, the Tongaat estate evolved its own sense of heritage and dynastic claims, in what appears to have been a more or less overt response to this manifestation of borrowed tradition. The Saunders family have been proprietors, in part or in whole, of the Tongaat sugar estates since the 1850s. The representation of the estate by its own commentators makes the Saunders family out to be a kind of benevolent fiefdom with a self-validating family tree, lineage, and set of local traditions. Thus we are given detailed accounts of the early history of the Saunders family from the sixteenth century on, with a family tree running from the sixteenth century directly to the current chairman of Tongaat, Christopher Saunders.[25] In 1953 his father, Douglas Saunders, presented to the Tongaat Sugar Company the Saunders art and antiques collection which is of considerable value and a material index to the implicit ideas of tradition, continuity, legacy and public bequest that underlie the period concept of heritage. The main purpose behind his gift was concern at the breaking-up, in the 1950s, of many distinguished collections of antiques and Africana, on the deaths of their owners, such as the sale of Sir Abe Bailey's collection that same year.

Douglas Saunders built up the Tongaat collection with his personal interests in Chinese porcelain and antique Cape furniture. He purchased many Cape antiques during the Second World War when these were available at reasonable prices, and after the death in 1957 of Sir Ernest Oppenheimer, chairman of the huge mining concern of Anglo-American, Douglas Saunders was able to become first client of the noted Cape Town antique dealers, Friedland and Sons, being offered thereafter exclusive choices on old furniture. Until then, Sir Ernest was Friedlands' primary client, accumulating his family collection at Brenthurst, in Johannesburg. In 1951 Saunders

---

[24] For a discussion of the cultural aspects of the idea of the Cape as 'Mediterranean', see Peter Merrington, 'A Staggered Orientalism: The Cape-to-Cairo Imaginary', *Poetics Today*. 22,2, 2001:323-64.

[25] Watson, *Tongaati*: 29.

visited the Ashmolean Museum at Oxford for advice from Professor Cohn on his interests in Chinese porcelain.[26] A son who, as eldest, was to take on the chairmanship of the company in the second decade of the century, was killed in France in World War I, and his Coldstream Guards uniform and accoutrements are mounted in a life-size montage in a glass case at the main building. The impression of a patrilinear dynastic continuity is reinforced. James Renault Saunders, the first of the Saunders family at Tongaat in the mid-nineteenth century, received the appellation *Nkosi Bomvu* or 'Red King' from the local Zulu. Douglas Saunders was nicknamed 'the hare' in IsiZulu, for his habit of appearing and disappearing at any moment on inspection tours through the canefields. This kind of benevolent nomenclature was typical of colonial relations between Zulus and white people in positions of leadership in the province. It reinforces a sense of relationship between tradition and personality.[27]

The achievement of Tongaat might be described in terms of 'tradition', but the concept of heritage is arguably more apt. First, heritage implies a sense of agency, of stewardship, trust, and entailment for the future; it includes the sense of the dynastic or family role of the Saunders family; it encompasses the material tradition, built environment, and collections of artefacts, as well as the handing down of traditions of belief and attitude; it translates into cultural terms the legal aspects of ownership and incorporation of the land and the industrial and commercial activities; and in particular ways the concept of heritage reflects the internal policies and self-image of the company. For instance 'heritage' embraces the very distinct use, at Tongaat, of discourses concerning social Darwinism, cultural evolution, and genetics.

The company has for several decades produced an annual magazine, *The Condenser* (cleverly named from the process of sugar-refining), which is a show-case for the Tongaat estate activities and policies. Each issue has articles on technical and economic matters, sugar production, soil, machinery, global trends in the industry, and global economic matters, as well as articles on the social and educational development of the workforce. For all its years of production the magazine has carried an equally prominent amount of articles on art, poetry, and architecture (notably 'Garbled Gables: A Note on the Use and Misuse of Cape Dutch Architecture'[*The Condenser*, December 1953, 11-17]), on cultural identity, and philosophy. 'The Importance of Art in the Development of South Africa', (*The Condenser*, 1952:5) sets the tone. There are recurring studies of Gwelo Goodman, on Mitford Barberton and his influences from the baroque Cape sculptor Anton Anreith, on the Tongaat collection of antiques and

Africana, on Katharine Saunders's botanical sketches made at Tongaat in the nineteenth century, on horticulture and garden design, on Goya, on the Impressionists, on Chinese porcelain, and on other loosely related topics such as the work of the Edwardian art collector and critic Hugh Lane, who brought to South Africa the nucleus of the Johannesburg Art Gallery in 1911. There are articles on Indian women's dress, on Indian culture, on Zulu folk tales, and on the history of the Zulu people in Natal. There is a regular page of quotations from world poetry, including frequently the work of Rabindranath Tagore, following themes to do with beauty, ethics, and the human spirit.

Significantly there are several articles over the years on the 'nature of humanity', notably 'The Nature of Tomorrow's Man' by the eminent South African palaeontologist Phillip Tobias.[28] Tobias's article focusses on the shift, in human evolution, from a physical to a cultural and spiritual emphasis, that is, from biological to psychical development. ('Undoubtedly, the future evolution of man will lie fairly and squarely in the psychological, intellectual, cultural and spiritual realms'.) Tobias uses the metaphors of genetic 'inheritance', 'endowment' and 'heritage' to root his discourse on human 'development', and emphasises the role of consciousness, appreciation of beauty, and of compassion, in this evolutionary path.

Tobias's universal humanist reading of palaeontology is wholly in line with the general philosophy of Tongaat, and of Douglas Saunders in particular, who, however, brings to bear on questions of community management a decidedly elitist application of the concept of cultural evolution. Douglas Saunders, the many-talented Cambridge-educated chairman of the board from the 1930s to the early 1960s, reflects his personal viewpoint strongly, citing Ruskin, William Morris, Bernard Berenson, and Friedrich Nietzsche, in his insistence that good community management, open discussion, and the overriding role of the arts, should stand before what he sees as the folly of modern democracy. With an enormously patriarchal, insistent, but benignly intentioned perspective he argues the need for the total 'Europeanization' of the community, at a philosophical level, where idealistic standards of both tolerance and spiritual aspiration should draw all members of the community into harmony and into higher levels of 'humanisation'.

Recurring among these articles is the theme of a common humanity, a common faith in a Supreme Being, which transcends particular religions or creeds, and topics dealing with evolution and cultural or social evolution, which are an exploration of the theme of 'heritage' in its biological-cultural guise. Teilhard de Chardin, Aldous Huxley, and George Orwell are some of the authors cited in this regard. The entire force of the very many articles on art and aesthetics is dedicated towards a loose philosophy on the improvement of humanity through culture, and in particular, through beauty and beautification.

---

[26] Information on the Tongaat collection comes from M.G. Mackeurtan, 'The Tongaat Collection', appendix to Watson, *Tongaati*: 250-52; Bruce Lezard, 'Living with the Tongaat Collection', *The Condenser* IV,3, December 1960: 20-23; Barbara Wray, 'Some Shapes of Beauty', *The Condenser* VI,1, December 1968: 39-43.

[27] Senator Marshall Campbell, referred to above, had a black township in KwaZulu-Natal (KwaMashu) named in his honour, a similar dynamic which seems peculiar to the old Natal, where a particular relationship of at least nominal respect existed between the governing class of English settlers and the Zulu nation (who are, in the first instance, in their present identity, largely the product of colonial British genealogical, administrative, diplomatic, and tribal invention).

[28] Phillip Tobias, 'The Nature of Tomorrow's Man', *The Condenser*, December 1968: 44-48, this article being condensed from his 5th Raymond Dart Lecture, read to the Institute for the Study of Man in Africa.

Douglas Saunders's dated and race-based emphasis disappears with the change of chairmanship of the board in the early 1960s, but the pre-occupation with cultural evolution, social upliftment, and ethnic cultural traditions continues. An article, 'Superman and the Superhorse: Some Thoughts on Selective Breeding', by the board member Graham Ellis, diplomatically refutes Douglas Saunders's long-held Nietzschean views by arguing, from the experience of race-horse breeding, that there is no exact science in breeding a winner, that too many variables are entailed, and that, in the end, the 'Superman' concept is nothing more than a fantasy:

It would seem then, that when applied to any advanced or complex form of life, selective breeding enjoys no apparent advantage over the process of nature. If this conclusion is correct, then the argument of the Superman theorist is disproved, and the genius of the future will not be the result of some genetic computation, but will remain as the outcome of natural selection. In humans, the proportion of excellence to 'averageness' has been consistent for many centuries – thus genius is recognised as extraordinary, brilliance unusual, and mediocrity commonplace.[29]

Ultimately, in the context of a changing South Africa and the intensification of the anti-apartheid struggle, idealist and speculative philosophy gives way to sociological discourses such as 'The Housing of a Sugar Community', by P.T. Garland (*The Condenser*, 1962:16-20), and 'The Human Being in Tongaat' (G.H. Mitchell and S.S. Savage, *The Condenser*, 1978:3-8), and a particularly important essay by the United States Senator Daniel P. Moynihan, 'The Politics of Human Rights' (*The Condenser*, 1978:17-22).

It is arguable that this peculiar mixture of industry, social relations, and cultural patriarchy could only emerge and endure in the province of KwaZulu-Natal. Natal has tended to be more preoccupied with colonial tradition, and with family traditions, than other regions of South Africa. Until fairly recently a distasteful car bumper sticker declared 'Natal: the Last Outpost'. More seriously, Natal has pockets of very distinct cultural continuity and variety. Mount Edgecombe, a sugar town close to Tongaat, is distinctively built in Victorian red brick, with colonial verandahs, and corrugated or wrought iron. Verulam, a similar town in the region of Tongaat, has a long-standing Methodist tradition, having been founded by a party of Methodists in the nineteenth century under their leader Lord Verulam. Zulu national identity and prestige is vigorously promoted by the Zulu royal family and their *indunas*. British colonial military history is a prominent topic in Natal, with the famous Zulu War battlefields of Isandlhwana and Rorke's Drift as well as the much-promoted battlefields of the South African War of 1899-1901, such as Colenso, Spion Kop and Ladysmith. Parts of Natal are sacred to Afrikaner national memory, in relation to the experiences of the Voortrekkers in the 1840s, and the battle of Blood River. Natal Indian culture is a topic of particular interest, with various language groups and religions in some instances still jealously maintaining their separate affiliations.

A conservative English preoccupation with class, combined with the caste system of the Indian population, and the intense tribal or ethnic national pride of the Zulus, differentiates Natal from any of the other provinces of South Africa, where relations in the past have tended to be either far more crudely racist along simple white-black divisions, or (as in the Cape) based on a 300-year process of more or less inclusive creolisation. Questions of heritage are re-emerging in the post-colonial New South Africa, usually with a conservative and separatist cast to them, notably in the emergence of a very vocal 'Khoi-San' first-nation political and cultural lobby in the Western and Northern Cape provinces. This paper argues that the idea of heritage needs exact scrutiny for the remarkably conservative range of concepts and attitudes which it entails. It is a concept which properly exists in material case-studies, rather than as an abstraction. Each case study, however, will give new inflections to the range of meanings carried by the idea of heritage. The example of 'Cape Dutch Tongaat' is presented in this light, as an exemplary instance of the early twentieth-century preoccupation with heritage. Tongaat is, however, a continuing experiment in industrial, social, and cultural relations where earlier understandings of the project are now being recontextualized within a postcolonial society. The board and trustees of Tongaat are, for instance, investing largely in the work of local black artists, as a deliberate policy of transformation in the aesthetic and cultural sphere. Tongaat-Hulett, as the sugar company is now styled since a merger in 1982, has 'sweetened the pill' for its workers for seventy years, and has embraced the need to refine its cultural product in line with the times. Within the Tongaat 'family' of engineers, fieldworkers, and social workers there are many particular personal and household stories, many cultural perspectives, and remarkable achievements. There are, too, undoubtedly various oppositional perspectives. The intense struggle years of the 1980s touched all aspects of life in South Africa, but to explore against the grain must be the material of another study.

Acknowledgements

To the Tongaat-Hulett Group archivist Anne Dean, for sending me, on the recommendation of Yvette Hutchinson, lecturer in performance studies at King Alfred College, Winchester, copies of original material from the Tongaat archives, as well as copies of *The Condenser*, and for showing me around on a visit to the estate in 1998. Illustrations from Trotter (1903), and a copy of *Tongaati: An African Experiment*, by R.G.T. Watson.

Peter Merrington, Department of English Studies, University of the Western Cape.

Bibliography

Baker, Sir Herbert, 'The Architectural Needs of South Africa',*The State,* May 1909, 512-24

Beit, Sir Alfred, and J.G. Lockhart, *1906-1956, The Will and the Way; being an Account of Alfred Beit and the Trust which he Founded,* London: Longmans, Green, 1957

---

[29] Graham Ellis, 'Superman and the Superhorse: Thoughts on Selective Breeding', *The Condenser* IV,5, December 1962: 12-15.

Bruce, W.S., *Our Heritage: Individual, Social and Religious*, London: Blackwood, 1903

Cape Times, 7 November 1929

The Condenser, annual magazine of Tongaat-Hulett Ltd, 1953-1968

Correspondence between R.G. Goodman, Douglas Saunders and R.G.T. Watson, 1938, Tongaat-Hulett Ltd archives

Gutsche, Thelma, *No Ordinary Woman: The Life and Times of Florence Phillips*, Cape Town: Howard Timmins, 1966

Huxley, Aldous, *Grey Emminence*, London: Chatto and Windus, 1941

Jaff, Fay, *Women South Africa Remembers*, Cape Town: Howard Timmins, 1975

Merrington, Peter, 'Pageantry and Primitivism: Dorothea Fairbridge and the "Aesthetics of Union"', *Journal of Southern African Studies* 21,4, 1995, 643-56

Merrington, Peter, 'A Staggered Orientalism: The Cape-to-Cairo Imaginary', *Poetics Today*, 22,2, 2001, 323-64

Nash, Andrew, 'Colonialism and Philosophy: R.F. Alfred Hoernle in South Africa, 1908-1911', unpublished MA thesis, University of Stellenbosch

Newton Thompson, Joyce, *Gwelo Goodman, South African Artist*, London: George Allen and Unwin, undated, c.1960

Newton Thompson, Joyce, *The Story of a House*, Cape Town: Howard Timmins, 1968

Semmel, Bernard, *Imperialism and Social Reform*, New York: Anchor Books, 1968

Stead, W.T., *The Last Will and Testament of Cecil John Rhodes*, Bulawayo: Books of Rhodesia, 1977 (reprint of original edition of 1902)

Trotter, Alys Fane, *Old Cape Colony: A Chronicle of her Houses and Men*, London: Country Life, 1903

Watson, R.G.T., *Tongaati: An African Experiment*, London: Hutchinson, 1960

a. Bosch en Dal, a typical eighteenth-century Cape homestead

b. Side Gables, Groot Constantia, home of Governor Simon van der Stel

c. Wine House at Groot Constantia, which was the model for the Tongaat Municipal Market

d. Main façade, Groot Constantia, 1685

e. Meerlust, Eerste River, circa 1700

f. Farm Bell, Meerlust, Eerste River, typical design, of which there are 16 replicas based on another original, on the Tongaat estate

g. Hen House at Meerlust

h. Façade of Gwelo Goodman's Community Centre, Hambanati Village, Tongaat, based on the design from illustration 'g'

SIDE ELEVATION

i. Architect's drawings for worker's cottage, Tongaat

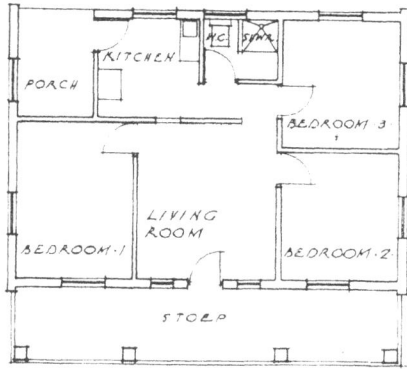

STANDARD PLAN

j. Old artisan's cottage, the 'Malay Quarter', Cape Town, which is the model for the Tongaat workers' houses

k. Two-storey Cape townhouse with roof room or *dakkamer* behind gable

l. Another façade of Goodman's Community Centre, Hambanati Village, Tongaat, with his 'Gwelo Colonial' circular gable window

m. A view of the Adderley Street façade of the old Slave Lodge, Cape Town

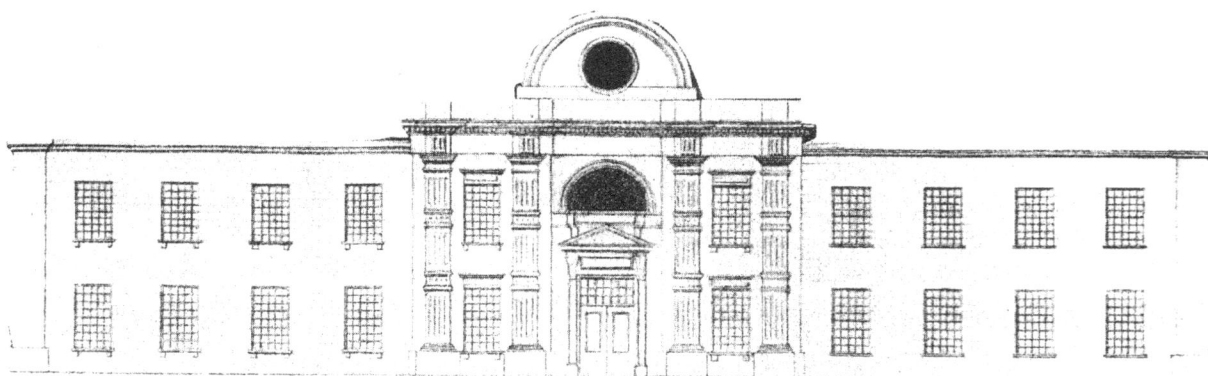

n. The High School, Maidstone Village, Tongaat (1956), based on the façade in illustration 'm'

MASSIVE WALLS AND DECORATED ENTRANCES:
AN ARCHAEOLOGICAL APPROACH TO PRE-MODERN ARCHITECTURE

Dragos GHEORGHIU

Abstract: The study of pre-Modern architecture reveals a tension, between the interior and exterior spaces. Evidence of this are the physical and symbolical barriers, examples of which are the door and the gate as well as the thickness of the walls, the position of decoration and the proportions of the entrance in the building's façade. The most common pre-Modern metaphor was that of "solidity" and "weight" of the built screens in a building.

Every void left in the façade has to be 'filled' in as an effort to counteract the weight of the wall. The most dramatic example of this being the metaphor of Caryatids.

Motto: "They left no writing, but they did leave all those houses". (Glassie 1975: 178)

INTRODUCTION

Although very close to the present time, Modern style in architecture is an unknown subject mainly because the historical data are insufficient.

In the spirit of this volume, an archaeological approach to a global problem (see Giddens 1990: 63) such as the emergence of Modern style in Europe is a necessary undertaking, because Post Medieval styles had a large geographical dissemination.

Parallel to the history of events and of the history of art, there is an "unconscious" history (Braudel 1969: 63ff.): that of rituals. This history of rituals is itself outside material evidence, and requires the historical archaeologist to arrive at conclusions from a global perspective such as the comparative ethnological studies (see Leone and Potter 1988: 336-355), material culture studies, or from artistic representations or literary texts.

An episode of the "unconscious" history is the "jump" (Gould and Eldredge 1977) or "catastrophe" (Thom 1983) that occurred in profane everyday ritual and in the styles and metaphors of the beginning of the 20th century, and generated in architecture the style labelled "Modern".

In spite of an archaeology of industrial society or of Capitalism (see Johnston 1993), there are no archaeological attempts to analyse the sudden emergence of Modern space in architecture; rather, there are only histories of Modern buildings. Indirect evidence from the history of art demonstrate the occurrence of a change in visual perception, by the substitution of the Renaissance perspective with that with many focal centres (points?). (Lowe 1982: 114). The material evidence of the "jump" in spatial perception and daily rituals is available through analysis of the architectural style of the entrances in buildings.

Bearing this in mind, the question could be asked: what kind of data could provide an archaeology of space?

As a point of departure the archaeology of space could be considered to be the genuine archaeology of architecture, because the main function of architecture is to generate spaces, and archaeology of buildings should not be reduced to the simple description of the material form of the construction.

Architectural space is the phenomenological result of the configurational and symbolic-ritual relationships produced in an interval of time, imposed by the constructions barriers and technological thresholds, such as the walls or entrances, in other words, the result of a relationship between the rites of passage and style. In this perspective, an archaeological study of architecture becomes a mixed research of ritual and style, namely of the immaterial and material borders that define the interior of a building after an individual enters it (see Johnston 1993:341).

As ethnological studies in contemporary cultures (Kaufmann 1996) demonstrate the importance of the entrance in the daily ritual, so, it can be contended, an archaeological analysis of a space should start with the analysis of the entrances and of the ritual passages that define that space.

Map

THE ENTRANCE – AN UNIVERSAL

As archaeological remains from prehistoric enclosures to the buildings of the last century demonstrate, built space was defined using the opposition interior-exterior (Edmonds 1993: 111), by means of physical and symbolical barriers (see Lawrence 1997: 89). The basic element of architecture, the wall, is a physical and symbolic barrier that divides space into a binary opposition: interior and exterior. Therefore, the openings made in the wall, such as the entrance or the windows, are, at one and the same time both attributes of the wall and physical and symbolical barriers.

The entrance and the doors are the most important architectural constituents in the large majority of pre-Modern facades. In the conception of the edifice the constituents of these openings such as proportion, width, decoration, positioning in the wall economy, is probably the most important architectural decision made by the architect, after that of the structure.

No matter what the material of construction, pre-Modern entrances were characterised by height, width, and thickness. Every empty space in the massive structure of the wooden, stone or brick wall was the result of an effort to counteract the load of the wall that pushes down, therefore any aperture was limited to the dimensions of the lintel. The width, the attribute of the "solidity" of a building, (see Vitruvius 1536), and of its protective function, reveals these characteristics by uncovering the real thickness of the protective screen.

"Whether the entrances be single, triple, or manifold, it is a constant law that one shall be principal, and all shall be of size in some degree proportioned to that of the building. And this size is, of course, chiefly to be expressed in width, that being the only useful dimension in a door [...]" wrote Ruskin (1921 [1851]: 158).

A second important attribute of the entrances, apart from those mentioned above, was the support of emblems, allegories and (bi and three-dimensional) narrativities, displayed on the exterior surface of the separation plane of the wall over the liminal zone of passage.

THE ENTRANCE – A RITUAL

In pre-Modern societies the entrance seems to have been a symbol of protection from and the repeal of risk and fear (see Kaufmann 1996: 282). This is because the pre-Modern environment was one of risk (Giddens 1990:106). This generated an imaginary of fear, materialised in architecture through metaphors of protection. A building with massive walls would protect more efficiently its interior than one with thin walls. Therefore, the ritual importance of the entrance of the first would be greater. To stress the sheltering role of the wall, the opening of the entrance could have additionally protected by the presence of anthropomorphic, zoomorphic and phytomorphic characters. All these figures could also be interpreted as the materialisation of the protection of the passage. The protective symbolism of the gate and of the entrance is present in Europe in an uninterrupted tradition since the Neolithic (e.g.: the Chalcolithic architectural models of Cucuteni culture, in Monah 1997: 260, fig. 8), up to the beginning of the 20th century AD (see Frampton 1992: 80, fig. 60).

As one can perceive from the archaeological remains, historical bi and tri-dimensional representations of buildings, and from ancient preserved buildings, all pre-Modern buildings made use of various technological methods to produce the rite of passage. All were reduced to two vertical elements that permitted a passage through them (see van Gennep 1969 [1909]: 25). Every entrance involves the performance of a rite of passage, "a process of symbolic action focussed upon the body", through which "performers of the ritual passage find and resituate themselves in cosmological space" (Richard Werbner 1989: 1).

In European pre-Modern cultures, the "passage" as a "re-situation", represented a strong metaphor used for the world of the living and for the world of the dead as well. Pleasing examples of the latter could be taken from Roman funerary iconography depicting the figure of the deceased positioned in front of an entrance (see Cumont 1966).

A rite of passage does not reduce itself to a simple repositioning of the body; by entering into a built space, the performer has to suffer a "jump" between two perceptual and emotional states of stasis. Additionally, the decoration of the separation plane between two spaces filled with meaning or with social value (see Edmonds 1993: 111) produce a psychical effect upon the visual perception of the individual (see Thomas 1993: 87).

With few exceptions (Edmonds 1993: 116), the daily rituals of sacred or profane passage were not studied by archaeologists, the field of research being quite virgin.

Generally rituals had a structured form, for instance the rites of passage observe three stages, one of separation, one of liminality, and one of re incorporation (van Gennep 1969: 25; Turner 1967; Edmonds 1993: 114). This structure is not fixed in architecture.

Sometimes separation is preceded by an additional pre liminal stage, materialised under the shape of stairs or porticoes that stresses upon the entrance. The positioning of a "frontispiece (i.e. the pediment of the portico) in the main front of (...) villas and (...) town - houses (...) show the entrance of the house, and add very much to the grandeur and magnificence of the work" (Palladio Bk. II, chap. 16, cited in Wittkower 1971: 74).

In many European folk cultures this sort of liminal space, and particularly the threshold (Turner 1967), was metaphorically associated to 'death and rebirth', because individual is moving from one category to another, by rebirth (Rosman and Rubel 1998: 229).

Fig. 1. The Arch of Septimius Severus with false columns and emphasised cornerstones.

The dimension of the threshold is determined by, and determines the nature of, the re incorporation space: there are rituals with a short passage and rituals with a long passage, that allows the performer to prepare himself/herself psychically before entering into a new space. One can conclude that the liminal phase materializes in the façade of the building the coefficient of risk and protection of its content.

In every building the liminal zone is materialised under the shape of the door - frame, that limits itself to the width of the wall, or, in an extended form, under the shape of covered passages. The funerary corridors in prehistoric tombs are, ritualistically speaking, a hypertophic liminal space of protection. Sometimes this space also is preceded by a preliminary passage under the shape of steps or inclined planes. All these examples of pre-Modern architecture display a rhetorical link between the exterior and the interior spaces. A grandiose heavy door, difficult to pull open, a high and wide threshold, a decorated lintel, together with the door handles, door knobs, joints and loops are all metonymies of the quality of the space hidden by the gate. Ethnological or

historical examples (see for instance *Gilgamesh epic*: 11-14) demonstrate that the axiology of pre-Modern society rhetorically stressed the importance of the content of the building in the proportion and in the decoration of the entrance. This statement is the most explicitly expressed in the case of the symbolic or "triumphal" arch, where all the space of the building is reduced to the perimeter of the entrance, allowing the performer to enter into a virtual space delimited by the contour of the gate. By passing through the arch, the performer could live a psychical experience similar to that generated by the ritual of passage in a real building.

A particular aspect of the rite of passage to be discussed is the metaphor of the separation stage by embodiment, sometimes the vertical architectural elements that define the passage displaying anthropomorphic characters. In this respect the entrance and the gate represent a case of embodiment, exemplified by human sacrifices under the threshold (Josua: Gen.), or by the assignment to various protective deities, for example, the god Hermes was called "the threshold protector", Vernant 1990: 157). All pre-Modern European history of architecture has examples of iconic projections on the separation plane of the wall of the entrance. An additional example in support of the above mentioned identification is, in folk cultures, the strong link between the entrance and the basic ritual moments in human life as marriage and death(see Marian 1995 [1892]), the latter being associated especially with the symbol of threshold and liminality in funerary rituals (see Florea Marian 1995 [1892]);. Paul-Levy and Segaud 1983; Kaufmann 1996: 281).

THE ENTRANCE: RITUAL AND STYLE

What viable approach should be adopted to carry out an archaeological investigation of pre Modern buildings? A possible method could be the analysis of ritual and style through an evaluation of the visual importance (cf. Renfrew and Bahn 1991: 359-360) of the space of separation and of the liminal space. This should be carried out in relationship with the rest of the built space, namely the analysis of the proportion between the decoration of the entrance and the decoration of the other important elements of the building.

A further method could be the analysis of ritual and style through the analysis of art representations (see Renfrew 1997: 52) of the building studied. Bi- and three-dimensional representations of the space such as paintings, drawings, photos, tapestries or models could offer complementary data to the basic data gleaned from diggings or restoration.

Both methods imply the analysis of style that represented simultaneously in the structural and the decorative (cf. Shanks and Tilley 1987: 92) attributes of the building.

Because in the rites of passages, the rite is in fusion with the technology of construction, and consequently with style, the ritual is stylistically determined, and therefore the archaeological approach imply a reading style as a starting point and following onto to ritual.

The large variability in the succession of styles in public and private buildings is due to technological and social changes in Post Medieval Europe. By means of the decoration and of the proportion of the voids in the facades, a continuity of the rite of passage until the beginning of the 20th century, is demonstrated.

METAPHORS OF PRE-MODERN SPACE

Traditional pre-Modern materials as bricks, wood or stone produced a massive architecture whose metaphors of "solidity", "weight" and "protection" (expressed in their facades, especially in entrances) would change only with the introduction of the new building materials such as pig iron and reinforced concrete. The dominant metaphors cited above, that characterised pre-Modern space, were supported by a number of subordinate metaphors. In the present study, for the sake of the economy of space, the discussion will be restricted to those specific to Classicism and Neo Classicism,

namely the cornerstone, the triumphal arch, the false column, and Caryatids. The cornerstone supported the metaphor of "solidity" by visualising the force hidden in the arched openings, in Neo Classicism its use as plastered decoration hypertrophied its original functional shape. An analogous case to demonstrate the forces hidden in the wall's structure were the false columns plastered on the facades that stressed the force of sustaining and of effort.

The metaphor of solidity was also supported by the width of the triumphal arches, their hypertrophied dimensions trying to emphasise the great massiveness, and subsequent solidity, of the (virtual) building.

The "openings" i.e. the overcoming of the weight of the heavy wall screen were visualised in Classicism and Neo - Classicism also by iconic narratives, with references to the Greco-Roman mythology. Sometimes the false columns were replaced with images of human beings, the Caryatids, that, similar to the columns, expressed the effort to counteract the descending pressure of the weight of the walls. This narrative, more or less iconic, persuading on the attributes of "solidity" and "weight" of the buildings, is to be found in relationship with the entrances and passages, i.e. with the ritual component of the buildings.

All the metaphors discussed disappear at the beginning of the 20th century, and are replaced by the metaphor of the "machine", that took two centuries to become finally established.

THE DOMINANT STYLES IN POST MEDIEVAL EUROPE: THE ARCHAEOLOGICAL AND THE INDUSTRIAL STYLE

In the 19th century, "the present become more mechanical and external" and the "[b]ourgeois society tried to consume the past, in order to attenuate somewhat its estrangement in the mechanical, segmented present" (Lowe 1982: 40). The recycling of the styles of the Antiquity, from the 15th to 19th century, and the idealisation of the Middle Ages in the 19th century enabled some to ward off the threats of technology and industrialisation"(Lowe 1982: 42).

All these styles, inspired from the past, that influenced the architecture of Europe, could be considered to be the result of a global process of cognitive archaeology. Specific to all of them is the emphasis on rituality, mainly visualised in the design of entrances.

An explanation for the emergence of the archaeological styles could be the "separation of the context of production of material goods and services from the physical and social context of household relations" (Johnston 1993: 331). This process that would be inverted at the beginning of the 20th century, becoming an 'export' from industry to the household. The transfer of the 'export' or *chaines-operatoires* from industry into the habitation buildings produced a change in the rituality of the pre-Modern household and in the cognitive way the buildings were designed. If pre-Modern architects designed the building determined by its entrances (in fact depending on the exterior space), Modern architects started to design from the "inside" of the buildings, starting from one object, for instance the bathroom or the fireplace (Buckminster Fuller 1963 [1938]: 23), as in the design of a "machine". The compacted configuration of the functions of the building resulted from such a design process, as well as the new multi-perspectival perception of space (Lowe 1982: 110). This led to the genesis of a new architectural style after the first decade of the 20th century which invalidated all the previous metaphors. Therefore the industrial style would invalidate the barriers and separations of pre-Modern buildings and, subsequently, the rituals of passage. It would also invalidate the metaphors of "protection" and "weight", Modern buildings ignoring pre-Modern statics. Reinforced concrete would substitute all the pre-Modern materials and would allow for larger openings, in this way diminishing the value of the rites of passage.

THE FOLD MODEL

The synchronically and diachronically analysis of the genesis and development of two styles shows the presence of two stylistic directions, one, "industrial" evolved dramatically in the 17th and 19th centuries. A second one "archaeological", evolving in the opposite direction, starting with the Renaissance, and disappearing suddenly at the beginning of the 20th century. In my opinion, this complex historical process as the development, the returning to the past and the sudden disappearance of styles and rituals in architecture could be visualised with the help of the fold /cusp catastrophe model [Thom (1983: 22), Zeeman (1980)], the model being used by archaeologists to explain such complicated situations as the collapse of complex societies (Renfrew 1984: 377-379; Bintliff 1997: 67 ff.).

One can imagine the historical process of the development of the two styles from Late Antiquity up to the 20th century as a surface characterised by a directional vector. Beginning with the Renaissance, on one of the edges of the plane surface a fold emerges, changing the direction of the vector, due to the turning to the past of the archaeological style, a curve in the plane that disappears slowly during the emergence of the Baroque. The same fold is produced in the 19th century as the Neo - Classical style turns backwards again. The process of the disappearance of the fold suddenly like a 'catastrophe" or a "jump", occurred when the industrial style replaced Neo -Classicism. This "jump" in the style is evidence of the ritual crisis due to industrial style and metaphors in the context of an unparalleled industrial development at the beginning of the 20th century. Architects, under the influence of industrial technologies changed the philosophy of building design by a sudden renunciation of the metaphors of "solidity", "weight" and "protection" conferred upon the building by the separation of walls. It also resulted in the new "Modern" style being not only stylistic, but also ritualistic, by promoting a continuos space, without (obvious) physical barriers.

CONCLUDING REMARKS

The conclusion of the present paper is that an archaeological approach to buildings is needed that shall examine the available material evidence and historical data and also discuss concepts as space or ritual that are not discussed in the archaeological record. One of the main aims of the paper is to promote an archaeology of the immaterial in buildings, that of perception, of metaphors and of rituality. The subject chosen, the archaeological study of entrances involves a combination of the studies of material (implying style) and the immaterial studies of space already mentioned.

An approach to the archaeology of the cusp catastrophe that developed at the beginning of the 20th century should be, at one and the same time, an archaeological and a phenomenological approach. This involves, not only the description of material shapes, but also an archaeology of the sight and of the invisible ritual barriers crossed by the movement of the body in space.

Acknowledgments

I owe a great debt to Ruth Tomlinson who helped me to improve the English translation.

Dragos Gheorghiu, University of Arts Bucharest
dgheorghiu@digi.ro

Bibliography

Bintliff, John, 1997, Catastrophe, Chaos and Complexity: the death, decay and rebirth of towns from antiquity to today, *Journal of European Archaeology*, vol.5, no.2, pp.67 - 90.

Braudel, Fernand, *Ecrits sur l'histoire*, Flammarion, Paris, 1969.

Cumont, Franz, *Recherches sur le symbolisme funeraire des Romains*, Librarie Orientaliste Paul Geuthner, Paris, 1966.

Edmonds, Marc, 1993, Interpreting Causewayed Enclosures in the past and present, in Christopher Tilley (ed.), *Interpreting Archaeology*, Berg, Providence/Oxford, pp. 99-142.

Frampton, Kenneth, 1992, *Modern Architecture, A Critical History*, Thames and Hudson, London/New York.

Buckminster Fuller, Richard 1963[1938], *Nine Chains to the Moon*, Southern Illinois University Press.

Gennep van, A., *Les rites de passage. Etude systematique des rites*, Mouton & Co and Maison des Sciences de l'Homme, 1969 [1909].

Giddens, Anthony, *The Consequences of Modernity*, Stanford, Stanford University Press, 1990.

Gilgamesh Epic (French transl. Rene Labat, Lucien Mazenod, Paris 1961)

Glassie, Henry, *Folk Housing in Middle Virginia*, Knoxville, University of Tennesie Press, 1975.

Gould, Stephen, and N. Eldredge, Punctuated Equilibria - The Tempo and Mode of Evolution Reconsidered, *Paleobiology*, 3, 1977, pp. 115-151.

Johnston, Robert, The Paradox of Landscape, *EJA*, vol.1, no.3, 1998, pp. 315-325.

Kaufmann, Jean-Claude, Portes, verrous et cles: Les rituels de fermeture du chez-soi, in *Ethnologie Francaise*, 2, 1996, pp. 280-288.

Leone, M. and Potter P, 1988, *The Recovery of Meaning in Historical Archaeology*, Washington D.C., Smithsonian Institution.

Lowe, Donald, *History of the Bourgeois Perception*, The University of Chicago Press, Chicago, 1982.

Monah, Dan, *Plastica antropomorfa a culturii Cuuteni-Tripolye*, Memoriae Antiquitatis, Piatra Neamt, 1997.

Lawrence, Roderick, Public collective and private space, in Susan Kent (ed.), *Domestic architecture and the use of space. An interdisciplinary cross-cultural study*, Cambridge, Cambridge University Press, 1997, pp. 73 -91

Marian, Simion Florea, *Inmormantarea la romani. Studiu etnografic*, Bucharest, Grai si suflet, 1995 [1892].

Paul-Levy, F. and M. Segaud, *Anthropologie de l'espace*, Paris, Centre Georges Pompidou - CCI, 1983.

Renfrew, Colin and Paul Bahn, *Archaeology, theories, methods and practice*, London, Thames and Hudson, 1991.

Renfrew, Colin, The Archaeology of religion, in Renfrew, Colin and Ezra Zubrow (eds), *The Ancient Mind. Elements of Cognitive Archaeology*, Cambridge University Press, 1997.

Renfrew, Colin, 1984, *Approaches to Social Archaeology*, Edinburgh University Press.

Rosman, Abraham and Paula G. Rubel, *The Tapestry of Culture*, McGraw-Hill, Boston, 1998.

Ruskin, John, *The Stones of Venice*, London, Dent and Sons, 1921 [1851].

Shanks, M. and C. Tilley, *Re-constructing Archaeology*, Cambridge, Cambridge University Press, 1987.

Thomas, Julian, The Hermeneutics of Megalithic Space, in Christopher Tilley (ed.), *Interpretative Archaeology*, Berg, Oxford, 1993, pp. 73-98.

Thom, Rene, *Paraboles et catastrophes*, Paris, Flammarion, 1983.

Turner, Victor, Betwixt and between: The liminal period in rites of passage, in Turner Victor, *The Forest of symbols: Aspects of Ndembu ritual*, Ithaca, New York, Cornell University Press, 1967, pp. 93-111.

Vernant, Jean Pierre, *Mythe et pensee chez les grecs*, Ed. de la Decouverte, Paris, 1990.

[Vitruvius], *Architettura con il suo comento e figure, in volgare lingua raportato per M.Giambatista Caporali di Perugia*, Perugia, 1536.

Werbner, Richard, Ritual passage, sacred journey. The process and organization of religious movement, Washington D.C., Smithsonian Institution Press, 1989.

Wittkower, Rudolph, *Architectural principles in the age of humanism*, The Norton Library, New York, 1971.

Zeeman, Christopher, *Catastrophe Theory - Selected Papers*, 1972-1977, Reading, Addison-Westey, 1980.